3 -

Northern Nurse

Writers' Federation of Nova Scotia
1113 Marginal Road
Halifax, Nova Scotia B3H 4P7

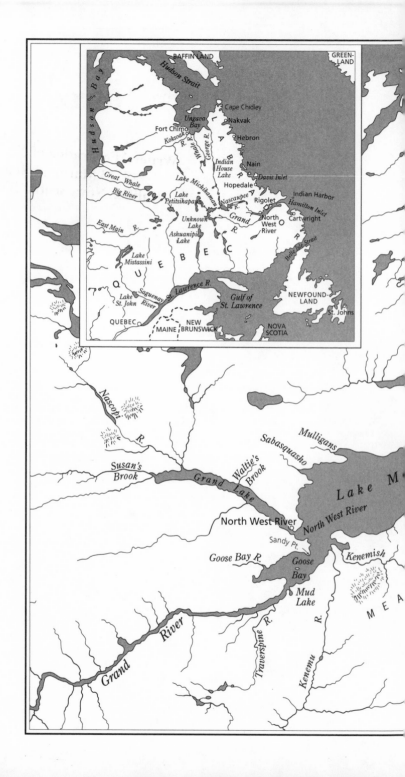

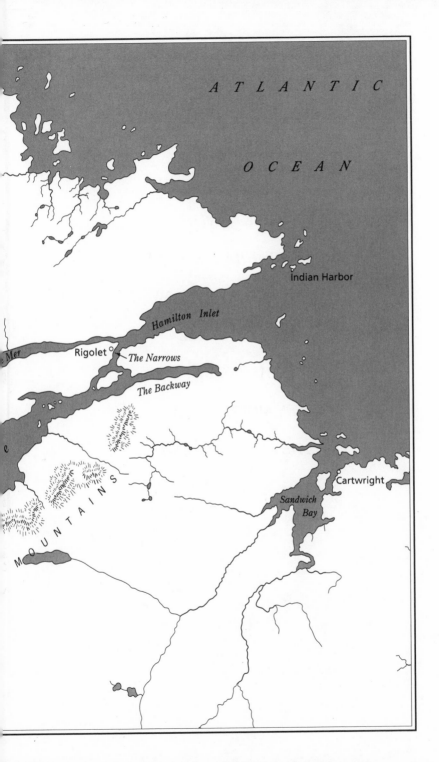

ELLIOTT MERRICK

Northern Nurse

Foreword by
LAWRENCE MILLMAN

NIMBUS
PUBLISHING

Northern Nurse was originally published in 1942 by Charles Scribner's Sons.
This edition was published in 1994 by Nimbus Publishing Limited
PO Box 9301, Station A
Halifax, NS
B3K 5N5
(902) 455-4286

Published by arrangement with The Countryman Press Woodstock, Vermont

Canadian Cataloguing-in-Publication Data
Merrick, Elliott, 1905-
Northern nurse
ISBN 1-55109-091-0
1. Austen, Kate. 2. Nurses—Newfoundland—Labrador— Biography. I. Title.
RT37.A88M47 1994   610.73'092   C94-950156-5

Cover design by James F. Brisson
Map by Mapping Specialists, Ltd., Madison, Wisconsin
Printed in Canada

10 9 8 7 6 5 4 3 2 1

Northern Nurse

FOREWORD

MORE THAN any other point of the compass, the North likes to fill its literature with heroic mythology. Intrepid explorers, life-or-death situations, unimaginably awful weather—mix them together, simmer, and serve. If you want a flavor slightly less rough about the edges, you might add a nurse to the ingredients. But be forewarned: too much nurse might make the dish a trifle too sweet. A few years ago I read a book called *Angel of Hudson Bay* that had me alternately squirming in my seat and yawning. It wasn't that the titular "angel," a nurse, was too good to be true. Rather, she was too good to be interesting.

Having said that, let me hasten to add that *Northern Nurse* is not a typical book about a northern nurse. That's because the author, Elliott Merrick, is not a typical purveyor of northern myths. Quite the contrary. He's a writer of uncommon talent more or less in the tradition of Thoreau. Like Thoreau, he upholds the belief that we humans ought to let Nature govern us rather than vice versa; a belief that makes the conquest of the Pole, among other conquests, wholly unnecessary. Also, his nurse may be a model of devotion, but happily she's no angel. She's a flesh-and-blood woman whose adventures in pioneer Labrador bring alive—dramatically alive—a way of life now gone forever. I have no hesitation in calling this book, which was first published over fifty years ago, a classic. In retrospect it is an elegiac classic.

The Labrador of the late 1920s and early 1930s—the Labrador of Elliott Merrick and Nurse Kate Austen—was one of the great inhospitable places in North America. Whoever fetched up on its adamant shores could be assured of one thing: hardship. Even today it is not the sort of place a person visits casually. As befits a subarctic locale, winters are frigid, summers bug-ridden, the coast mined with nautical hazards, and the interior all but uninhabitable. Southern Labrador is a frieze of dense coniferous forests rooted in the cold granite of the Canadian Shield. The north is treeless and consists only of that cold granite itself.

Small wonder that explorer Jacques Cartier called this "the land God gave to Cain." Cain turned down the gift, so it was accepted by others of a more stalwart disposition, Indian and Eskimo, along with latter-day settlers from Scotland. Inevitably, these people pooled both their genes and their skills. As described by Merrick in his first Labrador sketch, "Escape to the North," they were "Scotch-Presbyterian by religion, old English in speech and custom, Eskimo when it came to seal fishing and dog driving, and Indian in the way of hunting and their skill with canoes..." Subsistence trappers and hunters, never far from bone-grinding poverty, at least—in Merrick's view—they marched to the beat of their own drummers. At least they lived according to the dictates of Nature, albeit a Nature often downright hostile to their interests.

It's not surprising that Kate Austen should have turned up among such people. She was a tough-minded Australian nurse ("Cast-Iron Kate, the Boilermaker's Mate," Merrick called her) of Scotch-Irish extraction who refused to be merely a doctor's handmaid. Having recently looked after a would-be invalid in Paris, she must have felt as if she was going home again, or at least going to the boreal version of her own outback, when she joined Labrador's Grenfell Mission. Merrick, however, was casting off his home when he signed on with the Mission. Raised in affluent Montclair, New Jersey and educated at Phillips Exeter Academy and Yale University, he seemed destined for the world of business, his father's world. And he seemed to be accepting this destiny when he took a job as assistant advertising manager for the National Lead

Company, his father's firm. For almost a year he commuted daily to New York, sat in an office, and wrote copy for products like Dutch Boy Paint. But he detested it all heartily. Surely, he felt, there was something better, more healthy, more exhilarating *out there*. He found that exhilarating something far, far from the skyscrapers of New York.

By the 1920s the backbone of the Grenfell Mission was its summer volunteers, otherwise known as WOPs (Workers Without Pay), who chopped wood, dug ditches, put in plumbing, and even helped with medical chores. Merrick joined the Mission as one of these volunteers, but he was so intrigued by Labrador—so ill-disposed toward his own cozy, urban background, too—that he stayed on as a schoolteacher in North West River. There he met and courted resident nurse Kate Austen, with whom he shared an almost palpable love for the outdoors. Together they took wilderness canoe trips that would have made Thoreau green with envy. At one point they went on an extended winter trip into the largely unexplored interior with trapper John Michelin. It was a trip full of risk, cold, and discomfort, gut-cauterizing food and more cold, yet I suspect it did more for their relationship than candlelit dinners and evenings at the movies. Indeed, Merrick describes this trip so rhapsodically in *True North*, his first book, that even the ubiquitous cold takes on an appealing quality.

Whereas Thoreau took all of Nature as his bride, Merrick took Kate Austen as his and thereby brought to an end his two-year sojourn in Labrador. Much later he wrote: "When I went to Labrador I was young and strong and single and fancy-free...But when I had a wife, with a child on the way, I necessarily began to wonder how I was going to support them. I had to face the fact that I wasn't half as good a trapper or seal fisher or dogteam driver, etc., etc., as the native-born man, and even he, with all his

Indian, Eskimo, and Scotch arts, had a very difficult time of it to make ends meet. A major in English Literature at Yale and a minor in French were not very good preparation..."

It was 1931 and the height of the Great Depression when the couple returned to the United States. For awhile Merrick bit the proverbial bullet by driving a Mrs. Wagner's Pie truck to restaurants in and around Jersey City. Then he and Kate bought an old farm in one of the few parts of the country, northern Vermont, that could ever be mistaken for Labrador. In fact, it was probably Vermont that coaxed him into writing about Labrador. Not only did it have certain affinities with Labrador, especially in its wintered-up aspect, but the differences (farms, roads, and so on) quite likely helped him focus his thoughts on what made Labrador such an extraordinary place.

Merrick's early tales and sketches now seem like warm-up exercises for *True North*, a book that so enthralled its Scribner's editor, the legendary Maxwell Perkins, that he reputedly asked Merrick if there was anything *he* could do in Labrador. The book has a similar effect on readers considerably less exalted than Perkins. It is a *Walden* of the North, its lyrical, curmudgeonly voice now celebrating the boreal wilderness, now inveighing against the superfluities of the urban wilderness. Be thou like the doughty Labradorian, it suggests, and despite a life of hard knocks you'll still be happier than if you waste yourself "in the roaring city." *True North*'s anti-urban, anti-technological message perhaps speaks more eloquently today than when the book was published in 1933. Does that make it a call to arms? Not really. It is rather a call to lay down one's arms and live harmoniously with the natural world.

By the end of the decade Merrick was tapping several diverse economies—as a writer, a farmer, and an English instructor at the University of Vermont—in an effort to support his family. Occasionally, he would descend on New York and toss around book ideas with Perkins. Meanwhile Kate was giving talks about her Labrador nursing adventures to women's groups in Vermont. She forbade her husband to attend these talks because she was afraid that he'd make her self-conscious. But he sneaked in on one of them and sat in the rear of the room, whereupon a light bulb suddenly flashed on in his mind.

And so *Northern Nurse* was born. Here's how Merrick describes the initial forging of the book: "My wife and I worked together morning after morning, week after week, she telling and telling me, I making notes and asking her for more details. I'd discard a chapter because it was too unlovely, too bloody, too grisly...too inconclusive or damaging to somebody we knew, but always I'd be building and building (having faith, as one must). She would be baking bread, or tending her flowers, or picking peas and sometimes get exasperated with the whole thing and quit for a week." Later Merrick took over the work entirely, fleshed out its bones, shaped it, and then sent the manuscript to his editor. Perkins liked the work so much (no, he didn't ask Merrick how he could become a Labrador nurse himself) that he said he wouldn't change a single line of it.

Northern Nurse is such a crisp book, so often funny— *very* funny—that the reader may not notice that it is also a somewhat slippery book. Its wealth of hands-on medical detail suggests a straightforward nurse's memoir told in the first person by the nurse herself. Merrick would seem not to be in the book at all until the last few pages, when Nurse Kate discovers him "poking his nose into everything." But he is in fact everywhere in the book, in nearly every turn of phrase, storylike vignette, and philosophical aside. The voice is the voice of *True North*, a bit leaner, it's true, but nonetheless the same voice. He could never have adopted this voice or indeed written the book without his own experience of Labrador. All of which makes for a husband-wife collaboration highly unusual in the annals of literature.

Kate Austen is the "northern nurse," of course. In scene after scene she proves herself to be supremely capable at her profession, dealing with everything from *placenta praevia* to a child with a bean up its nose. But she's also a character created by Elliott Merrick and sent through the book with novelistic gusto, from one patient to the next, until she seems to be a nurse to Labrador itself. She heals, one might say, so Merrick can reveal. And what he reveals is a place fallen off the world's map, where a Murdock McLean can drag his toboggan 150 miles simply to have an infected molar removed or a boy might be named Noti because he was born when there was *no tea* in the house. It's a place where survival is a daily pursuit. I don't mean survival as practiced by certain explorer-adventurer types, who get heaps of grant money and then try oh! so hard to risk their lives. I mean the quiet, undemonstrative survival wrested from adversity by anonymous people, for whom life itself is a risk. At the core of *Northern Nurse* is this sort of survival, with a nurse and her charges kicking, or trying to kick, Death in the teeth.

The book was a success, although not a large one, when it was published in 1942. It got excellent reviews, spent seventeen weeks on the *New York Times* best-seller list, and came within a vote of being a Book-of-the-Month Club selection. Yet several factors kept it from establishing itself more securely in the literary firmament. First, it came out during the darkest days of World War II, not a very favorable time for a book seemingly unconcerned with contemporary events. Then Scribner's ran out of copies during the Christmas buying season and didn't get the book back in stock until the following spring. Last but certainly not least, *Northern Nurse* has as its heroine a woman who liberated herself long before Women's Lib became a cause. Books that are ahead of their time like that tend to play second fiddle to books that reinforce the status quo.

During the War Merrick worked for the Office of War Information, for whom he put together an illustrated booklet on the volunteer sailors of the activities of the merchant marine. His interest in these men led him to ship aboard a convoy tanker bound for bombed-out Liverpool, and from this experience came his novel *Passing By*. The manuscript of *Passing By* was turned down by Perkins, perhaps because the novel was such a departure from Merrick's previous work, perhaps because of its salty, waterfront language (Perkins, for all his virtues as an editor, was a notable prude.) Even though *Passing By* was picked up and published by MacMillan in 1947, Perkins' rejection, in Merrick's words, "rocked me."

The reader might wonder whether Perkins' rejection had a long-term effect on Merrick. After all, none of his subsequent work is quite as fine, as wonderfully rich and alive as either *True North* or *Northern Nurse*, with the possible exception of *Green Mountain Farm*, a chronicle of his Vermont years. Yet this falling off had little to do with Perkins. It had more to do with Merrick's decision to eschew writing, at least full-time writing, for work that would support his family somewhat less haphazardly. It might also have been the natural outcome of his distance in time and space from Labrador, the main source of his inspiration. By the late 1940s he was so removed from what he refers to as "that pristine, beautiful land" (he was now living outside Asheville, North Carolina) that he must have felt cut off from it. Cut off as if from his Muse.

And yet insofar as he pursued the subsistence ideal in his own life, he was not cut off from it at all. Even as he labored as an associate professor at Black Mountain College and then as an editor for the Southeastern Forest Experiment Station, he and Kate continued to live "as close to the wilderness ways as we could manage in our industrialized, urbanized society—always remembering Labrador, always hugging the wild days and ways to our hearts." Kate died in 1989 at age 94 and Merrick has since remarried, but his views on life, liberty, and the pursuit of happiness remain unchanged. "How can you *stand* living in a city?" he wrote me recently from his home in rural North Carolina.

What has changed, however, is Labrador itself. Gone are the trappers who in Merrick's time practiced the arts of canoe-and-portage and snowshoe-and-toboggan. Gone are the pioneer women who were often twice as strong as their male counterparts. Gone, too, is the fishery that was the original raison d'être of the Grenfell Mission. The Labrador of today is a brave new world crisscrossed by low-level NATO jets, roared over by Skidoos, and increasingly regarded by the rest of Canada as (dreadful concept!) a "resource." The Trans-Labrador Highway, Labrador's first real road, now makes it possible to drive a car all the way from Los Angeles to Goose Bay. As roads reproduce at a rate that puts rabbits to shame, no doubt there'll be more roads...and more roads...and more roads, along with the development roads always bring. So gaze upon this once-proud land now, friend, because when you gaze again, it may not be there. You might also read a remarkable book entitled *Northern Nurse*, which will give you some idea of what Labrador was like when the only roads were waterways and trails of a person's own making.

Lawrence Millman
Cambridge, Massachusetts
December 1993

This is the story of my wife when she was Nurse Kate Austen. She has told me many of the tales given here; others I saw for myself during the years we worked in the same Labrador settlements. Planning this book together, we have tried to give a true picture of one nurse's work, thought and adventure.

ELLIOTT MERRICK

CHAPTER 1

FROM AUSTRALIA to Labrador is quite a long jump, but even when I was little I knew I'd go somewhere. When we were kids in Australia my elder brothers and sisters put a pan of water out on the back steps one chilly night. In the morning it was thinly skimmed with ice, the only time I ever remember a freezing spell in Sydney's semitropical climate. But it was enough for me. "Some day," I said, "I'm going where there's more of this."

The World War and the returning soldiers influenced me to take up nursing, the finest job an adventurous girl can have if she must wander. Training at the Coast Hospital a little way out of Sydney on a bluff above the Pacific, I saw the ships go by. From the wide verandas all of us trainees watched with a sigh the P. & O. liners, the Japanese N. Y. K., Norwegian tramps and American Dollar Line ships sliding over the horizon. Australian training was long and thorough, for Australian nurses are second to none. But I liked the work and, wandering the beaches on my days off, I liked the thought that some day I'd be going on one of those vessels. The idea buoyed me when I got into difficulties with our Scotch matron for leading an insurrection against the food, and again when I was nearly fired for even arguing with a doctor. Heresy! It was out of hearing of the patient, naturally. I was right too, and that was why I was not dismissed.

I graduated and learned a bit about my country and its

deserts and out-backers, the never-never-land, the hot north, black trackers, 50,000-acre sheep ranches and the mines. The faraway job, the one that went begging, that was the one for me. I nursed through epidemics in the cities, and once by the lonely Murrumbidgee River I nursed a settler's wife who had borne her baby all alone with no one to help her but a five-year-old daughter. Nursing her made it worthwhile to have become an A. T. N. A. (Australian for R. N.), and to have doubled my knowledge since the great day when I graduated and thought I knew everything.

Finally, with a little money saved, I sailed away too on one of the ships. It was hard to make the break, to stand by the rail and see the water widening between me and my friends, my mother and father and my eleven brothers and sisters. Now both my mother and father are dead, and that day was the last glimpse of them I ever had. They knew how it was, and used to write me so, for such breaks had happened to them when they were young. The day of leaving, nevertheless, was rather sad than grand. I remembered Stevenson's lines:

"And all that I could think of, in the darkness and the cold,
Was just that I was leaving home and my folks were growing old."

It was later that the grand times came.

In France I got a job in the American Hospital of Paris. Prohibition was on in the States, and many of the hospital patients were American alcoholics who had fled the drought and done too good a job of it. For weeks my work was walking about with one of them and trying to steer him safely past barrooms. He said it was very kind of me to get him ready so quickly for his next bout. He was a lost soul, pathetic and wise and brave and humorous and tolerant, like so many lost souls.

Then I was assigned to Mrs. Solomon. Though I wasn't with her long, it was she who sent me north. If it hadn't been she, it would have been some one else; if it hadn't been Labrador, it might have been Finland. But, for some strange reason, I look upon Mrs. Solomon as a milestone in my life.

Her swarthy little face looked out at me from a nest of crepe-de-chine sheets and silken pillows. Mrs. Solomon had a suite of three vast rooms and her own chef at the American Hospital of Paris. There were silk shades on the lamps and at the windows, priceless paintings on the wall, carpets like sponges. A statuette, severe, by Rodin, stood in a softly illuminated niche. One of her staff was carrying out the evening pint of champagne, from which she had sipped a teaspoonful. There was a tray mushroomed with gold covers, gold the color of grain fields in Australia, but different.

"What is your name?" the woman asked.

"Kate Austen," I answered.

"You are an experienced nurse, my dear?"

"Yes," I said, "but I have never experienced anything like this."

It must have been the crepe-de-chine sheets or the gold.

Her staff shuddered, and the woman herself half closed her eyes as though to ward off another of life's unbearable blows. When the blue lids rolled back, her eyes gleamed at me. "You will do," she said.

Perhaps it was a whim.

Mrs. Solomon had three nurses working eight-hour shifts. Mrs. Solomon's husband never came to see her, though three specialists paid daily visits, and she received them clad in negligée of swansdown, à la Mme. Récamier. In her sitting room there was a mahogany case with glass doors which enclosed a few dozen books. On one of my first nights with her I pulled out a copy of *Tristram Shandy*. "Pretty good story, isn't it?" I said to her.

The familiar expression of horror came over her face. "They are all priceless first editions," she said. "You must put it back immediately."

Poor Mrs. Solomon had had three operations in the preceding two years, although there was nothing the matter with her except that most terrible of all things, neurosis. If only her husband had been a poverty-stricken invalid, and she had had to scrub floors to keep ten children fed, she would have been so much happier and lived so much longer.

I was the night nurse. Occasionally, in the evening for sociability, I drank a glass of champagne with her. Sometimes I read to her, and sitting there in the hush of that magnificent bedroom I thought I should feel like the serving woman of a queen. But I couldn't quite manage it; she was so pitiful, so at war with herself. At bedtime I changed the crepe-de-chine sheets and the silk pillowcase to fresh linen, since she did not like the silk at night. "Ah, roughing it; there's nothing like being hardy," I used to want to say, but never did.

Then, having turned the lights down dim, I massaged her feet with sweet oil while she tried to compose herself for sleep. "Have you ever massaged feet?" she had asked me the first evening, and I claimed I was an old hand at the business. "My feet are very beautiful," she said. "A famous painter once painted my feet."

I gently massaged them with the Syrian sweet oil and wondered if the painter was distantly related to those priceless specialists of hers; and I thought about the teeming slums of Sydney. It rested me somehow. She said I was the best masseuse she had ever known.

Gently, gently, at last I stopped the foot massage and stole from her bedroom. For a while I read my book in the adjoining sitting room. Then I composed myself upon the chaiselongue and slept like a top till morning, as did Mrs. Solomon. Never once in my time with her did the electric bell that connected her hand with my ear disturb our slumbers.

Daytimes I saw Paris, the Louvre, the Cluny Museum, Versailles, Notre Dame, the Madeleine, the Quarter, the Seine, the Rue de la Paix, the Bon Marché, and all the rest of it.

One evening after a particularly happy afternoon of wanderings, I said to Mrs. Solomon when I came on duty, "Oh, Mrs. Solomon, this afternoon I walked in the Luxembourg Gardens and it was so jolly. Wouldn't Doctor Pincette let you—couldn't you go for a stroll with me there some sunny day?"

She closed her eyes and spat, "Dirty little children playing in the paths! I *hate* the Luxembourg Gardens!"

For a while I thought that sleeping all night with pay and sightseeing by day was the softest thing I'd ever struck. But it was too soft. I'd had too good a training to waste it on Mrs. S. I expect I'd seen too many soldiers home from the war with something really the matter with them, too many Australian boundary riders with broken legs, too many hard-pressed mothers with their broods, to put up indefinitely with La Solomon. Some evenings at the massaging session I began to experience a desire to bite one of those white toes. Alone at last in the adjoining sitting room I kicked over the wastebasket and tore a magazine in half. But it didn't seem very constructive, somehow.

One morning when I came off duty I met in the corridor a lovely American nurse, a great friend of mine named Billy Smith. I happened to have in my hand Mrs. Solomon's gold-water glass which also had a gold cover. "Well, how does it go, gilding the lily?" asked Billy.

"I'm sick of it," I said.

She pulled a cablegram out of her pocket. "You know, I was in Labrador once, nursing for a fisherman's mission. They want a nurse to sign up for two years in their northern district. I can't make it. But would you like to go?"

"Is it *real* there?" I asked.

"The realest place you ever saw."

"All right," I said, "I'll go. You've got to tell me where it is, though, and how to get there."

While I was arranging passports and buying big heavy-soled boots and French winter clothing, most of which I later found quite unsuitable for Labrador life, I sent a letter home telling of my new plan. Pretty soon a cablegram came from my brother, saying, "Aren't you far enough away in Paris? Are we bothering you any?"

CHAPTER II

THE NORTHERNNESS began aboard the mail steamer plowing the coast of Newfoundland. I was so happy. What is the use of supposing that we are rational beings whose aim is comfort? Everything was friendly and chummy, and everybody was interested in everybody else aboard the crowded little steamer. The skipper in his cowhide seaboots and great ulster, walking to and fro on the bridge, said to me, "Wait'll you get to Indian Harbor. You'll be sorry. Oh a wild place, an island, never a tree, nothing but rock." I knew then that I should like it.

We had been crowded when we left St. John's with mission workers, Hudson's Bay men, fur traders, priests, a Northwest Mounted policeman and fishing families. But at every Newfoundland outport where we called, more fishing families bound for the summer codfishing grounds of Labrador came aboard with their barrels and boxes and babies; sometimes even their motorboats were hoisted to the boat deck. We were now so crowded there were three sittings at meals, and people were sleeping in boats, on the floors and even on tables in the dining saloon.

The chief steward was a jolly little fellow about five feet high. "Sure this is nothin'," he said. "You should have been with us last fall on the crossing to Nova Scotia when the sea stove in the mailroom door on the main deck. 'Tis two inches of oak bound with steel, and there was hardly enough left to make a toothpick out of. We only come up for air about twice the whole way over. This spring in the Gulf we got froze in the ice and was there five weeks. It was a mile walk to the shore and there wasn't even a house when you got there. We wore out five decks of cards, one a week. Oh my, what a life!"

"Pretty soft I call it," I said.

"That's right, have an orange," he said, and popped one out of the pantry like a magician. "There's always a mugup for anybody that wants, before bedtime, so don't go hungry on us."

One passenger who didn't deplete the commissary much was Rose Crunch, a twenty-three-year-old fisherman's wife with a new baby. I took a fancy to her, on account of the baby, and because she was so seasick. My mother used to say to me, "You're never really happy unless somebody's dying."

Rose was a Newfoundlander with blue eyes and black lashes and a bit of Irish in her, way back. The baby was only three weeks old, and Rose was so sick she couldn't stand. Consequently I moved into a bunk close by and took care of the two of them.

"A little boat don't bother me none," said Rose, "and many's the day I've jigged cod offshore. But this! Oh, hand me the basin."

The baby wasn't seasick at all; in fact, I've never seen an infant who was. To me it seemed strangely appealing that the father had never set eyes on this bonzer little boy. A month ago Rose's man had gone north to Whaling Cove on the Labrador to build up a summer fishing shack for his family. And now Rose was going to join him with the new prize package. I could imagine how he'd feel, seeing his son for the first time. "Won't he be pleased, Rose," I said, "to have you all together again?"

"I s'pose," Rose answered noncommittally.

Cape Bald, the Land's End of Newfoundland, was gray and stony as we headed across the Straits of Belle Isle. Out there lay even greater desolation. Way off across the huge mouth of the St. Lawrence we could see a dim line that was the southern coast of Labrador. Midway stood the little dot of Belle Isle with its lighthouse and the foghorn that helps transatlantic ships pick up the river. The gulf was strewn with ice, dirty chunks of broken bergs that the fishermen call "growlers." They were not so handsome as the huge glittering mass of whole bergs, but they were just as dangerous to a ship, for some of the pieces were thirty yards long. Small boats bound north hate this stretch because of the frequent fog. And then, too, the variable river current, tide current and wind set up such a side-drift that compass courses and dead-reckoning mean almost nothing.

The wind's song in the rigging began to keen like minor violins. And then, as though it had been waiting for us, the fog came down in gray wisps of tattered ghosts, moving fast. The dark water hissed, and the ship's long pitching quickened and intensified. It was evening, the light fading, the fog thickening, wind rising. The Labrador had disappeared. On the barren island we saw the lighthouse gleam, and then fog erased it. It was as though this gulf were not made for human knowledge, as though all the forces of destruction lived here. The old legends of terror and death that go back to prehistoric times had their beginnings in such places as the Straits of Belle Isle on stormy nights.

The passengers left the soaked decks. Portholes were bolted

shut. The bos'n poked about the winches, lashing things fast, examining the hatch covers, tapping here and there a wedge that held the battens down. The fishermen who were aboard seemed reluctant to go below. In their wet jerseys, with drops of water clinging to the wool, they gathered on the lee side under the bridge overhang, staring into the gloom. Through the flying fog were long clear lanes like the courses of Valkyries cutting the sinister dusk. "What makes them, Sam?" I asked a seaman as he brushed past.

" 'Tis ice, Miss. The growlers part the fog and leaves a path to le'ward." He hurried aft where they were checking the rudder cables and the emergency steering wheel on the poop. Rose Crunch came on deck, had one look and fled with a whispered "Ach! Horrors!" Then darkness settled in with a vengeance and blotted out the fog paths that had marked the ice. The ship's foghorn began its unearthly moan, and far away Belle Isle answered.

We were due to go in to Belle Isle, to an open roadstead there with mail for some fishermen and the lighthouse. But I heard the steward say at supper we were giving that up because of the weather and running straight across for Battle Harbor. The word *harbor* just then had all its true connotations of security and snugness, with a mental picture of a ship anchored quiet in a landlocked basin.

When the meal was over I went out on deck again, because it was so black and wild and scary. The foredeck was wet with heavy spray as I crossed it and went up the reeling ladder to the fo'c'sle head. Up there, climbing high in the air and then diving, I felt as though the wind would tear the skin off me. I hung onto a winch and saw in front of me the dark forms of seven men on lookout. Three were searching the darkness off the starboard bow, and three more gripped the port rail, lurching as she rolled. In the very prow was a skinny old man whom everybody called Uncle. I had seen him in the daytime, a regular ancient mariner with bony hands and hollow cheeks and a thin nose whittled by the wind. He was bent forward now, his clothes pressed back against him like the figurehead of a ship. They were all concentrating on the darkness, not speaking.

Uncle, I learned later, could smell ice; he was good at it as a result of many years on schooners threading ice fields in the night.

The wind screamed, and below us, knifing the waves, the forefoot seethed. I hung on there awhile, then went to my cabin to dry out and see to Rose.

Two hours passed. We could not find Battle Harbor in the fog and darkness. We could not anchor because the river current or the wind might drift a berg down on us and snap our chain or crush us. We steamed in slow circles somewhere in the gulf, going just fast enough to keep steerageway on the ship. Seven men continued on lookout, sometimes more. At two o'clock the stopping of the engines woke us all with a start. The ship began to tremble and then shudder violently. That was the screw churning full astern. Throwing a coat around me and running on deck, I saw dead ahead a big berg towering so high over the ship its top was lost in fog. We could see and hear waves breaking against its base. As the ship backed away, we smelled the ice easily, a cold clamminess like the dank breath of some monstrous cave, like the shuddersome chill of a tomb. We owed it to some fisherman's nose, Uncle's probably, that we weren't taking to the boats that very minute, with the bow crumpled in and the forehold full of water. Rose came panting out and stood near, fully dressed, the baby on one arm and a cork life jacket dangling over the other. "Ice, eh?" she said, looking at it. "Oh, the Devil is loose this night. Come, we'll go in and wait for the next one."

But there wasn't any next one. In the morning we steamed into Battle Harbor with the rocky islands lying clear and cold along the sharp horizon, and a lighthouse shining white in the sun. The growlers that dotted the Straits winked prettily. I could see what Billy Smith had meant when she said that Labrador was a real place.

Blue and silver days we had, devouring huge spaces of ocean and islands while a head wind buffeted the ship, making her vibrate as though she were a sailing fiddle. I leaned on the rail and talked with a Hudson's Bay Company factor, who, after a year's leave at home in the Orkney Islands, was returning for another five years' term at the Ponds Inlet post in Baffin Land.

"I've been at Indian Harbor and up the bay at North West River, where you'll be this winter," he said. "I was factor there once for a year. How long are you signed up for?"

"Two years."

"Two years. You will be lonely. What will you do for love in all that time?"

"Love?"

"Well, whatever you call it."

"I hadn't thought of that somehow."

"The Eskimos have better sense," said Mr. Harlan. "They don't pretend they're gods. They know a man can't exist happily or normally without a woman, and they know that woman's greatest happiness is satisfying man, because that's the way she's built. They make their lives happier. You make your life more miserable."

"I suppose, then, the Eskimo girls help you pass the time."

"There have always been half-breed children round the posts," he said, "and they're smart and everybody likes them."

"All the same," I said, "I'm glad they don't belong to me."

"No Eskimo's life is blighted so sadly as yours," he answered.

He spent less time talking to me as the voyage went on, and more drinking and playing poker in the smoking room with a priest. I expect he thought me a prig, and on my part I thought he was wise in a way, but so hard I'd pity a woman who was under his thumb.

I spent hours standing by the after side of the bridge out of the way, watching the shores change and the world and my life. Rock and grass, unending surf, cliffs, headlands, long ledges, caves, the sharp horizon seaward, a point of sail, the glint of ice; it was more like a story than real life. The wind was generally cold there, but I had some windproof clothes I'd bought in New York, and a new green felt hat that stuck on like glue and shed water duck-fashion. I was attached to that hat, and it seemed to return the compliment.

A quartermaster stood at the wheel, watching the compass, watching the bow rise and fall, twisting a spoke now and then. There was no rubber mat for him to stand on, no glass and mahogany wheelhouse round him, no metal mike, no dials nor any of the sanctuary atmosphere of a liner's bridge. There was only the compass and the wheel for him, and for the bridge officer, who paced to and fro, to and fro, the speaking tube and a brass engine-room telegraph. In front of them, chest-high, flapped the canvas wind screen, over them lay the sky. Often the wheelsman wore mittens for his two-hour trick, and at regular intervals both he and the captain stamped their boots to warm their feet.

And about then we were off a harbor where things began to happen. Below on the foredeck the bos'n was opening up the hatch. Round the tip of a point we could see a schooner dipping at her mooring, the mains'l half up to dry. Here and there along the lonely heathery shore among the rocks at the water's edge a fishing shack of whitened poles appeared, and a boat and a ladderlike rig for hauling her up out of reach of the tide. The captain went out on the bridge wing with his glass and peered ahead, then looked astern. "Port, PORT!" he called.

"Port," repeated the steersman, "port," and spun the spokes while the ship swung in a wide arc.

The skipper looked ahead to rock cairns on the hills, and astern for a bearing on the notch in the crest of an island, and all the while the ship swung till she was headed straight for a high rock headland. "Steady!" he called.

"Steady, sir," and the quartermaster spun the spokes back to hold her straight for the cliff.

Two rock piles on an eastern hill came into line.

"Starboard a little."

"Starboard a little."

"Steady."

"Steady it is."

The captain rang for half speed, and the bow sank. "Starboard."

"Starboard."

"Steady."

"Steady."

So we threaded our way through invisible reefs keeping close to deep water under the shadow of the cliff. We did this sort of thing not in one, but in scores upon scores of harbors, often at night or in fog or rain, and once in a snow flurry. When we rounded the point we did not know whether we'd see a little rock basin like a soup bowl, or a broad bay forty miles long, or a narrow run behind hundreds of rocky islands all snarled together and white-edged with breakers. Some of these places had names like *Run-by-guess*, *Come-by-Chance*, and *Nameless Cove*. If it was a port, the trap boats and dories would be coming off from all directions, rowing, sailing, chugging, sculling, till they sometimes lay round the steamer three deep.

CHAPTER III

LABRADOR FISHING stations have no wharves, so the steamer anchors off and sends the mail ashore in a small boat. Passengers could go along if they wished, but not many cared about it except me. At Wolf Cove our chain rattled down in the outer harbor at one o'clock in the morning. The blast of our whistle was snatched away so quick into the smoking blackness that it had a staccato quality instead of its usual moan. I crept out of the stateroom quietly so as not to wake Rose, and down the narrow lighted corridor, bumping into white enamel cabin doors both sides, the ship was plunging so. I did not know whether I should go this night, for it was truly wild, and I might be a nuisance in a desperate time. The lifeboat was lowered to the level of the main deck, the men aboard it. I paused in the shadow of the heavy oak door, wondering.

"Well, shove off," I heard the mate say.

"Where's the woman in the green hat?" said Sam, as though that explained everything.

So I climbed into the stern, the blocks creaked and we sat down soft as a feather on top of a sea—to sink immediately six feet below the steamer's red-lead water line. They had their oars out to fend off as we rose, or we would have been smashed. The heavy davit blocks, now hanging free, were swinging crazily with force enough to kill a man if they should hit him. But we were clear in thirty seconds or less. Blowing

16

straight into the harbor entrance, the wind kicked up waves as high here as in the open ocean. The following seas made us yaw a little in spite of anything the oarsmen could do, and one wave did break aboard, right over my back. I set to bailing, glad to have something to do that would help keep me warm. The shore was inky and roaring with breakers, but the men pulled for it, sure of their bearings, with a certainty that was as miraculous as the way that staunch double-ended boat cocked up her stern and rode the combers. We rounded a rock point and saw a light. Inside the point there was shelter as we drew in to the fish stage where a man in oilskins stood with a lantern. This was the post office. He had a beard that blew in the wind. His red hands were shining with wet. Behind him, above the gray roof of his fishing shack, loomed a black hillside across whose top the wind screamed. The principal impression was one of smell: cod oil, salt cod, cod heads, sea, a dash of wood smoke. Sea was the foe this night, and fire the friend.

Rising and falling beside the slimy piles, we handed up our mailbag, and he handed down his. By the weight of them I should judge there weren't ten letters in either.

"Any news up south?" he asked.

"Nothing much."

"Seen the *Sarah L. Hallett* from White Bay?"

"She got a clipper bow and a sawed-off jib-boom?"

"Yes."

"She was in Battle Harbor. She'll be along."

"I s'pose."

"Dirty night, ain't it?"

"Wonnerful."

"So long, b'y."

"So long."

That was all. While the boat crept off over the swells, he stood there in the cold and wet with his lantern raised, lighting us a little way. I would never know him, never see this place by daylight. For that very reason, the strange smells, the fish stage and the little pool of light, the sound of wind tearing through the grass high overhead were to me pure adventure. We had met and now we parted, each to fight the elements once more. It made me think of Conrad's *Youth* and the young ship's officer who woke in a lifeboat and saw strange Asiatic faces above him on the dock. I felt that this night I had touched the strangeness of a strange coast too, and been alive as one so seldom is. Danger, physical action, struggle, adventure, are nothing in themselves perhaps, but sometimes they open one's senses to the essence they distill. In danger I lose my stale self and find a new one. I give myself a good big pinch and say, *Here's to me and the rain and the ocean.*

The wind was dead ahead now, and as much as we could buck. My conscience hurt me at the thought of their pulling my added weight, but when I mentioned it, big Hurley, who pulled stroke oar, said, "This boat weighs nine hundred million tons and you don't make no difference."

Sam, the little seaman with the big chest, laughed and spat tobacco juice over the side. Then he spat spit into his hands and began to row again. We could see the steamer's lights, but we appeared to crawl no closer upwind to her. Our bow reared up toward the low clouds, as though the men were trying to lift this heavy boat to the sky; then shivered down with a crash that stopped us dead. The four oars dug and bent again. Even on the backstroke the great nine-foot oars vibrated in the wind. "Wind's comin' up," grumbled Hurley, wiping some spray out of his eye without missing a stroke. "Look's if it might come on to blow." Then they settled themselves on the thwarts and pulled some more. They rowed the same stroke when bucking a blow as when it was calm, a strong, unhurried pull with the fisherman's tug at the end. They rowed as you seldom see men row any more, and whether it took them five minutes or an hour and a half to row off to the steamer, you could see no difference in their attitudes, their faces, their stroke. They rowed, and sometimes the wind shoved them back, sometimes it flawed so they could punch ahead. They rowed just the same, no fuss and fury, no fireworks, just rowing, deep into the dark trough, up over the crest, their feet braced, shoulders back, and always at the end of the stroke that quick snap that drove the boat.

For once the wind was more than our four oars could buck. We were still abreast of surf that whitened the darkness. "Take it easy," said Hurley. "Just hold 'er."

As though the ship could see and sense our powerlessness, we heard her anchor winch take hold, and the slow grind of chain. Her tossing masthead light rolled farther into the harbor so we could drift downwind to her again.

"Is there water enough for her in there?" I asked Hurley who sat facing me.

"Yes, miss, water enough if ye know where it's to. The Old Man don't like to go in here in the dark, but 'ee kin if 'ee has to."

We whisked down to the steamer's side like a galloping horse, and even as they hoisted us aboard, the vessel was turning for the sea again, shivering in the wind, knifing the waves, hunched down close and throbbing into the blow as though she loved it.

I sneaked past the white enamel stateroom doors again and into my bunk. Rose pushed her emaciated face out between the curtains. She was getting so thin her eyes looked big. "My Uncle Small was drowned a night like this," she said. Then she put her head flat down again and began to gag.

I pulled the warm dry blankets around my neck and thought that being snug and comfortable so far off shore on a night like this was almost wicked. The ship creaked sharply in a way she had when the seas were steep. Poor Sam would be up there on lookout now, a two-hour turn at the forepeak with the rain and scud in his face.

The steamer was an hour in Fishing Cove, a beautiful harbor with high rocks and grass fields way back at the edge of the sky. I had time to go ashore and have a cup of tea with Mollie O'Shea who was nurse at the small mission hospital there. It was a white cottage perched on the bare rocks so close to the water that spray soaked the porch in a storm; it did well enough, however, as a summer emergency station for fishermen, and bad cases were shipped south to Battle Harbor or St. Anthony. Mollie was a black-haired little girl with a rich brogue. She weighed about ninety-eight pounds, I'd say, and could probably have licked her weight in wildcats.

"How have you been making out?" I asked.

"Ah, good enough," she said, "except forr the teeth."

"Teeth?"

"Yes, let me tell you, it was no joke."

This is the story she told:

No sooner I'd settled meself here a coople o' days than along coomes a fisherman with the toothache. And he wants his tooth puled out. A great stroppin' creature he was, with but one idea in his head and that mighty persistent.

"Maybe 'twill cure itself," I ventures to suggest.

"Ach," says he, "niver a chance. Forr a full week's time it's been murderin' me. Me vessel's come sixty miles off 'er course forr the sake of me tooth, and here I stay till ye pule it, me lass." He claps his hand over his achin' jaw and grins at me with the pure malice. A horrrid-lookin' mon like a lopsided walrus.

"My friend," says I, "I niver puled a tooth in my life."

"Well," says he, "time ye began."

I saw I was in forr it, and the thought made me heart coome up into me mouth. "Sit right there, me lad," says I, and I wint out in the next room and sat in a chair meself.

I took him in a glass of water, and then wint out and had a glass of water meself. There was a fierrce-lookin' pair of forceps, so I sterilized 'em and took 'em in me hond. I got me arm around his chin and started wurrkin' at the tooth. He yelled and I yelled, too. I gave a healthy tug an' out she coome. He fainted in the chair, and I fainted dead away on the floor meself.

CHAPTER IV

A JAGGED ISLAND of black rocks lying in the ocean—that was Indian Harbor, the place where I was to be stationed for the summer. Across the black was a band of green slope, topped with more black rocks and blue sky. No buildings were visible from seaward. We rounded the point and dropped anchor off a harbor sheltered by this island and another high one to the north. A few schooners, ice, some boats coming off, dotted the water. It was the first day of July.

The mission motorboat came alongside to load freight, tons of it, six heavy drums of gasoline, and me. Everybody knew Doctor Paddon, the silver-haired Englishman who was chief here. Twenty years he had been working for the mission, and as he hurried about the deck in his sou'wester and worn canvas coat, he seemed to have a smile for all his friends.

On the way in I met his crew: Jack Watts, a capable Newfoundlander in his twenties, who sat in the bow with the bills of lading, checking freight; Joe Kullinuk, an Eskimo who had been with the mission ever since he was orphaned in the 1918 flu epidemic; Graham Blake, a young Labradorman, expert hand with motors, who spoke in an extremely cultivated way as a result of four years' schooling in the States.

"You see the Indian Head, Miss Austen, which gives the place its name," said Doctor Paddon.

On the crest of the island was a perfect Indian profile gazing upward to the sky. "The forehead is our lookout. From there we can sometimes spot the steamer thirty miles away."

Way down below it was the hospital, flat-roofed, its clap-boards the gray of storm-scoured whitewash. Around it were buildings known as the Mission Room, Laundry, Doctor's Cottage. A long boardwalk led up from the shore. The place was quite an establishment, complete even to graveyard.

The landing stage was sagging, battered by the spring ice. Just off it lay the anchored ketch *Yale* in which they had ar-rived from the winter station this very morning. "We were five days coming down the bay from North West River," said Doctor Paddon, "on account of head winds and ice. It's 200 miles, you know, the bay is. We were taking the shutters off the hospital when *Kyle* blew."

He nosed the boat in toward some sloping shore ledges where the water lapped clear and green. The landing stage was unusable, so Jack took charge of unloading the heavy freight onto the rocks by means of log skids, crowbars, par-buckle hitches and other methods that were miracles to me, while Doctor and I went up the long boardwalk to the hos-pital. "Thirty years ago," he said, "Sir Wilfred Grenfell, who founded this mission, built the part that is now staff quarters and kitchen. I designed and built the present two-story hospital wing on this side."

We went into the hospital part which was cold as a morgue from its winter vacancy, and half dark with most of the shut-ters still on. I noticed water pipes, oil lamps, *a bathroom*, linoleum on the corridor floor, woodstoves, porches on the back or south side with netting in ribbons from the winter snowdrifts.

"Mosquitoes are bad here sometimes," he said.

The ground floor consisted of dispensary, doctor's office, a bath and a ten-bed men's ward. Mattresses were piled in a huge mound on one bed, covered with canvas. The roof had been leaking. Upstairs was a ten-bed women's ward, operating room with skylight, a couple of single rooms, another bath, an oilstove, kerosene sterilizer. There was a fine view of the harbor and the sea from the windows. Patches of snow still clung to the hollows of rock outside. Several miles to the north across the harbor on a hilltop was a tall mast with a little shack at its base.

"That's the Smokey wireless station. Admiral Peary, coming south, sent out from there the first news of his North Pole discovery."

What a day we put in! The men were stowing freight, carrying some of it up the long boardwalk on hand barrows. They took the shutters off and patched the roof. Doctor and Jack worked all day on the pipe line which came down from a rock reservoir up near the back of the Indian's neck. Though the pipes had been disconnected and drained, water had seeped into some, frozen and split the iron.

I had expected to find a primitive shack here, and had brought soap and towels in case there shouldn't be any; also many pounds of sweet chocolate for an emergency ration. The size of the place consequently staggered me. There were mountains of sheets and towels. In the storehouse were four cases of soap, ten barrels of flour, boxes, crates, food enough to feed an army. In another few weeks more staff, I learned, would arrive. The place was open for only two and a half months per year, but I could see that it hummed in the short summer. Soon more Newfoundland fishing schooners would arrive. As many as 150 were known to have anchored in the harbor at once.

I put the linen outside to air in the bright wind. I scrubbed and swept and dusted. Graham checked the long stovepipes for me so we could get a fire going in the men's ward. The mattresses had to be distributed, and medical supplies unpacked. Joe chugged out of the harbor to catch some codfish for dinner while I went to the staff part of the building and descended on the kitchen. Hunters had made themselves at home there in the spring before the ice went out. "They come down here from the mainland in April to trap white foxes," Graham told me.

Anyway, they had left the kitchen pretty dirty, and the stove crammed full of ashes. But we got it dug out after a while and the soot cleaned out of the stovepipes. Joe appeared with a string of cod, all cleaned. "Sure, Miss, I catch 'em that way," he said. He was always laughing. I rolled them in cornmeal and fried them. It was a good smell, making the place seem alive again, and as the kitchen warmed up we all began to feel more cheerful. It was winter in Australia now, but summer here was colder than winter there. Jack and Doctor were about frozen from working on the wet pipes, but Jack was hopeful. "By tomorrow, with luck," he said, "we'll flood the kitchen." He pointed to a crack in a pipe that ran across the ceiling.

Joe helped me scrub the operating room, and then left to get up a pile of stove wood with bucksaw and axe. I'd never had anything to do with oilstoves before, but we must get the sterilizer going, so I had a whack at it. It was rusty and carboned and gummy with grease, and of course wouldn't light. I started taking parts off it and cleaning them, but when I finally got them together again, it still wouldn't go. Graham came and showed me how to drain out the main feed pipe, which was full of rust.

Quantities of the hospital's rubber and thin-glass equipment had been taken to North West River for the winter to save the rubber from perishing and the glass from cracking here in the cold. All those tubes and beakers and funnels and vials had to be unpacked and washed, the dispensary set to rights, blankets aired, the beds set up. It was evening by the time I got around to checking up on the stock of dressings, making more and sterilizing them to be sure of a minimum supply, at least. I went over the instrument cases, sterilized everything, made ready the injection and other trays, and finally took it into my head to prepare some saline solution and the apparatus that goes with it. It's quite a lengthy job to make up saline solution for intravenous injection, but you never know when a hemorrhage will arrive on the scene and need it quick.

At bedtime, too tired to tackle another job, we sat around the stove a few minutes and had a mugup of tea and ship's biscuit. "They swell when they get wet, these biscuits do," Jack told me. "Once I was out in a motorboat a long ways from anywhere, and we stove her on a reef. We shoved a bag of this hardbread into the hole and it swelled up tight as a bottle."

"It's been a big day," said the doctor, leaning back in his chair. "But the biggest opening day we ever had, we arrived late in the evening, properly soaked and thoroughly numbed, and no sooner had we come up from the wharf than a boy with acute appendicitis was brought in. We hadn't even lit the stove. We got ready as best we could, and Mina—that's my wife—held the lamp. The Lord must have been on our side, for the job went so well the boy was fishing again in two weeks."

As I looked at the four men, it struck me we were quite a conglomeration. Doctor Paddon had back of him a traditional English classical education, with medical training at London's famous St. Thomases, relatives who lived on estates, and now for many years his job had made him sailor, dog driver, hunter, surgeon, builder and Heaven knows whatnot.

Jack Watts had already been a sailor, fisherman and sealer. He'd been radio operator at several of the lonely Labrador stations, including Smokey, could build a house or a boat, lay cement foundations, and thought nothing of running-in a new main bearing for a motor or repairing a Delco generator. Having spent his life in and out of the sea, he couldn't swim, of course, and in a land where the snow is more than half the time neck deep, he couldn't snowshoe either, but he blithely tackled such chores as knocking together a dog sledge, breaking a balky horse, salvaging a schooner or stepping up milk production on the mission's growing farm at North West River.

Joe was a pure-blooded Eskimo and owed his life to chance. Doctor had found him on an island, everybody else dead from the influenza scourge that decimated communities along this coast in 1918. Only six years old then, Joe had been living on seal fat and nothing else for a month. His sealskin boots were shrunk so hard and small they had to be snipped off with scissors. He'd grown so wild in his solitary state that he ran away and hid. It took them half a day to catch him. "If it hadn't been an island, you'd be loose yet," Jack said to him.

Graham had been such an outstanding student in the mission's schools that a well-to-do American had taken him out to the States for further education, as well as training in a machine shop. After four years as protégé of the American,

Graham got lonesome for his country—which nearly always happens—and returned, bringing among his other effects a Tuxedo and wing collar.

Englishman, Eskimo, Labradorman, Newfoundlander, and Australian, we were an assortment.

I went to bed, and the bed swayed in the whistling wind. Those were the rockingest quarters I ever lived in. Most every day all summer somebody crawled under our end of the building, had a look at the underpinnings and came out shaking his head.

Early next morning a motorboat arrived with a man, a woman and a child. They had come a long distance from over Cartwright way, and the woman was in bad shape. She had had a miscarriage, and nothing but a curettage of the uterus could stop the hemorrhage. We immediately got ready, and I was very pleased that sterilizer, stove, instruments and dressings were mostly shipshape. I had a last look around, hoping against hope that everything was right in this as-yet disorganized place, for it is the nurse's responsibility and not the doctor's to have equipment and supplies in perfect order.

"You are accustomed to giving anesthetics, Miss Austen?" the doctor asked.

"Yes," I said, getting out the ether. In Australia and warm countries ether is one of the simplest and most effective anesthetics, and I had given it hundreds of times.

"Hold on," said Doctor Paddon, seeing the ether. "Can't you give chloroform?"

"I am used to handling ether," I said.

"Then we'll have to get the room hotter."

I had never realized it before, but ether does not volatilize readily unless the temperature is well up. At zero, ether would have no effect whatever.

We removed the ether and set the oilstove going full blast. When the temperature was high, we started administering the ether and put the stove out because one must of course keep ether fumes away from open flames if the roof is to stay on.

The patient had bled so long, and was so bloodless that she collapsed on the table while we were operating. Now she was white as a sheet, her pulse weakening fast, and as the cooling room diminished the ether's efficiency, she commenced to stir feebly and moan. "Doctor, I'm afraid I can't keep her going much longer," I said.

"All right, I'm nearly finished," he said. "We must stop this bleeding if she is to have any chance whatever."

I did what I could and hoped we would not lose our first patient. In two minutes more he had finished the operation, stopped the hemorrhage, called Joe to take one end of the stretcher, and we were tucking her into a bed filled with hot water bags. The warmth revived her a trifle, but even so she was scarcely breathing.

"The shock has been more than she can stand," said Doctor Paddon. "She may not come round."

He listened worriedly to her heart. "I wish we had some saline for intravenous injection. I don't suppose you've had time to make up any?"

I was happy to produce the tray with everything complete.

"Good!" said he. "You're going to be useful here."

That started us off on the right foot, that and the fact that the woman began to gain from then on.

CHAPTER V

As soon as they knew the hospital was open, people came from all over. Hidden away in the jagged coast, in spite of its undiscovered look, were coves with hundreds of people. One of our visitors was a woman with three small children, set ashore by a motorboat which immediately steamed away and left them.

Here comes another patient, I said to myself as I hurried down the walk to help her with her big bundle. One of the children could walk, but the other two were in her arms. They were bedraggled-looking, and their yowls made the place resound as tears streaked their dirty faces. Their hair was long and oafish, and they were wet and thin. They looked utterly destitute.

"Can I help you? Here, let me take your bundle," I said. "Is some one sick?"

"Oh, no," Mrs. Peters beamed. "We ain't sick. Us just aims to stay awhile. We're on a cruise."

They were going on what was apparently an annual visit to Brother Evan's at Horse Harbor, and they had come from Ragged Islands. Three different fishermen, just happening to pass by, had brought them various stages of the journey.

"How will your brother know you're here?" I asked.

"Oh, we got it all arranged," she answered. "He said he'd

come soon as he heerd the hospital was open. He'll hear pretty soon, likely."

"Well, come on up and get warm anyway," I asked her. I was a bit nonplussed, though I didn't let on. I hadn't yet realized that the mission hospitals serve also as hotels, and that that is part of their purpose.

Right away I took to the children. For all their travel-worn grubbiness, they were cheery as larks once they got moderately warm and dry. The mother bustled around helping us set the hospital to rights as though she'd been there all her life. Between the two of us we finished rescreening the back porch. I told her she might as well take advantage of the hot water and tub while she was here to scrub the kids and get organized. She set right to it, washed them all till they glistened, and then went off to the laundry to wash all their clothes. To dress them meanwhile, I got out pink wrappers and sweaters and things from the clothing store, cut their hair, set them in cribs on the back porch in the sun, tied ribbons in their locks and fancied them up till they were the handsomest youngsters you could imagine. Their mother had a good hot bath too, and finally washed and dried and ironed every rag they owned.

In the three days before Brother Evan came, Mrs. Peters helped me cook and clean no end. "I believe I'll buy them pretties for the children," she said one day, indicating the finery in which her young were dressed. She opened up her bundle to disclose quantities of handwork she'd been manufacturing all winter: sweet-grass baskets, hooked rugs, knitted mittens, sealskin moccasins and beaded bags. The industrial worker was not here yet to value such products, but Mrs. Peters said she'd leave them and settle all that on the way home from Evan's. Pay for handicraft work was very good, whereas our clothing store material was cheap, so I knew she'd have a substantial balance coming to her.

She went away as unexpectedly as she had appeared. I got up early one morning and she was gone. That was the way here; people came and went, and the hospital was open house to any one travelling the coast or waiting for the steamer. Some of our useful work never appeared in the in- and out-patient casebooks. Sometimes there were five or six fishermen bunking in the mission room waiting for some boat or other. They always pitched in to help us while they stayed. I soon became accustomed to it and thought it the best system that ever was, but at first it seemed strange to be actually living in a land where any one is welcome anywhere at any time. In many hundreds of miles' travel you would be asked to spend the night in every house you passed. They mightn't have a whole blanket in the house, but you could have what they had.

It was foggy and a big lop was on from the recent blow when out of the fog, pitched high on the swells and tossed so her sail shook, came a little skiff with four people aboard. They were from Bluff Head, twelve miles in the bay, and how they found their way among the islands and reefs in that thick fog, and how they dared make six-mile crossings exposed to the open ocean in that eggshell, Jack said he couldn't figure. In the stern, steering, was an old lady with smooth, golden-bronze cheeks. She was Mrs. Oliver, and this was her fine Hamilton Inlet family, part English, part Eskimo. They lived at Bluff Head or thereabouts all the time. They were "livyeres," very different from the Newfoundland fishermen who went south in late summer. The Olivers were more like pioneers. This was their country, and they loved it and thrived on it. They hunted the rivers and the inland as well as the sea and the coast; they ate caribou with their seal meat, and trout as well as cod.

When all the Oliver children were little, Mrs. Oliver had been widowed. Somehow she managed. Now the children were grown to be a fine capable daughter and two black-haired hunter sons who were men. "Ma's still our pilot, though," said one of them. "When 'tis t'ick, or a breeze a wind, there's nobody like Ma."

The daughter, Sarah Jane, was our cook that summer at the hospital, and she was a wizard. Mrs. Oliver had her winter's output of craft work to sell, such as parkas trimmed with fur, baskets, mittens, hooked rugs, and nearly a dozen pairs of boots and moccasins. They were done with such exquisite bright color and perfect needlework that I bought two pairs of moccasins myself, unable to resist. The boys had a polar bear skin to sell and some carvings of walrus ivory. They had done fairly well with fur that winter they said. Apparently it was their habit to catch trout by the barrel instead of by the inch.

As soon as I grew used to Indian Harbor I saw that above everything else, above our doing and even our duties, it was the sea that counted here. It was more than any of us, and anyone who forgot the sea that lay around us and made our climate and our days and nights and moods was only half alive. Storming or sleeping or hiding itself in fog, it was always up to something new. At night when storms were on, it was fun in my new oilskins and boots to climb the black path to the Indian Head. Crawling over the crest and hearing the surf on the exposed shore was like getting the full-throated roar from ten thousand lions' dens. Flattened and torn by eighty- and ninety-mile winds that blew spray even this high, I sometimes smiled to myself as I lay on the wet rock with rain running off my nose. The ocean took itself so seriously, surely it was serious enough for both of us and I could just do my job and at other times be gay. Why should I fret or rage or smile or weep when it was being done on such a gigantic scale all around me? On my few hours off duty I would just live, just be.

Sunny quiet days I spent my off hours knowing and breathing the sea and being as impersonal as any wave. What if the bacon slicer was broken and the oilstove belching smoke. Dust thou art, oilstove, to dust returneth. A few more winters of rusting would settle that one's hash. Meanwhile from the forehead I watched great white icebergs sailing by across the ocean. They had silver pinnacles and purple caves and green iridescent ice beaches where the waves broke. Some were squat and smoothly sculptured, others Gothic, lacy, tall, and all of them glittered and changed color as they rolled on the long swell. All around the compass such wild space fell away from the smooth rocks of the forehead as would surely rest the tiredest heart that ever beat. And when the vastness was too much, there were caves for climbing down and sitting in, and clusters of bright wild flowers in hollows of gravel, fighting for life, pretty and strong and resilient. The far or south side of the island showed no sign of man whatever as I went down below the "rockline," through the green grass of the slope, through the wild peas and bake-apples to long rock ledges by the surf. In the miles of rock, some sharp, some smooth, some gray or red or black, there were special spots for swimming and for thinking and for sleeping. There was one gray ledge with a black dike of traprock running down its center where I often lay with my face close to the waves, watching them come and go, feeling their cold breath. And there, somehow I was renewed. It was nothing I did. It was the ocean's doing.

CHAPTER VI

MORE STAFF came on the next steamer. The housekeeper, Martha Gibbons, a grand red-haired woman from Philadelphia, had been here other summers and knew every one for miles around. She also handled the clothing store business. Martha worked in collaboration with Annie Baikie, a pretty Labrador girl who was Industrial Worker. Annie had been out to the States where she was trained in weaving, designing, sewing, carving and native arts. These skills, added to her natural ability and taste, as well as her intimate knowledge of local conditions, made her an ideal boss of handicraft activities in this region. She gave out materials, criticized and demonstrated techniques, made patterns and suggestions, and bought finished products from people who were all her friends and relatives and acquaintances. Over the course of years the mission had built up a large market for rugs, embroidery work, fur-trimmed slippers, etc., which enabled men and women here to earn some cash in their winter evenings. The two outdoor workers, or wops, who were to chop wood, run errands, stoke stoves, dig graves, man boats, were Bill from Princeton with leanings toward the ministry, and Hoppy from Yale with leanings toward laughter and girls. Even as they came ashore they were ragging Mabel, the Chicago Junior Leaguer slated for Doctor's secretary. "Two evening dresses! Ho, ho, she brought two evening gowns. Look at all the rocks!"

Doctor Paddon smoothed that over by assuring her that lots of strangers arrived here in the middle of summer with skis, snowshoes and ice skates, convinced they were going to have to live on raw seal blubber. "Maybe we'll find an occasion for the evening gowns. You never know," he said. "One of the southern mail steamers is the former yacht of a Russian Princess, and a British man-o'-war was here twelve years ago with lots of gold braid."

So evening gowns became the rallying cry.

The jolliest of them all was a young interne named Jeffrey James from New York, who had been here before as wop several times. "How's the water system behaving?" he wanted to know. It seemed that he personally had carried several tons of cement and sand up to our high rock reservoir when the dam was being built. Medically he was keen for experience, interested head over heels, marvellously trained, with a strong sense of responsibility. We got on famously and worked well together, which was fortunate, as Doctor was often to be away in that battered little ketch *Yale* on medical trips, and Indian Harbor hospital might soon be full to the brim. Even in that steamer came our first T. B.'s, beriberi children, septic hands and rotten teeth. There was also a sick sailor from the 7000-ton freighter now lying at Cartwright. She had a freezing plant and was loading Birdseye salmon for England.

We soon settled down. Martha began demonstrating for us her thousand and one ways of cooking codfish, fried cod, cod with fried salt pork, cod hash, codfish cakes, fish chowder, fish and brewis. On all this coast *fish* meant *cod*. It was a staple of life, almost more so than bread—for there have been times when fish were available and flour was not. Salmon were salmon, trout were trout, and similarly with pike, whitefish, caplin. But fish meant codfish. Now and then our codfish diet was varied with whale steak, seal livers or tongues, porpoise which tasted like a delicious combination of liver and beefsteak. Martha was adept at the mixing of Klim, the use of egg powder and the handling of food by the case and the barrel. Our tea came in hundred-pound chests and our beans in fifty-pound sacks. I had never seen a barrel of cocoa before, but it's quite a lot of cocoa. Now and then she called in the wops to wrestle a 250-pound sugar barrel for her. The island abounded in wild mushrooms, every variety of which Sir Wilfred had once upon a time had analyzed. They were all found safe and edible except one reddish variety which Martha knew all about, so we had mushroom sauce; also puffins, bake-apple berries, blanc-mange made of seaweed, and some wild greens known as alexander which had a flavor like wild parsnips and were supposed to be very good for us. The boys finally begged for mercy when the green mound of spinachy alexander appeared.

On the subject of food, Doctor told us one evening, "We had a splendid nurse one year, named Kimber, with whom we had a great deal of fun. In the spring she arrived here via *Kyle* before we came out from North West River. The afternoon we pulled in, she set about preparing a meal she'd been saving in our honor. Among other delicacies she had gulls' eggs, half of which blew up spontaneously during the meal, and the other half on being opened were found to contain full-fledged gulls with feathers, just ready to hatch."

There were now ten schooners anchored in the tickle, and more coming every day. A fourteen-year-old boy was brought in off one of them. His name was Albert Hutchins, but he called it Halbert 'Utchins, so that was what we called him too; a slim little tow-headed chap with blue eyes, pale as a ghost, a hand dripping blood, mashed in the anchor chain. The accident had bodily removed the tip of one finger and part of the joint, as well as lacerating, crushing and bruising the whole hand. Under a general anesthetic which I gave, Doctor with Jeffrey assisting took off the damaged joint in order to get a long enough flap to make the suture line come on the back of the finger. Jeffrey had never done an amputation as yet, though he had seen a great many. Doctor said he would let Jeffrey do the next one and be assistant himself.

Several fishermen came in with terrific teeth, which Doctor Paddon extracted. Jeffrey and I watched very closely to learn what we could, for he must soon leave us to face the tooth problem ourselves, a problem caused by unbalanced diet, poor food for the mother during pregnancy, dearth of milk in childhood.

Kyle arrived bound south while we were doing a T. B. peritonitis operation on a hopeless fisherman case, and subsequently seven new patients were treated. A Hudson's Bay Company motorboat arrived in the evening from Cartwright, thirty miles southwest, with a man who said his wife was dying in childbirth, so Jeffrey had to go, though it was very foggy and "t'ick." Doctor had too much work here to leave.

Two days later when Jeff popped ashore again in his oilskins and mittens, carrying his little black bag, we told him he looked almost like a real doctor. "By jimminy I am," he said, "and you have to be a pilot around here too." He was full of good spirits and full of his adventure. In his former summers as wop he had travelled around quite a bit as crew of *Yale,* so that when Coomb Williams headed the motorboat off due west, Jeff knew they were headed for Bluff Head in the bay and would fetch up at Rigolet instead of Cartwright. After considerable tactful expostulation, he got Williams to head off south-southwest. They brought George's Island abeam and knew they were on their course. The fog lifted, stars came out, and northern lights too. Jeff slept in the bow from two in the morning till seven, rolled up on a blanket and a tarpaulin. He found Mrs. Williams perfectly normal and the baby thriving.

"I did get a tooth, though. Fellow with a fearful jaw. If you don't believe me, here it is." He pulled it out of his pocket as proof. "Came from an oldish chap named Ned Broomfield. I walked to his place over a rough portage path that crosses the point to Nooks Cave. It was dusk yesterday and I was kind of uncertain about the trail when I started back. 'Too bad you haven't got a fish with you,' Broomfield said, 'to throw to Joe Senish's dogs if they should all go for you at once.'

"Luckily, they only came at me separately. When I got back to town, I scoured the place for more patients, but nobody else in Cartwright even felt faint. Ran into a funny scene this morning, though, before we left. Old man Siverak decided to try out his son's motorboat. He didn't know much about it, not even enough to turn on the water-cooling system. But he twisted the flywheel a bit and off she went. After making a couple of fine circles off the wharf, the engine began to get hot and he wanted to turn her off, but he didn't know how. He began to holler, and people came to the wharf. 'Pull out the wires,' they shouted. So he pulled off a stiff galvanized wire that was screwed to the side of the engine house for hanging rags on, and threw that overboard, but it didn't do any good. 'Stop 'er! Stop 'er!' all the town kids were shrieking, fit to be tied. The boat was chugging round and round, and people were going off in skiffs, trying to catch him. Old Siverak yanked out all the ignition wires next, and threw them overboard, but that was no good either, because the engine-head was red-hot and the thing pinged right along without any ignition. A skiff caught hold, but the man had to let go or capsize. All the time the town kids were yelling 'Stop 'er,' and the old man was getting wild. Finally some one jumped aboard him from a skiff, leaving the skiff behind, and turned off the gas-feed cock. There was still gas enough in the carburetor to run her awhile. The engine-house wall began to smoke from the heat, and they were so scared she'd explode they steered her alongside the empty skiff and tumbled into it as she went by. The boat stopped soon after, and the old man came ashore. He had a small burn on one hand which I fixed up for him. 'Never trust them engynes, b'y,' he told me. 'Never trust them engynes!' "

From Pax Harbor or somewhere south a little girl with a badly burned back came in with her mother. She was six years old, and in terrible shape, with so large an area raw that she stood only about a fifty-fifty chance with the best of care. The doctor of a passing ship had seen her and left with the family some iodine and alcohol, telling them to dress the burn once a day with that. Nothing could have been worse than such irritation. It was enough to kill her, and in fact it almost had. She was a nervous wreck from so much pain, and so young it was hard for her to understand why people were all the time hurting her. She was afraid of everybody, refused to be moved out of bed, and, once in a chair, refused to be taken back to bed again. She never let go her mother's hand, and she screamed when any one touched her. The walls were flimsy and the rooms all close together, as a result of which we always found the wards very much disturbed when a patient's treatment was so painful that he cried out. We heated the room very warm, the mother sat and held her child's hand, and while the little girl alternately moaned and sobbed and shrieked, we did the best we could. It was a wearing business, and Jeff grew very pale, as well he might.

To reduce shock we decided that we must henceforth dress that large area in small sections. We got the child back to bed, and I brought a doll from the clothing store and started making friends with her. Since these dressings were going to go on for a long time, we must try to get her to accept them somehow.

CHAPTER VII

UNDER DOCTOR PADDON's supervision Jeff had done his first operation on a finger, a terminal phalanx. Jeff did very well too, and soon overcame his initial nervousness. That very day Doctor had sailed away to answer the calls that kept coming from north. He was also going to pick up patients for an operative clinic that was to be held at Indian Harbor as soon as two visiting specialists arrived. We had packed the little ketch full of supplies, and cooked up enough beans and bread to last them a few days at least. We had filled a chest with dressings. She hoisted sail and leaned out of the tickle, leaving us to it.

Yale had only been gone an hour when one of the stout little Norwegian whale ships, of which there were six operating out of Hawkes Harbor some distance down the coast, rolled into the harbor and landed a mate with a broken leg. He was a grand old man named Mathison who had been on two- and three-year whaling expeditions in every ocean in the world. He had broken this same leg before in the Antarctic, and in the same way—just slipping on the greasy iron deck.

In the days that followed, Mathison was the only jolly one among us. The weather was bad, and the atmosphere depressing. The hospital was full, and many out-patients came each day besides. The wards throbbed with bare, unstoppable pain—one of those things there is no use talking about. In the white iron bed by the door lay old man Wade, and next to

him Halbert 'Utchins and beyond that the fellow with the
gone thumb and the dying T. B. and more; upstairs two
blind Eskimo women and burned Agatha and so on, for miles
it seemed. Jeff stepped around the wards briskly in a nice
fresh white coat doing a splendid job of cheering everybody,
talking boats and fish and sea things.

"Yes sir, 'tis a fact, the *Giant King* had a main boom seventy
feet long," the T. B. assured him as though it mattered.

But outside, the fog was flying and the surf was grumbling.
The eaves were dripping and the wind howled high and in-
consolably through the screens. The wind and the pain were
things you couldn't stop.

Jeff's cheerfulness was a front. It was morning and time to
do dressings. Little Agatha's raw back, Wade's wrist, the
thumb and the rest were waiting for him. It was cold outside,
and the wind was whistling, and the boardwalk gleamed in
the wet. And inside one by one the patients must shuffle to the
dispensary and suffer.

"Well, Doctor, here I be agin."

"Sit right there," Jeff said, "and we'll see what we can do
for you. Let's see now," and I guardedly handed him a probe.
"I'll try not to hurt you any more than I can help. How's
it looking this morning anyway?"

"Don't look too good, do she?"

"Well, it could be worse. Now hold fast for just a second."

The patient grabbed something with all his strength.

The color drained out of Jeff's face and he began to sweat.

I didn't mind so much. I was used to things like this. I
knew you must do what needs doing and get it over with.
But I knew what Jeff was up against and how he felt.

"Oh, Doctor," breathed the fisherman, "no more."

"Okay," said Jeff. "Rest on the bench there for a bit." And then in a firm voice, "Halbert next."

Halbert 'Utchins slid his slippers along the cracked linoleum, the oversize hospital bathrobe and pajamas trailing a few feet behind. He sat down in the chair and laid his hand on the white table with a gesture that said, *"Do what you like with the blasted thing."* It was just brave bravado.

As the bandages began to come off, an expression of horror unconsciously stole over the young interne's face. He made talk to make the minutes pass. Halbert's foot began to tap the floor. That was his way, tapping his foot, faster and faster.

"What do you do in winter, Halbert, down there in Newfoundland?" Jeff asked as he started dressing the crushed hand.

"I mend clocks."

"Clocks, eh? What kind?"

"All kinds. Big fellers, grandfather clocks, little 'uns, 'larm clocks, all kinds."

"Who taught you to mend clocks, for goodness sake?"

"Nobody. I took 'em abroad and seen all them little machines in their inwards. Bimeby I could do it good."

"Have you special tools to do it with?"

"Not many, not many. Not so many as you got here for people's inwards."

Faster and faster the foot tapped. Jeff was sweating again. On the bench the reprieved man had his eyes closed, trying, I suppose, not to think of anything.

When I was in training to be a nurse, accident cases were the worst. That bloodless feeling of the head, goose flesh, feeling the color go out of my face. How to stand it, other people's pain. How not to run away and hide and hide. One never feels any different. They used to have to take me outside to lie down. Old Doctor Lawrence, our House Surgeon, would look around the operating room and say, "Take that young nurse out." And I'd go out and somebody would ask me, "Do you feel all right?" and I'd say, "Yes, I only feel pale." Then I'd go back again.

One never feels any differently facing smashed legs and groans. It is forever unspeakable that men must suffer so. But you learn to control yourself, to work efficiently. You see great doctors calmly mending all this, while silly little pigtail nurses faint, and you see how criminally ineffectual sympathy is. I used to cry and want to cry. But what do tears do? I was so proud when first I began to conquer—not the feeling, but the unnerving goneness that makes you useless. Your cheeks go white just the same, but inside, not outside. Nobody can tell to look at you, nobody.

Jeff was getting a huge sudden dose. This was so different from making rounds in a tidy institution with the resident explaining. I knew what Jeff was up against when Halbert's talk of clocks ended in poor piteous cries. It had been a foregone conclusion the mangled hand would go septic.

Jeff was whiter, his lips blue. Laymen think we are callous. They do not know how much we have suffered to gain the power of keeping the pink in our cheeks when we are hurting a child.

It was done now, what we could do to Halbert's hand today.

"Doctor James, somebody wants to see you outside," I said.

He went into the dispensary and sat with his head in his hands. There was still that half-finished fisherman to do, and

Wade and the thumb and the back, beside three outpatients who wanted teeth pulled. As it turned out, more teeth arrived, so that that day Jeff pulled nine teeth, with me as head-holder. Two of those were so hollow and gone they broke. But we did the best we could.

The stormy days went by one after another. "Harbor days," the fishermen call them. Somehow, people don't get well on stormy days. And the dressings went on and the teeth. More in-patients with bad hands were admitted, and a very sick man with a high fever and a number of significant symptoms.

"Do you know what the man has?" said Jeff after a while.

"Yes," I said. "Do you?"

"No idea. But I'll try to figure it out if you think there's time."

"Yes, there's time," I said.

"Very well. Now watch the Visiting Quack from Vienna get busy and you'll see a miracle."

He worked away, eliminating this and that, suspecting and making tests for all sorts of rare and peculiar maladies. Finally he said, "What is it? I'll bet it's something simple. Medical students are always thinking measles is leprosy or calling a sprained ankle a marvellous illustration of elephantiasis."

"Probably in Massachusetts you've never seen a case of typhoid fever," I said.

"No, I never have. Great Heavens! Say, I'm the Visiting Quack all right."

"You've never seen typhoid before, that's all," I said. "I've seen lots of it in Australia."

The typhoid made me a great deal more work, for he was

very sick, and typhoid with its starvation diet and its dangers of complication is always a matter more of endless care than of doctoring. I had also to disinfect the typhoid's utensils and sheets, to use a special apron and rubber gloves for tending him, and to take every precaution for preventing the germ's spread in this crowded place.

Then, as though our responsibilities weren't worrying enough, came Ben, a young skipperman from Ailik, with blood poisoning. A month ago when the fish struck in, his crew had not yet come down from the head of their bay, so he and a boy of seventeen rowed thirty miles in a heavy twenty-five-foot boat against a head wind to get them. Ben had a big sculling oar over the stern, and the boy a pair of smaller oars amidships. They rowed for two days and a night, almost without a stop. Ben said the other chap fell asleep several times, "but I let him sleep, because he was only a young fellow." Ben's trouble was that he had worn through a callus that was a quarter of an inch thick on the palm of his hand, and raised a big blister. This had rapidly become infected, until now he had such an arm as neither Jeff nor I had ever seen. His arm was three times natural size, and aflame with colors; Ben was so sick with general blood poisoning he could not stand. It was considerable for a young interne to handle alone, but it must be incised, nevertheless.

We gave him a general, and Jeff opened the arm to try to make it drain. He was worried, and so was I. Ben's temperature shot up to 105 and over. Jeff paced the floor. His face grew grayer. He could not eat.

Next day Ben was worse if anything. His arm did not drain. He was in a delirium. Lymphangitis set in and spread to his entire shoulder, while the underarm gland continued to swell till it looked as though it would burst. The man hovered between life and death.

At two o'clock that night I was still at work in the dispensary. There was so much to do all day, so many beds to change, so much routine treatment. It was almost a full-time job doing special carbolic washings to keep the typhoid case isolated. I sat on a bench in the little bare room, reflecting that I had never worked so hard anywhere as I was working now for the $500-a-year-and-found that the mission was paying me. It was satisfactory anyway, and I wasn't kicking. I looked at the bare, crude shelves around me, some of the boards not even planed, and I wondered what amateur carpenter from Yale or Harvard had nailed them together. Some of the shelves were crooked. I could imagine the amateur standing off and viewing them with pride, so much more pride than a professional carpenter would take in a finished set of shelves.

Until midnight Martha had been helping me patch torn sheets; then she had gone off to her room to spend a half hour working on baby clothes for some unfortunate she knew up the bay at Rigolet. Since we were nearly out of dressings, I was making some now, but I was getting pretty sleepy. Suddenly I heard a step in the ward and saw a flashlight's glow.

Jeff looked in. "Hello, what's going on?"

"Dressings," I said.

"At this time of night?"

"It has to be done. This is all we have."

"My lord, why didn't you tell me? May I help?"

"Sure, sit down."

We worked awhile. "Couldn't you sleep?" I said.

"No. Look here, Austie, what about that fellow Ben? He's not getting on. I don't believe he's going to pull out of it."

"You've got to grow a shell, Jeff," I said. "What if he doesn't pull out of it? You shouldn't feel responsible if he dies. He'd gone three weeks without treatment and was practically dead when he arrived."

"I know, I know, but he's getting worse."

"Well, that's not our fault. Do you know what I think you should do?"

"No."

"Tomorrow you should go and row a boat. Row out to sea a ways."

"Oh, I couldn't," he said. "I haven't time."

We worked awhile. "You think I'm hard, don't you?"

"No, Austie. I have a big job here, that's all. Too big maybe. I don't think you're hard." He hesitated a moment. "Let's go outside and sit on the steps."

We sat out on the steps, with the night wind blowing over us, bringing the sea smell and the sound of surf. It was a romantic setting, and we couldn't help feeling it. We sat close together. It was nice to have companionship; one always craves it.

"Austie," he said, "I don't know what I'd do without you here, and it's not only with the work either. You're such a help. You keep me going."

"I've had a lot of experience, Jeff."

"I'm not usually so fond of nurses," he said. "I don't know what's come over me." He put his arm around me, and it didn't seem merely the immemorial way of a man with a maid.

I was happy, but sad too if he was serious. I made a move to go, but he gave me a kiss first. "Do forget it now, Jeff," I said, and left him sitting on the steps in the night wind.

In the morning things were no better with Ben or with Jeff. Jeff took the man's temperature hoping with every nerve in his body for an abatement. Ben did not speak or eat. Jeff had grown visibly thinner in the past few days. He carved the codfish at supper in a formal, absent-minded way. As boss here in the doctor's absence, he told the wops what to do in a cold, impersonal voice, as though they were strangers. They wondered at it, but said nothing. Jeff had nightmares. He lit the lamp in his bedroom at one o'clock in the morning and thought he saw rows of patients lying on the floor.

Forty-eight hours passed, forty-eight hours of foments and constant work on Ben. And then, "Ben is down to normal!" Normal, just like that. We could hardly believe it, but that is the way with blood poisoning, which rockets out of sight or drops like a stone. The gland began to shrink, the crimson streaks retreated. "I think I'll take a walk," said Jeff, casually. He went up over the rocks and lit out over the crest, lost down the sky, running like a child.

We celebrated, we rejoiced. The wireless man's old demin pants were flying from the faraway mast on Smokey Head (sign of a message for us), and Bill made a record trip to the wireless pole, forty-seven minutes over, forty-four back, bringing a radiogram from Doctor Paddon who said, "Hope all goes well wire me Hopedale." Hoppie ran the good news back while Bill was chopping ice off a berg in the harbor. Martha was making ice cream. The codfish was fried extra brown. Mabel was prevailed upon to wear one of the famous evening gowns in honor of the occasion. Jeff ate like a bullock. He informed us with extreme modesty that he hoped to save another patient some day. Annie cooked up some fudge. We sat around the little iron stove in the parlor telling stories of the places we had come from, while the building rocked in the wind as usual. Jeff told us about a two weeks' trip once in winter out to the banks on a Gloucester fisherman. I told about bush nursing on the edges of the Australian desert, sheep stations, an old man who got lashed almost fatally by a bull kangaroo's tail, and a sundowner who crawled in once with his feet full of prickly pear thorns, till I almost made myself homesick except that it was so snug and satisfying here.

The wind roared in the stovepipe, the little stove snapped and the building rocked.

"Peace, perfect peace," said Mabel, "with loved ones far away."

CHAPTER VIII

NIGHTS when we'd heard by wireless that the steamer was near, we kept watches so she would not catch us unprepared. We had patients well enough to leave by her, and there were nearly always others arriving to take their places. We had mail and clothing packages and messages, and a thousand things to see to at steamer time. Often it was night and storming when we heard her blow in the outer harbor, but even in daylight it was a wild scramble, for she stayed but half an hour at most, and sometimes half that. They say that once during a Sunday service, Sir Wilfred was in the midst of a prayer when the exigencies of the situation forced him to suddenly break off: "Lord, please excuse us. The mail steamer is in. Amen."

I had the two-to-four watch for *Kyle,* the "graveyard watch," but it was pleasant up on the Indian Head alone in the dark breeze that was so full of ocean scents. The night was crystal clear, with a brilliant aurora. I was watching it light the sea when I saw a ship's row of portholes pass George's Island, bound in the bay for Rigolet. To me in all that loneliness she looked like a liner, and I thought of Kipling's, "Oh, the liner, she's a lady." It would be awhile before she touched at Rigolet and could steam out here. Now I knew she was near, we'd be ready all right. So I sat and watched her, and let the others sleep awhile. The breeze was fresh and salty, and the northern lights kept walking around.

Doctor Mount was due to be aboard, a surgeon specialist

from Ottawa who had travelled the coast before on summer medical cruises. It was for him that Doctor Paddon had been collecting patients north and bringing them back on *Yale*. We were all keyed to a high pitch at the thought of working with so distinguished a man. The wards were specially scrubbed, and the trays laid out with even more care than usual, if that was possible. Jeff had collected all the movable men patients on the back porch one sunny afternoon and put in a session cutting their hair. We had even made Bill fix up the stovepipe that sagged clear across the breadth of the women's ward. We'd been bumping our heads on it for weeks, but such was not for Doctor Mount. Mabel had wild flowers set around in vases. She also had a new hair-do. Martha had relented once again and completely refurbished Joe in a new outfit from the clothing store. He had an ungovernable passion for caching good clothes in undiscoverable places, and appearing in old rags. Martha had also ferreted out of an ancient cookbook still another obscure way of serving codfish, so we were completely ready, or almost.

The whistle shrieked in the outer harbor just before breakfast, and of course it had breezed up since the calm night. Jeff took over while we went out to the steamer with a fractured rib patient, Doctor at the tiller, Joe at the engine and Bill handling lines. In my new cap and special socks and a fresh white uniform under a beautiful sailor coat with brass buttons, I was tickled to be going aboard, because the steamer's visit was one of our red-letter days. Such a beautiful taste of civilization she was; she brought us half the things we wanted, and the rest we forgave her because of the civilized ills she left behind.

It was roughish when we came alongside the heavy companionway stair. The men handed our patient aboard while our boat waltzed around, shoving in against the fending poles and yanking back on painters while the companionway jangled its chains and slammed the ship's side. Now it was my turn. I did a hop skip and jump along the thwarts and landed square on the wet companionway stair, right side up and twice as cheerful, and there was Doctor Mount holding out a hand to me. Doctor Paddon was shouting up an introduction from the motorboat: "Miss Austen, our aquatic acrobat and Eskimo interpreter from Australia—Doctor Mount."

"Some title!" said Mount. "Come on up."

Safe on the steamer's deck, I said, "I'm happy to meet you, Doctor. They speak of you ten times a day here."

"Oh, pshaw," he answered, "I'm happy to meet a woman who's a sailorman. I've seen so many come aboard with a scream and a flounder."

It was a good thing he didn't know how many times I had barked my shins while toppling in and out of small boats.

There was a pink-and-white German girl standing near, to whom he introduced me. She spoke hardly any English. She had come from Germany en route for Hopedale where she had agreed, as the Moravian missionaries do, to serve for life. Most of them never see their homes again. In addition to that, this shy young girl had contracted to marry on arrival, sight unseen, one of the missionaries there. I was awed at the thought of so much bravery or foolishness. She looked young and fresh, like a porcelain image of a dairymaid, and here she was staking her life on one toss of the dice. I hoped with all my heart she'd win.

We went ashore for breakfast. By noontime Doctor Mount

was well acquainted with every one of the twenty-three patients in the hospital, with Joe, the cooks, the whole staff, a couple of fishermen and a little boy, eleven years old, off a schooner, troubled because he wanted to send a letter home but neither his skipper-father nor any of the crew could write. Mount wrote the letter, and the boy had him sign it *Hermit*. "Ma says it is a lonesome name and most everybody is lonesome, so that's the name she give me."

Doctor Mount had time for everything and was never busy. This was his "vacation." The most difficult cases along the coast, or operations so big one surgeon couldn't handle them, were saved for him. A dozen tonsils here, a thoracotomy there and he breezed on north. A day or so ashore catching salmon, and then a stop to mend up another six or eight broken lives. It sounds debonair. Watching him do a plastic operation on a bad shotgun leg wound, I knew it was miraculous. In the case of a surgeon like that, the hand is not just a hand but the visible concentration of centuries of learning, a natural aptitude and a lifetime of training.

Among other operations he removed a large abdominal tumor from a woman of Baffin Land whom Doctor Paddon had taken aboard at Nain. He also did a repair of a recto-vaginal fistula for little Mrs. May Shepherd from up the bay. It was a big job, as the condition had been going on for a long time. The fistula had resulted from a four-and-a-half-day labor two years ago, a time of such ignorance and bravery and terror that it all might have happened in the prehistoric days of cavemen. I hereby spare you the tale, gentle reader.

So much for Doctor Mount and his good work. In the same class were Doctor Paddon, an eye specialist named

Phinney who visited us from Cincinnati, a bone specialist whose name I forget, the dentist who travelled the coast fixing teeth and teaching nurses (like me) what he could. And there were others who had been north in other years.

Doctor Phinney came to Indian Harbor on a pleasure yacht named *Zavorah*, lent him by the mission, a slim white craft very different in build from the boats we usually saw. He did six eye operations, three of them being cataract removals, on the Eskimo women Sabina Muktilik, Barbara Mugasuk, and Lin Tupin, whom Doctor Paddon had brought from the north. From them Doctor Phinney, who was making a study of Eskimo snowglasses, plants and a number of other things, learned the Eskimo words *atsuk* (I don't understand), and *auction aye*, a greeting which seemed to connote "be strong," or something similar. *Auction aye* became the password between Jeff and me, particularly when work was heavy.

None of the Eskimo women had even a working knowledge of English, so we called Joe in to be interpreter when Barbara Mugasuk came out of her anesthetic. "You must tell her," said Doctor Phinney, "that it is very important to remain quiet. She must stay quiet, not move, and above all she must not sit up."

Joe nodded his head sagely. He turned toward her, where she lay in the half dark, her face bandaged, and at first he spoke slowly in that long-worded language of theirs, for he was a bit rusty with his Eskimo, not to mention a slight shakiness in English grammar. Faster and faster he spoke until the polysyllabic words full of k's and t's were pouring from him in a flood. She answered with a speech which took a full three minutes. Joe began to speak to her again.

"What does she say, Joe?" Doctor Phinney broke in.

Joe babbled Eskimo for another sixty seconds.

"Well, Joe?"

He scratched his head. "He say she will lie up."

"Lie up?"

"No, no," Joe corrected himself. "He will not sit down."

Doctor Phinney discovered from Joe, or thought he did, that there are no Eskimo prepositions for *up* and *down*. The custom is to point. But since the woman was blind at the moment, Joe was faced with a nice linguistic problem.

At any rate the Eskimo woman seemed to get the idea, for she remained perfectly quiet and progressed nicely.

Hardly had Doctor Phinney left us when the little black steamer *Strathcona* came in off the sea, tooting her shrill whistle. She was bound north, way north, perhaps even to Cape Chidley, on a combined medical and charting cruise. They had two dories nested on deck, one of which Sir Wilfred had overboard and was rowing ashore almost before the anchor was down. He was bursting with energy and ideas as always, and had all kinds of plans for more cooperative stores along the coast, more schools, a new mission boat, and improved greenhouses at St. Anthony to provide the whole coast with cabbage plants.

The crew, with the exception of a Newfoundland mate and engineer, was composed of college boys from Harvard and Yale and various other places. The cook was a stockbroker's son from Princeton who had never so much as boiled an egg before in his life, so most of the ship's company, including Sir Wilfred's secretary, Eleanor Cushman, weren't long in ferrying themselves ashore in the remaining dory. They had a hungry look which Martha understood. They were full of fun, dressed in boots and sweaters and flannel shirts, and had already been through some exciting days of fog and storm and difficult passages in and out of the little harbors that Sir Wilfred dared even when fishermen wouldn't. The *Strathcona* has a wrought-iron bottom lined with cement, which has many times stood her in good stead. It is well dented, mate Sims told me. "They do say that *Strath* has been ashore more than she's been afloat, but that's not true."

Sir Wilfred's bronze face and white hair were everywhere at once, and everybody who talked with him felt useful and happy. He scoured the island, he crawled under the hospital and looked at the props, he chatted with the patients and held long consultations with Jeff and Doctor, and with Annie on industrial goods. Then before you knew it he was out back of the hospital on a little flat patch of ground setting up a deck tennis court, and had a game in full swing. Seeing him play reminded me that once in mid-Atlantic during a small vessel crossing, he dove overboard after their last cricket ball. In the course of *Strathcona's* forty-eight-hour stop we had a fast mixed-doubles tournament. Jeff was very good, and I was not so bad myself, as I had played the game day in and day out on the eight weeks' voyage from Australia round the Cape to England.

We had an enormous supper, with twenty-five at the staff dining table, and the visiting sailors liked even alexander. I managed to get out to *Strathcona* for a little while to see the ship and meet the two Newfoundlanders who lived aboard. Real sailors they both were, Will Sims, the mate, a big, jolly, sharp-eyed man, and Styles, a thin chap. "Worn out by worry, Miss," he said with mock mournfulness. "I never get enough coal." On the foredeck were a sawhorse, bucksaw and a big pile of polewood. *Strathcona,* a narrow, yachtlike ship, mostly cabins, couldn't carry enough coal for a very long voyage, unless they piled it on deck as was done when she crossed the Atlantic. But anyway, Sir Wilfred liked to buy wood from settlers along the Labrador to help them out.

"Six knots is all I can get out of her with wood," said Styles sadly.

Will Sims, it developed, was still not resigned to college-boy crews for manning mission vessels, though he had survived many years of it. He felt they weren't dependable and that they asked too many questions. "You know what? Once we were outfitting at St. Anthony. *Strathcona* was on the ways and we were painting her. One coat, you understand. A boy was sitting next to me in a bos'n's chair slappin' on the paint, and he says, 'Will, what color was she last year?' and there it was in front of his eyes, a half-acre of it. 'Pink and yellow,' I says. I've learned how to do it. I tell them nothing but tall yarns, and they catch on after a while."

"Now tell me, Miss," he said with a twinkle. "You haven't any hens here, have you? Styles and me ain't ate a egg for weeks, seems like."

"No. No hens," I said.

He brought out a half-empty cardboard box with six eggs in it.

"Mrs. Curtis sent these to you from St. Anthony. There was another dozen, but they got broke." He smiled blandly, a culprit unashamed of his crime.

"Mm," said Styles. "They hit on the edge of the frying pan. These almost got broke too. We've had some starvation times already."

I found out later that all the men who manned mission boats, including Jack Watts and Graham, had an irrepressible craving for hens' eggs (as distinguished from gulls' or ducks' eggs) and that the only way to have such luxuries survive a voyage was to mark them GLASS, FRAGILE, or VICTROLA RECORDS, HANDLE WITH CARE, as Mrs. Paddon quite methodically did when she was able to send down a few dozen from the farm at North West River.

There are so many tales of *Strathcona* and Sir Wilfred's narrow escapes that it almost seems as though the Lord had been looking out for the two of them. Even before *Strathcona's* day, Providence was on the job, as witness the adrift-on-an-icepan adventure when Sir Wilfred was rescued off Hare Bay in the nick of time; also a late return from the coast in the little steam launch *Princess May* in the autumn of 1894, when they lost their compass and flagpole overboard, ran out of fuel, and stoked the furnace with chopped-up pieces of their cabin to get themselves at last into a harbor on the French shore. Once, in a fog in the Straits, *Strathcona* ran up on a sloping ledge with a horrible crash. She heeled over and stuck there. As nothing could apparently be done for her, they lowered a boat and started rowing to a village ten miles away for help. They hadn't gone far in the fog when they heard the ship's bell ring. They rowed back to see what was up. A big swell had lifted her; she had slid off the rock and was now peacefully afloat. They climbed aboard and steamed off again, none the worse. Time and again, running into little settlements to see sick people whose lives depended on a visit from the doctor, *Strathcona* has touched a shoal. And it is no wonder, considering the intricacy of the coast, the lack of buoys and lighthouses, the inaccuracies of the charts. But she always seems to get off, as if she were too useful to be wrecked.

Sir Wilfred on his voyages along the coast is always giving away his clothes. If he sees a ragged, cold fisherman he gives him his coat, his sweater, anything. This he has never mentioned in his books, but it is a well-known fact. Usually he is not very far down north before he is suffering from exposure. And when his own clothes begin to run out, he starts giving away those of his crew and passengers. Anything that is lying around, Sir Wilfred picks up. "Here's a jacket," he'll say to a fisherman. "Keep you warm."

"Thank you, sir," says the fisherman.

"That's all right," says Sir Wilfred.

After a while his crew begins to get a bit naked too, for there are so many fishermen and they wear out clothes so fast.

Once many years ago Sir Wilfred took the Bishop of Newfoundland north to give him a look at the Labrador. Right from the start the lop ran high, and *Strathcona,* narrow craft that she is, rolled like a barrel. The Bishop was very seasick all the way up and across the Straits. Sir Wilfred was in fine fettle, and there was hardly a little fishing harbor anywhere that he didn't poke into. He soon had most of his own clothes given away as usual, and the Bishop's sou'wester, and a few other odd articles had also disappeared. One day, it is said, the poor seasick Bishop roused himself from his bunk just in time to see Sir Wilfred tiptoeing out of the cabin with some black broadcloth apparel slung over his arm. "My dear Sir Wilfred," said the Bishop, "I would give you anything I possess, but how can I conduct a Sunday service without trousers?"

The second day of *Strathcona's* stay was Sunday, and the sun was shining. Sir Wilfred held a morning service on the rocks, his white hair blowing in the wind. There were more than eighty fishermen on hand. The theme was faith, faith in men, and the gains, material as well as spiritual, that grow from cooperation. "Consider us here," he said, "helping one another, instead of stabbing one another in the back, as we might."

It was compelling, with the sea beside us splashing on the rocks, and the fishermen listening so silently, those fishermen whose lives in small sail craft are never very far from fundamental verities. It was true that they share never-ending dangers, and it was true that they save one another's lives. The salt wind entered in and made it true too. I've seen places, people, settings that made the same words pure hypocrisy, but here it was so true it made us weep.

In the afternoon *Strathcona* sailed away.

CHAPTER IX

MOST OF THE PATIENTS who came to us were so grateful and inarticulate that at leaving time the struggle for words nearly gave them a relapse. However, the exception to the rule was a boatload of interrelated men and boys who fished about ten miles north of us. We called them the Horse Harbor crowd. Every Sunday their dirty white motorboat rolled into the harbor packed full of heads that were stretched toward the hospital. They made me think of a flock of crows moving in on a cornfield. There was only one blessed Sabbath when they didn't show up, and that was because a fine nor'-easter was on.

Sunday afternoon was one of our big times anyway, particularly for outpatients. A long line of rubber-booted men sat on benches along the hall outside the little room full of shelves and bottles that we dignified with the name "Dispensary." The island swarmed with fishermen who, if they had nothing the matter with them, came to have a look at the hospital and its inmates anyway. In the midst of this busy time the Horse Harbor crowd intruded themselves prominently, not asking but demanding new books and magazines for their old ones, more attention, borrowing tools, begging clothes and supplies and generally making nuisances of themselves. "Here come the Horse Harbor boys," we'd say. "Nail down the carpets and chain the pictures to the walls." Even the pasty-faced young boys had a rapacious look as they wandered aimlessly about looking for something to cadge. My private opinion was that when they got around the point on the way home, they stopped the boat to compare loot and see who was high scorer for the day. We were their regular Sunday excursion. They were led by a ravenous old patriarch named Uncle Job, with a yellow-white beard, a hand like a claw, and the rheumatiz. Uncle Job's rheumatiz each week needed new treatment, new liniment, new pills, new salve, new tonic, until it almost seemed that Uncle Job's aim in life was to see how many bottles he could collect from us. We'd not have minded, except that our drug supply was never very plentiful.

One Sunday in August when Doctor Paddon and *Yale* were a long way north on a medical trip, Jeff and I were particularly busy with a stream of outpatients. Chief among those waiting on the benches was Uncle Job, and every time I'd have to pass to and fro for supplies or instruments he'd have something to say about liniment, pills, etc. Uncle Job had one very bad stump of a tooth. Jeff thought that the removal of that tooth might do a great deal for the rheumatiz, and he was planning on the extraction that day. He had done a great many extractions this summer with considerable success, but we had had so many teeth cases our supply of novocaine was exhausted.

Having a moment between patients, and wanting some kind of local anesthetic for Uncle Job's tooth, Jeff took from the dispensary a bottle with a single label and a patent name which indicated that it was a bona fide local anesthetic. He was exceedingly capable and thorough, so, being uncertain as to the strength of this stuff, and having no guinea pig at hand, he mixed up ten minims and injected it into the back of his own wrist to ascertain how large an area would be desensitized.

As I passed by the doorway a few minutes later, he remarked, "Say, Austie, I've just given myself a shot of this stuff. It's certainly working. Why, it's got my whole hand!"

His voice had an overtone that was different. "It's mighty strong," he said, half to himself.

I was immediately alarmed, and rushed in. "What have you taken?" I asked him.

Already his color was changing and his voice becoming thick. "This bottle," he muttered.

It was a little bottle of white powder. The name told me nothing whatever. There was no analysis, no indication of substance or strength. His head was wobbling. Not four minutes had passed, and he was going out.

I've seldom known fear like the panic that came over me as I held him in the chair and shook him a little and begged, "What shall I give you? Quick, quick, Jeff, what is the antidote?"

Uncle Job's shaggy face appeared in the doorway at this precise instant and whined, "Doctor, I been waitin' a long time and I got awful backaches."

I held up my hand to hush Uncle Job, and put my ear close to Jeff. "Give me adrenalin," he murmured, and those were the last coherent words I could get out of him.

"Go away," I said to Uncle Job. "Doctor's very sick and can't see you."

I felt so weak I could hardly hold Jeff's limp body in the chair, but fortunately Bill passed by with an armful of wood for the ward stove. I summoned him in to lift Jeff onto the table. Bill's mouth fell open at the sight, but I blessed him that no questions came out. That done, he stood by very helpfully.

Jeff was sweating profusely, his heart was pounding in great erratic leaps and tattoos. He suddenly came to again looking wild and unfamiliar. He took my hand and said, "Austie, you're all right, all right." He dropped it, glared at Bill, said in an icy voice, "Oh, I beg your pardon," and fell sound asleep. Twenty seconds later he was awake again, frenziedly pulling imaginary money out of his pockets, smoking imaginary cigarettes, talking a mile a minute, giving contradictory directions for the care of every single patient in the hospital, all so rapidly, so crazily stimulated that the torrent of unintelligible words rose almost to a scream. His head sagged. The babble of talk was cut off short as he went under again, this time to stay.

I had one more glance at that beastly bottle. "Give me adrenalin." Well, he must know. But how did he know? And had he known what he was saying when he said adrenalin? Jeff was getting worse before my eyes. I'd have given anything I owned or ever hoped to own for an analysis of that white stuff.

There are decisions that have to be made. Even while I was giving the adrenalin, Uncle Job shoved in again. "Doctor, we been waitin' a wunnerful while, and——"

I was frantic. "Go away," I said. "Can't you see the doctor is very sick?"

He had a good look, and grumbled, the wretch, that it was breezin' up and he had a long way to go.

Some of the other fishermen patients had a look too, and saw, and went away. But not the Horse Harbor boys. As I stood by him holding his pulse, I knew that Jeff was sinking every moment. The adrenalin was the wrong thing. It must be, for it had made him worse. Any one with a trained eye could see that Jeff was dying.

Martha came in with Mabel, and Hoppy stood beside Bill. The Horse Harbors murmured in the hallway. I asked the wops to tell them again to go home. "And, Bill and Hoppy, if they don't go at once, throw them out."

They were a grand big pair, over six feet both of them, footballers and bursting with energy. All their lives they'd had plenty of good food and exercise. Unconsciously they flexed their muscles as they marched out. And the Horse Harbors disappeared. I got the wops to reading through some medical books then, tracking down poison symptoms. But whether or not they found anything useful I've never been able to recollect, for, after all, the central fact was unknown, and so no book, no authority could help. I had to treat by trial and error, though an error might be fatal.

Some one suggested we ought to radio Jeff's family, and then thought it through to the conclusion that such a message helped no one. And anyway, the radio station was an hour from here. And what would a message say? "Jeff is dying"? "Jeff is living"?

He continued to sweat. The heart action had changed. Quicker and quicker his pulse beats came; and as the taps increased their tempo, they grew lighter and fainter, more like flurries of twitches than beats, until they were so weak and rapid they ran all together and became uncountable. He was in a low muttering delirium now. If only he could have told me. At any rate, adrenalin was wrong. I was sweating and trembling myself.

Not knowing the antidote made it horribly dangerous to give anything, since it might be just the wrong thing. I had no idea what to do, but what helps you make those fearful decisions is the certainty that the patient will die if nothing is done. If I shouldered the blame for his death, he might live.

The symptoms made me guess that a form of cocaine was in that bottle. His pupils were enormously dilated. Whatever he had taken, morphia might be the opposite, for morphia contracts the pupils to pinpoints. And so, while Martha and Mabel walked softly up and down in the corridor, and the two boys stood like statues in the corner, I gave him a very small injection of morphia. Something kept telling me it might kill him, it might finish him, but I did not listen. It was a desperate time, and it was up to me to do what I thought best, and this was what I thought best.

I hardly let go his wrist for an hour. During that time we carried him to bed and wrapped him in blankets and hot-water bags just before an intense rigor set in, with chills and icy extremities. I sat by the bed and thought of all the funny stories he'd told us, and how the fishermen took to him, and how quickly their shyness melted under his charm. And a horrible presentiment came over me that the good die young, so Jeff was to be the one. Only yesterday Jeff and Joe had been laughing together like brothers on the cliff below the Indian Head. Jeff the Yale graduate, and Joe the Eskimo orphan. It was an Alp, Jeff said, and they were doing rock climbs. He had a rope, but Joe said, "What's for that little old rope?" and wedging his feet and hands in a fissure, went straight up a vertical face. Jeff, who had once scaled the Matterhorn, rolled on the top with joy. "I've been studying this problem for an hour, Joe," he said. He was what I call an aristocratic democrat, a rare phenomenon. He had had a great many advantages such as Yale Medical School, travel abroad, internship at Massachusetts General, some post-graduate work at Johns Hopkins. But he was also Halbert 'Utchins' pal, and could split fish almost like a Newfoundlander. It was something for an interne of twenty-four to shoulder the responsibility he was taking, and I'd seen him change under it from a boy to a man. Now, on the verge of realizing his capacities, it looked as though his time had come, for an hour had passed since the morphia attempt, and he was no better, and he could not live long with a heart behaving that way.

But wasn't it something, I figured, that an hour after the morphia he was still there? Until I gave the morphia hadn't he been sinking every minute? To be sure, he hadn't improved since then, *but what do you want for tuppence*, I said to myself.

I took my courage in my two hands and gave him another and larger shot of morphia. Time dragged on. Nobody had any supper, and I never even thought of tea. But I did think how awful it would be to tell Doctor Paddon and to tell Jeff's family.

The wops were walking up and down the boardwalk outside now, and it was so quiet I could hear them strike a match to light a cigarette. Usually they didn't smoke because they were in training for something or other.

Martha and Mabel were in the wards fixing up the patients for the night. The bed springs squeaked as they straightened the sheets. It was one of the few evenings the whole summer when no wind blew.

Jeff had taken the shot of white mixture at five in the afternoon. It was not until two in the morning that I felt encouraged and thought he might live. He had had three doses of morphia by this time. I know now that the morphia saved his life. The clock seemed to shake the sand out of its bearings and move its hands around after that. Martha brought me a cup of tea which I drank standing up by the operating table. At nine in the morning, after a whole night of it, I saw he was out of the woods.

Martha stood guard with numerous written instructions, among them one to call me immediately if there was any change, and to wake me at noon anyway. At noon the word was, "He is better." I had a look at him which was so reassuring I slept again till suppertime.

He was conscious then and smiling. His voice was so fuzzy and drunken it was extremely hard to understand his unformed words. He realized that, for his comprehension was keen again. He was pleased to see me, and as for me, it was a miracle. He was very curious to know what had happened to him and what I had done for him. Doctors and their symptoms!

"Nurses," I quoted from a martinet who ruled the hospital where I trained, "never diagnose, and never, *never* suggest treatment."

"Never min' 'f I talk like a sot," said Jeff. "I know." So I started to tell him all about it, but he fell asleep again while I was talking.

With Jeff out of commission, there was so much to do around the hospital that it was nearly noon of the second day when I went to sit with him for a few minutes. His eyes were strange, and he took my hand eagerly. "I was hoping you'd come," he said. "Why didn't you come sooner? Couldn't you even spare a minute?"

"I've been mighty busy."

"Gee whiz," he said, smiling and looking up, "imagine your thinking of that morphia. Imagine a mere nurse figuring that out with no visiting quack from Vienna to think for her."

He was quite weak, and I felt a pang that I had disappointed him. I told him how things were going, and all about the patients, but that didn't seem to satisfy him or make him let go my hand. After supper I went and sat with him again, for he had had a great shock and plainly needed comforting. He had been put into my room, that being handiest to the ward, and temporarily I was bunking in his room in the old part of the hospital. It did look strange to see him in my bed, surrounded by my things. Though weak, he was regaining strength, and I wasn't worried about his health. But his mental state was a different matter.

He continued holding my hand. "Austie, I keep waking up with a start and saying to myself that I wouldn't be here except for you."

I moved a few inches and tried to look severe. "You mustn't worry now that you're practically well again— Doctor."

"Austie," he said, "how is it that you aren't married? You're the kind that marries very young. Do you remember the day that Doctor Phinney and you and I were operating on Sabina, and Doctor Phinney was feeling good, looking at you and saying, 'Jeff, my boy, are you aware of a pair of brown eyes around here this summer? I'm an eye expert, you know.' Well, I was flustered, and thought it silly of him, but, Austie, I can't help it, here in the midst of your dresses and your powder on the bureau, I think of you all the time. Tell me why you aren't married already, or am I being too personal?"

"Oh, Jeff, what a question!" I said. "I've liked lots of men. It must be that I'm too choosey or adventurous or something. I want so much in a man, such a fine body and mind, such wholeness. Lots of times I've fallen in love with one aspect of a man, but there was always a hitch, sometimes a last-minute one. What a funny thing to ask me! Shan't I get you a glass of water?"

"No, no, let's talk about you. Tell me some more, tell me what is your idea of a man for you?"

I felt like telling him how many men patients talk of love, when they are sick and the everyday world is blurred. The woman in white, the cool hands, the dream—when you are a nurse you know about men and how they need to love and be loved.

"Don't you want to take off your nurse's cap?" he said. "It looks so stiff."

I thought it might help him if I rambled on. "Lord knows, I'm affectionate and want to be loved as much as the next one, and a lot of people have been in love with me, from a seventeen-year-old schoolboy to a seventy-year-old bank manager, mostly patients, whose names I've fortunately forgotten. But here I am, happy the way I am. Don't ask me why. I don't know."

I felt sorry and humble that a tenderness was flying in and out of his eyes, and his pulse was accelerating. I was touched too.

"Do you think you've run across anybody lately?" he

said. "Anybody that meets your idea of a man? Austie, what makes your cheek so smooth?"

"Jeff, you want to remember that you're a doctor and not just a sick man patient whose nurse seems charming. You'll soon be well again."

He was disappointed, but they always are. And what is a nurse to do?

We never ceased wondering how that deadly white powder had come to be on the dispensary shelf. The hospital having been here more than forty years, abandoned in winter as most of this barren coast is, opened again each July, a new staff every season, some confusion was inevitable, and we decided we probably would never know. Jeff was convinced, as I was, that the patent stuff was some superpowerful cocaine compound. He carefully labelled it "POISON," and wrapped it up to take home so he could have it analyzed when he got to New York.

He was hale and hearty the following Sunday to cope with the Horse Harbor excursion.

"Well, Doctor," said Uncle Job, "I hopes you'll be a little more lively about gettin' this tooth out than you was last Sunday."

Jeff grinned. "Yes, I do hope so myself."

"It won't hurt, will it, Doctor?"

"It might, a little."

"Whyn't ya put some stuff in it to keep it from hurtin'?"

"We haven't any," Jeff said, and went to work.

CHAPTER X

Doctor Paddon returned and had to go away again. The northbound steamer stopped again, and longingly, thinking of the coast that lay beyond, we watched her smoke fade toward Horse Harbor and Emily. We thought of *Strathcona*, and hoped the reefs she grazed would be the bouncing kind.

The steamer left a letter for me postmarked Hopedale, but it also had a Battle Harbor stamp. It was from Sabina, one of the Eskimo women whose sight Doctor Phinney had restored. I remembered she had asked me where I lived, and that I had given her my home address. She had sent the letter to Sydney, Australia, but some knowing postmaster a mere 400 miles away had seen the name and readdressed the letter back to Indian Harbor. Sabina wrote:

Dear Miss Austen. God Loves You. I am well. God Loves You.
Sabina.

We'd heard Doctor Paddon say that he had received letters from the States simply addressed *H. L. Paddon, Labrador*. Even though he might be travelling, people on the coast kept tabs on him and delivered the letter promptly, to Nain or Gready; a few hundred miles made no difference.

There was a letter too from whaler Mathison, the dear old man, all of whose w's were v's. He embraced one and all, saying "Dear People." His leg was stiff, but strong. He was grateful for the care he had received at Indian Harbor,

75

and said that he had been in hospitals in South Africa, New Zealand, Chile, Iceland, but never a better one than ours.

> Even Oslo is not so good as yours. I vould like to be in Norvay to show you my land. Write me Seviken, Kyob-mandskyer, Tonsberg, Norvay. God bless and revard you.
>
> HAROLD MATHISON

Among Martha's mail was a clothing store note from a Labrador daughter of Eve who sent sweet grass baskets, and wanted in return, a coat.

> Please, Miss, don't pick me one of them thick old warm coats. I wants one of the lately styles for wearing to church and going aboard the steamer.

Jack and Graham with some freight and a couple of patients and a trapper named Jed Bird came out of the bay in the mission's home-made motorized scow *Capella*. She was a big, high-sided green thing, so hard to manage in a wind that it was always a noteworthy achievement to get from one end of Hamilton Inlet to the other in her. But she could carry an immense load. The trapper fellow was a twenty-year-old stalwart very powerfully built, with a round face that should have been jolly, but now it was getting hollow. He sat on the wharf most all day long playing a sad mouth organ. A song about a locomotive engineer who died in a wreck was his specialty and he could tongue it most lugu-briously. Often Joe would sit beside him with his feet hang-ing over the water and sing in melancholy tones.

Neither of them had ever seen a locomotive, but that did not lessen the plaintiveness of their wails by any means. Jed hardly spoke to any one.

Jack told me what the trouble was. Jed's girl was in Cartwright. She was going to have a baby.

"Jed's baby?"

"Yes."

"Do you think it could do any harm to talk to him about it?"

"No," said Jack. "It couldn't be any worse than it is."

So I cornered Jed one day. "Jack tells me your girl is going to have a baby?"

"That's right." His eyes were down so low you'd think it was the only baby in the world and that he had invented the process.

"Don't you like your girl?"

"Yes, I like her well."

"Then why is she in Cartwright?"

"That's where her folks live."

"So you sent her home to her folks?"

"I didn't send her. Mr. Darnage sent her home."

Mr. Darnage was an itinerant minister from Newfoundland. I had never heard anything very good about him.

"Mr. Darnage said she was bad and he said I was bad too," Jed continued. "My mother didn't like any of it either."

"It's not your mother's baby or Mr. Darnage's. You think about your girl, eh?"

"Yes."

"Suppose you went to Cartwright and got her?"

He raised his eyes. "You think I could?"

"Why not?"

"Mr. Darnage said he wouldn't marry us."

"Then somebody else will, that's sure. I'm a good hand with babies, and I'll take care of her when her time comes."

"I'm going to go," he said.

"Do. Now's the time she needs you."

When next there was a boat going, Jed left for Cartwright.

"Jed is a wonderful hunter," Jack said. "You wait till you get to North West River and you'll see. That's twice as good a place as this anyway."

I was glad to hear it, because I was looking forward to my winter in that up-the-bay-land I'd heard so much about. Doctor Paddon called it The Eden of the North.

Sure enough, *Strathcona* came back one day in late August, and the Lord had been watching out quite faithfully for Sir Wilfred as usual. They had been churning along through a thick fog way up above Cape White Handkerchief one day when Sir Wilfred said to mate Sims, "Do you know where we are, Will?"

"No, Sir," said Will. "I dunno where we're to."

"Well, keep 'er going," said Sir Wilfred, and pretty soon rocks jumped out of the fog and the ship struck a smooth ledge that ran out under water. She touched abeam, a glancing blow, and slid neatly off, sidewise, without so much as breaking a cup in the galley. Some of the off-watch crew were asleep and didn't even wake up. But Will claimed that was no criterion. "They'd sleep through Judgment Day, the whole bunch of 'em."

From sawing so much wood the college contingent had developed arms and shoulders which they said were more like those of gorillas than men. They looked at the bucksaw ruefully. "We've got to saw our way home from here, too. And all because Sir Wilf likes to buy wood from Labradormen."

Their departure south marked the beginning of the end

of summer here. Soon we would all be gone, leaving the sea land alone again with the gulls and ocean. Sunny days the livyere fishermen were making their fish, spreading it on the gray ledges, and piling it up at night under covers, like some valuable crop of hay. There was always a sail on the horizon, and sometimes from the Indian Head we could count as many as twenty dotting the ocean, leaning south. In one day from Cut Throat Islands, to seaward of us, three schooners left for home, one with 900 quintals of green fish, caught in eighteen days' fishing by eight men.

Every night a few of the loaded schooners from north came in to anchor during the darkness, and were gone again at daybreak. Every day one or two of the vessels that had been moored here for six or seven weeks hoisted sails and stood away. There was one little gray schooner with a white jib-boom and a green topmast, loaded so deep her deck was level with the water. Even rocking at anchor, water flowed in and out of her scuppers, and I did not see how men dared to sail her so many hundreds of miles.

A white, birdlike craft came in one bright forenoon. It was MacMillan's schooner *Bowdoin*, eight days out from Iceland, and this was their first landfall since Greenland, where they had not touched because of an unusual amount of ice. She'd been north all summer on one of her annual 7000-mile cruises. With some scientists and eight boys from Chicago, MacMillan had been studying volcanoes in Iceland, banding birds, charting arctic harbors, ocean currents and ice-drift, collecting minerals and fossils. They came to dinner and told us tales; they stayed the night, and MacMillan invited us aboard to see some of his arctic movies. He is friends with hunters who live a nomad life beyond the Arctic

Circle. Some he has known well, made trips with, shared hardships with, and never seen again. But there are others whom he meets now and then by chance on summer cruises to the north. In a bay along the Baffinland shore or a Greenland inlet or a cove in Davis Straits he will come across a family or two of friends, and they will rejoice.

MacMillan told us an interesting episode in the early days of his four-year Crocker Land Expedition, 1913–1917. He was saying that although he had taught a number of things to Eskimos, they were pretty good teachers themselves. Commander Donald B. MacMillan, famous explorer, awarded a Congressional medal for his feats, said, "At first we had trouble with sea ice. It doesn't crack and give you warning like fresh-water ice. But our Eskimos seemed to have a sixth sense by which they could spot a weak place. They only had to look at it to know. One day I was crossing a bay with one of our best Eskimo hunters. 'We must circle round this place,' he said. 'The ice is bad.'

"It looked all right to me, and I said to myself, *Rubbish*, and started across. Sure enough, it was mush with a crust on it, and I went through. He had to pull me out. He looked at me, sheathed in ice already. Now we would have to make camp and waste half a day. He was very angry. 'You know nothing,' he said. 'After this, if you do not do what I tell you, I will leave you. You are too much trouble to me.' "

MacMillan laughed happily at the memory.

Blocks creaked aboard the *Bowdoin* early next morning. There was frost. Like all the other ships she sailed away.

Doctor Paddon sailed to North West River and brought back the summer staff and his wife, all to wait for southbound *Kyle*. Mina Paddon was going to have a winter outside in Massachusetts keeping an eye on three sons who were in school there. She had with her a younger son, Johnny, who was only three years old. He amused us all, and his father too, by telling us, "My daddy knows the rocks in Hamilton Inlet better than anybody. He told me so. He's been stuck on every one of 'em."

Doctor chimed in with a story about a nervous lady passenger aboard a steamer who said, "Captain, do you know where all the shoals are?"

"Nope," said the captain.

"Then how do you manage to pilot the ship?"

"I know where they ain't."

While our crowded menage waited for the mailboat, rain came down in torrents, beating, lashing rain that made the sea roar. During one of those rainy afternoons Bill was sent to the Pole for word of the steamer's whereabouts. He brought back the news that she'd be here in the morning. "Oh what a dreary day, what a dreary day out there in the bogs!" he said when he was pulling off his oilskins. "And over at the Pole, my Lord, you should hear the wind howl. But you know," here he rubbed his hands over the stove and smiled apologetically, "it's so confoundedly dreary and wet and cold I enjoyed it. The wireless man was telling me what it's like in October when the last boat comes to take him off. Snowstorms, frost, doesn't see a soul for three weeks at a time."

Mina Paddon was knitting by the fire. "We were here at the hospital one fall in late October, the Doctor and I and two of our boys who were five and seven, and a sixteen-year-old lad from Cartwright who was crew. We were waiting to get up the bay in *Yale*. The last steamer had gone, the wireless operator had gone from Smokey, the patients had gone, all the schoonermen had gone. There was nobody. Head gales had been blowing down the bay for weeks, so we had to stay till they let up. *Yale* didn't have an engine in those days, and we were too short-handed to beat against a fall gale. Oh, dear, why do I bore you with these old yarns?"

"Go on, Mrs. Paddon, please do," said Bill, and we nodded our heads.

"Well, there really isn't any yarn to it. The season grew later and later till we were almost desperate. We were beginning to run short of supplies, and it did seem so lonely here. First of November came, and that night at two o'clock in the morning the wind changed. We were up and gone in half an hour in the pitch dark. At sunrise we passed Bluff Head and gave a toot on the foghorn to the Olivers. That night we anchored in Rigolet. We anchored because the Doctor was worn out from so many hours at the wheel in the cold. The boy didn't know the bay well enough to steer much, and I kept busy cooking, stowing gear that went adrift below, and minding the children. Next day we made it to Pelter's Island, where another northwester swooped down on us and held us windbound for a week. Finally we came into Mud Lake, where our head-of-the-bay station was then, in a snowstorm, having just missed a shoal in front of Blake's house in the rivermouth. Malcolm McLean was about to start down the bay looking for us in an eight-oared trap boat with a sail. He thought likely we'd been wrecked on one of the islands and might be starving. All the men in the village had gone up the rivers to their traplines long since, but Malcolm had collected five boys, the eldest fifteen, and the boat was provisioned ready to leave in the morning. "We had such a time at Mud Lake that winter. The hospital was badly built, and our two little stoves couldn't heat it. We wore fur coats most of the time, even indoors. On one prize occasion at dinner I sipped at my water tumbler and found it frozen.

"But don't suppose we haven't had some grand times too. Once we sailed the bay, North West River to Indian Harbor without a stop, a frosty moonlight night in the spring with a strong westerly boosting us along at nine knots or better. We were here in twenty-one hours, and that's pretty good time for 190 miles in *Yale*, not to mention the fun of it. We saw not a soul the whole way down, nothing but the moon and the mountains and the sunrise. We ticked off the points and left them astern as regularly as though they'd been railroad stations, and we had a hard time remembering there was anybody else alive on earth."

While Mrs. Paddon had been speaking, I hardly followed many of the small points of her story, for I was caught with the same hope of a far-off place that had filled me when I cleared the heads of Sydney harbor for the first and perhaps the last time. The same ache to know a distant place and people that had been with me when I left Paris was with me again, now that I was on the verge of leaving here. One always wants to go and see and know, but to be actually going—that is something else again. I saw myself driving dogteams, and learning to snowshoe, and travelling the woods and the frozen lakes that Jack had told me of. This place had been so fine, the patients so friendly and worthwhile; if it was even better there, I didn't know how

I'd be able to stand it. For when the work is interesting and the place is fascinating too, it keeps you mighty busy.

It was the last night at Indian Harbor for most of us. Mabel was big-hearted enough to wear her second evening dress to supper for a lark. She came in squired by Hoppy, whose limp white tie was made out of an old sheet, and whose tails were pinned on. Bill made a speech about the invaluable services of wops in general, and two in particular. Martha gave us bake-apple shortcake, with condensed milk for those who liked it. Doctor read a poem he had made up.

It was a happy time in the parlor of that old Indian Harbor hospital. We had worked together and worked very hard. Some of us had never known before what it was to work selflessly to the point of exhaustion, and those were the ones with tears in their eyes at the thought of leaving. Doctor shook us all by the hand and thanked us for our work. He said he'd seen a good many summer workers come and go, but never a better crew than this. Then he and Mrs. Paddon went off to their cottage on the rock.

We broke up, there was so much to do getting patients ready for the boat and packing, closing shop. They all envied Annie and me that we were staying the winter up the bay.

I lay in my bed and thought about the summer. You would suppose that on such a lonely isle as Indian Harbor nothing could ever happen. You'd think to look at it that it must be a sad place with its rocks and surf, the crying gulls, the salt grass blowing in the wind. All around was the sea, with nothing but a sail or berg whose point of white only made the distance longer. But out of those distances came people rich and poor, dilettantes, bunglers, whalers, Eskimos, sailors, sufferers, and miracle workers like Phinney, Mount, Paddon, Grenfell. A thousand stories and heartbreaks and happinesses had filtered through here in one short summer. Instead of being bleak and sad, life had been warm and bright. On this remote chunk of rock there'd been so many comings and goings the place was like a crossroads of the universe.

Even that last night, at 1:30 in the morning, a motorboat came from Cartwright with the familiar message that some one was very sick. Incidentally, the boat brought Jed Bird and his new wife, all married shipshape and en route for North West River. Jeff must go to answer the sick call. Since he would catch the southbound *Kyle* at Cartwright, this was good-bye for keeps. We tumbled out, sleepy-eyed. I felt the wrench of parting, so we spoke in banalities. Jeff threw his things together and snapped his bag. He turned to us all, huddled in the hall. "My Lord!" he said with a hopeless gesture, and ran, calling out, "So long," as he went.

Kyle slipped in at ten the next morning. Twenty-eight of us went out to her in the twenty-eight-foot motorboat, sitting very still because the overload made the boat topheavy. There were ten patients leaving, also Mrs. Paddon and Johnny, the summer staff from North West River, the Indian Harbor staff except Doctor and Annie and me. Captain Clark, leaning on the rail, said to me, "When I see ye in the spring, I s'pose ye'll have yer nose froze off." Sam, the seaman, was in evidence too, and my other friends of the lifeboat crew. There were so many good-byes to say to Martha, Bill and Hoppy and Mabel. It was hardest to say good-bye to Agatha, for I was like a second mother to her now. She was going to St. Anthony for a skin graft to close

up the last rawness of her back. Mrs. Paddon said she
would take good care of her on the way. The child put her
arms around me and gave me one last hug. The heartless
blast of the steam whistle (which made Agatha cry) and
the thump of the anchor winch sent me flying for the boat.
Down the companion stair, a jump into the tossing boat,
tears in the eyes, a banged shin, outraged feelings all in
tatters, and then it was "Good-bye, Good-bye," over the
water, with Mrs. Paddon on the ship's deck waving to Doctor, and Agatha beside her waving to me. The ship gathered
way, the last ship I would see till next July, and I had a
curious feeling that I had lost my equilibrium and imagined
it all, that it had never been.

At the hospital, working like galley slaves, we finished
the packing, and then commenced to load *Yale* and the motorboat with our quantities of gear. Doctor asked Jed if he
would help Joe to take the motorboat up the bay, and Jed
agreed. They had a tent and stove, and intended to go ashore
and lay up nights. They chugged off, and we didn't see them
again for some days. In the afternoon I also sailed away
with Annie, Jed's wife, our cook Sarah Jane Oliver, Doctor
and Jack in *Yale* to the westward. All that, cut off short,
erased and finished suddenly by the arrival and departure
of a boat, as is the Labrador way. I looked back at the hillside and the shuttered white hospital and the familiar old
rocks which were already changing to a formless heap in
a thousand miles of rocky coast. So much fun and sadness
there; could it be that it was over, sinking into nothingness,
many of us scattered never to reassemble?

Farewells are casual because they must be. Soldiers'
good-byes are that way, and sailors' too. The more they

mean, the more casual they are. You grab your bag and run. You shout, "So long," in a harsh voice, and the thicker the tears the faster you run. If you are a nurse, what are you running toward but new affections which will be broken off by new farewells?

Spray was wetting the forward deck. The bow went up and down on a cold, steely picture of the bay mouth. Now for a new start ahead there, new ways, new friends, which would also be cut off short one day. Where was I going and why, I asked myself as a point shut Indian Harbor from sight. I felt like a lonely wanderer, as wanderers sometimes do.

CHAPTER XI

IT TURNED out to be a beautiful evening, crisp and clear with that long transparency that makes you seem to have hawk's eyes. Sailing to the west among lonesome islands, I sat up in the bow and commenced to feel better. The boat heeled nicely, with her gray sails taut and lovely. I had never been on a sailing vessel before. I sat there getting wet, imagining as I stared ahead into the broad bay that I was a Viking out of Iceland looking for a place to settle. And when I couldn't quite manage that, I fell back on the reality that this voyage was my reward for a summer of hard work. Nobody could buy a trip like this with money.

But there's never much time for being a figure-head. Below in the little four-bunk cabin was complete confusion, with blankets, sails, crates, barrels, boxes of hospital supplies, tools and last-minute freight filling the space where we were to eat and sleep for some days. We were towing a dory astern. Jack was lashing our deck-load of four drums of gasoline so they wouldn't shift, we hoped. "I believe I'll put you in the dory," he said, "and that'll get us rid of one of the women anyway."

"You wouldn't cut the painter in the night, would you?"

"No, but the axe might fall on it."

Annie and the girl Sarah Jane Oliver who had cooked so valiantly for us all summer were trying to make something of the tangle below. Jed's new wife, a charming, intelligent girl, was there too. She was about twenty-four, with brown eyes. Since her baby was only five weeks off, the motion of the boat made her nauseated. She was apprehensive about the reception she would get from Jed's mother, but the pitching of the boat made her feel so sick she said she'd be glad to get there no matter what. She smiled at her own discomfort, and then she was quiet and wouldn't speak any more. Her name was Naomi.

Sarah Jane had decided that some one could bunk way forward in the tiny cuddy by padding the anchor lines there with a spare sail. Annie was shoving rubber boots under bunks and stowing lanterns and tools in the little space aft of the engine. This engine, a small greasy affair, took up about a third of the space below and was separated from the rest of the cabin by a partition of boards with wide cracks. Annie, who knew considerable about such things, said the motor was good in a calm, but not powerful enough to drive us against a blow.

On a small block of cement near the bunks was a tin-box trapper's stove arrangement with a pipe through the deck. When the weather was rough we had to take the pipe down and put a wooden plug in the deck hole, but now all was serene. We lit the fire with driftwood sticks, put the kettle on and began to feel at home.

We sailed into a flaming sunset that filled the sky all across, except where a great humpbacked headland blocked out the color. "That's Bluff Head, that's where I live. We're goin' in for supper and see my folks," said Sarah Jane.

We anchored off, went ashore in the dory and up a rocky path in the frosty dark. The sea was all around us as we climbed to the lighted window in a fold of the hill. There was no other light in all the miles of sea islands; for this was the most easterly house in the bay. The Olivers were like that.

Mrs. Oliver welcomed us with a quiet sort of dignity. Seeing her again, I wished I might have a portrait of this pioneer widow woman's face. The two tall black-haired sons were home, and from their nets there was salmon for supper. They gave us thirty pounds more of it and some berries to take along with us. Doctor and Mrs. Oliver chatted like the old friends they were from more than twenty years acquaintanceship. He told me later that they had some Indian in them and were in some ways the most remarkable family in the bay. But the bay was full of remarkable people.

Sarah Jane bustled around getting together clothes to take with her to North West River, where she was going to work in the hospital all winter. There was a shy little girl to be got ready too, Druscilla, Mrs. Oliver's granddaughter. Druscilla's mother had died when the child was born, and her father had been drowned just the spring before, sealing on the floe ice not far from Bluff Head. They found his boat but they never recovered his body. Druscilla was going with us to the mission's school at North West River, where I was surprised to hear there was a grade school with sixty pupils.

"We must shove off," said the Doctor. "In the autumn you have to take a good time when you can get it, day or night."

We piled aboard again, started the engine and chugged out of the cove. There was no breeze, and the black water was glassy except for a long swell. Stars were out bright and sparkling in the frosty air. Doctor stood at the wheel in a canvas dickie with the hood up. He didn't even need a compass on such a fair night as we ran past more looming great black islands. Wood smoke drifted from the funnel. A band of jagged northern lights began to rise out of the whole northern hemisphere like an overture set in jet solitude. The bow wave whispered. The aurora gathered force till it lit the bay and gilded the water through which we were sailing to the heart of an unknown land.

This was too fine a night for sleeping, I decided. This was the finest night since I had left home. To be alive in all this seemed so enchanting I was afraid my heart would burst. "Oh Annie," I called down, "come up and see the northern lights."

"Thanks," she said softly, and put her head up through the hatch so I wouldn't be offended by her gentle rebuff, "I've seen 'em before."

Jack finished tinkering with the engine, put on his sheepskin and came out on deck. When Annie followed a little while after, he sat beside her. Doctor had a fine bass voice which he began unlimbering now. For a long time we sat on deck making harmony out of "Silent Night," "How Can I Leave Thee," "Stars of the Summer Night," "Annie Laurie."

Druscilla was sound asleep when we went down. As I looked at her wide-open mouth, I thought, *Here's another tonsil case for Doctor Phinney next summer.* Then we leaned against something and went to sleep.

At midnight, so they told me, we anchored in Rigolet and Doctor bunked in his sleeping bag on deck. All I know is that I was awakened by a stirring at daybreak, looked out, and there we were off a poor little town of gray houses and a wharf. A few husky dogs prowled the shores. What I noticed most were the trees. It was a long time since I had seen forested green hills.

There were coffee and bread and butter, fried salmon, berries and Klim for breakfast as we got underway. The sun had risen and was melting frost off our decks when we entered a tide-rip known as the Narrows where the great bay closes to a breadth of less than a mile before opening again to an expansion ninety miles long and sometimes twenty miles wide. "People think of a bay," said the Doctor, "as nothing much, but this one is as big as the English Channel and sometimes just as rough."

By early afternoon we were beating with motor and sails against a strong westerly which raised a heavy chop. As we thrashed and pounded into it, *Yale* began to leak. It wasn't anything special; she had a rotten spot somewhere forward. But it meant that some one had to pump a lot. Annie and I, and then Sarah Jane and Druscilla took turns, for Doctor and Jack were busy. Poor Naomi was sick nigh unto death. The dory was yanking around with such violence it was in danger of breaking its painter; consequently Doctor let Annie and me steer while he and Jack were getting it aboard. Annie had such a soft voice, such gentle eyes, such a flower-like face, that her iron competence always surprised me. It turned out that she knew all about steering a vessel in a quartering chop, and the only thing I had to do was keep out of the way. She told me that she and her father had been blown onto a reef once in a little boat and shipwrecked on an island for ten days before some one came looking for them. "We got plenty of berries and partridges and fish, so we were all right. It was kind of cold, though, on account of we had no tent and stove, or any blankets."

Getting nowhere except up and down, we were all mighty glad when Doctor took us into the shelter of a place called Snooks Cove where Annie's two uncles, Willie and Freeman Baikie, lived with their families. Flimsy and weatherbeaten and full of chinks their homes were too, since these were only "summer houses." First thing in the spring they came down here in their little boats for the duck and goose hunting, the sealing, and then the codfishing.

Willie was a great talker and tall story teller. "Sure, Miss, we wouldn't live in a place like this in winter. Forty miles beyond North West River at the head of Grand Lake, that's where we lives in wintertime. The woods is thick, and the fur is thick and everything is thick up there. The rabbits is so thick they lean up against the door to get warm, crowds of 'em. All we got to do is open up and let 'em fall in. You come up there this winter and you'll see. 'Tis only a nice snowshoe walk from North West River."

It did me good to get my feet ashore on a fertile land after such a long time among the barren rocks of Indian Harbor; to see the warm fall sunshine slanting through green spruces in patches and lanes of light. I don't think I ever in my life appreciated trees so much. I touched their bark and felt their needles, and Annie showed me how to chew spruce gum. By the chopping block was a great pile of new white spruce chips, and two little boys laboring with a cross-cut saw, or supposed to be. Everything about the place smelled and breathed of trees.

We roamed through the forest picking blueberries and

mushrooms. It's hard to believe, but in a little while three of us had a twelve-quart pail filled with berries. To go with these the Baikies gave us a lard pail full of fresh-caught smelt, so we were all set for supper. On our tin stove aboard the boat we cooked the mushrooms with the smelt and had a delicious meal, some of us sitting on deck and some on the rocks close alongside. Poor Jack had a boil on his neck which was getting worse all the time. Now and then he'd let me poultice it, but not often. He wasn't very hungry and he wouldn't eat any mushrooms anyway, being a Newfoundlander. He said they'd poison us, and he s'posed he'd have to work the ship alone all the rest of the way home like some blinking Ancient Mariner.

Doctor kept his eye on the wind and the clouds, wondering if we'd be able to get on another hitch. Sure enough when the chill of evening settled in, the wind dropped sufficiently so we could make a start.

It seemed so kind of them to pull in the dripping anchor rope, to crank the engine and start us swinging and creeping away toward something new. I felt like a child who imagines that if a locomotive blows its whistle or the auto gets a flat, it is all being done solely for his benefit. We looked back at the gray houses. There is something so natural and so right about a house in a cove, a secure harbor-home sheltered by two outer points like arms, the blue wood smoke, the forest, the meeting of land and sea and a living, that it has a picture-like perfection. Later on in the winter when I visited the Baikie brothers by dogteam I remembered this picture, for I found the same thing at the head of Grand Lake—two little gray houses side by side in a cove.

Instead of quieting down as it had on other evenings, the

bay was getting rougher with a rising breeze and whitecaps jumping out of the dark. We punched and bucked against the wind for hours, with somebody pumping all the time, Naomi sick again, Jack miserable, Doctor wishing on account of Naomi's condition that we had never left Snooks Cove. However, he knew all the available anchorages, and after five hours of terrific thrashing to windward, he shifted course toward an inky group of islands. There were no stars, the wind was simply whistling, and how he could find his way I didn't know. Jack was in the bow peering, for he was an excellent pilot too and knew the bay like a book. Between the two of them they brought us nicely in, past a breaking point of rocks to a lovely protected place in Pelter's Island. It was too black for seeing much, but to have two anchors down, a line ashore, the waves stilled, the hatch closed, the stove going, the teakettle coming to a boil and a mugup of hard bread and peanut butter laid out, was very blessed indeed.

In this pleasant round harbor under a wooded hillside there was no sign of wind in the morning. We swung at anchor as dreamily as a lily pad in a pond. But by the time we had breakfast ready, Doctor and Jack were back from a walk across the island with the news that outside on the bay a northwest wind was snatching the tops right off the seas. Had it been fair, we would have put out and galloped and wallowed all day. But we could not gain in the teeth of it.

"Windbound," "laid up," "moored in the lee"—the words had a delicious sound. I tried to conceal my pleasure, since it's not ethical for a sailor to exult in a head wind, but I couldn't succeed very well. In fact we were all so pleased it was hardly any use pretending. For Naomi it was a particular blessing. Though she never complained, she had had a mean time of it. "Miss Austen would have fits if we were marooned here for a week, eh Jack?" said Doctor with a twinkle.

"Yes. Women!" Jack answered. He hated the creatures, though he had been known, on dark nights, to hold Annie's hand.

Doctor told us about the three terrible W's at North West River in winter: women, water and wood. The women of the staff squabbled; the water barrel was always empty or frozen solid; and no matter how much firewood was cut and stacked during the summer, there was never enough to last till spring.

That was all the same to me. This was my vacation, I loved it, and I only hoped we wouldn't get up the bay too soon, because work would surely start again then. I had never been on a cruise like this before and I wasn't sure I'd ever have another.

The sun came out by the time we had the dishes washed and the dish towels drying in the rigging. I poulticed Jack's neck, and then the gals all went ashore while Jack and Doctor turned in to catch up on sleep a little. Annie and I roamed all over that beautiful island. We found a steep-walled cove crammed full of hundreds of cords of driftwood, and decided it would be a good place to replenish our fuel supply —later. The slopes were carpeted with millions of redberry and blueberry bushes, the berries darkened and sweetened by a touch of frost, the leaves bronze and gold and russet and crimson-red like acres of bright oriental rugs. We climbed to the top of the island and saw the deep-blue bay rolling toward us in ridges, an inland sea with shores so far apart they were scarcely visible. "It always looks calm to le'ward," Annie told me, and sure enough, when we looked downwind in the direction of Rigolet and Snooks Cove, the bay appeared to be flat. "When I was little and scared in a small boat," Annie said, "Pa always told me to watch the waves goin' away, not comin'." She had a funny little silvery chuckle that was light and almost inaudible.

In the harbor below, *Yale* was swinging like a toy. We followed a brook down over small cliffs till we came to a pool, such a pool, with water tinkling, grass beside it, sunshine! It was the spot to bathe in. We went back to the boat for towels, soap, blankets, and spent the rest of the morning bathing in the pool and lying in the sun. After working hard at Indian Harbor for so long, it was Heaven to lie in warmth on my Australian steamer rug doing nothing, watching the clouds sail out of the northwest.

"This is the best time of year," said Annie. "The frost kills the flies, and the sun is warm, sometimes."

To work hard and then loaf, to know hardship and then luxury, to learn about society and then color it with a dash of the wilds—is there anything quite so fine as alternation? I never could see how consistency might be called a virtue.

Our gorgeous day couldn't last forever, though. We set sail again at evening, according to our habit, when the wind veered round to the east. The breeze was so chill and damp that we put on all the clothes we had, and so we sailed, wing and wing with a tight-stretched sail out on either side and the strong wind boosting us in surges. Naomi found the motion rather better than the pitching against a head sea, but it still wasn't comfortable for her. I couldn't help reflecting that a premature birth would rather complicate matters at this point, but nothing serious seemed to be happening so far.

We hadn't gone a great way when a cold fog came down, making the night strange and clammy. Jack had the wheel for a while, but his neck was in such dreadful shape that Doctor soon took over. The rest of us went below out of the cold and wet. Down there with the lantern swinging from the beams, the teacups jangling back and forth on their little hooks, the tin plates sliding to and fro in the locked cupboard, I tried to make Jack as comfortable as possible, and got him to let me poultice his neck once more. The game was for me to claim the cloths were cold, and for him to say that I was scorching his hair off.

After a while Annie put on some coffee, and when it was done she filled a cup for Jack.

"No, no, leave me alone," he said. "I couldn't lift my head to save my life."

I took a hot cup out to Doctor Paddon. It must have been very cold for him at the wheel, careening along through the fog hour after hour. He had a little compass box, dimly lit in front of him, a watch in his pocket which he looked at now and then, and a chart in an isinglass case to keep the water off it. The chart was all covered with pencilled lines and notations of former trips, such as: "WNW & ½ W one hour & 42 minutes, Green Cove to Eagle Point, engine alone, against head wind estimated 5 knots."

"It's going to snow," he said. "I know this curious cold fog, and it always brings snow. Ha! That tastes good. Bring me up a dry pair of mittens, will you?"

The wind was dying down a bit. I brought the mittens and went below again, shivering.

We were all asleep in our various niches below when *Crash!* Druscilla fell out of her bunk, a frying pan stood on end, the floor bent beneath us and all the hung-up clothes danced a jig. Then the boat stood utterly still. Jack couldn't move, of course. He couldn't lift his head. Nevertheless, almost before I opened my eyes, I saw his feet disappearing up the ladder in one smooth and lightning lunge. I jumped into my great, clumsy lace-up Paris leather boots (just the thing for the north woods, Madame) and was only about four steps behind him.

"We're on a shoal," said Doctor Paddon calmly. "Sand, I believe. I think it's that long shoal off Sabasquasho Islands, Jack."

Jack was everywhere at once, sailor fashion, lively as a cricket, letting go the halliards, hauling down sails. In no time at all he and Annie were in the dory sounding the water around us, Annie at the oars and Jack heaving the lead. "Make a noise so we can keep our bearings," he said. They disappeared into the fog. I whanged on a gas drum with a piece of pipe while Doctor started the engine to pull us off astern. But she wouldn't come.

The boat was alongside again in a few minutes. "It's Pig Shoal all right," said Jack. "Deep water astern, sir. A kedge is the thing."

"Righto, Jack, good." They loaded an anchor and a long hawser into the dory and splashed away with it into that eerie darkness. Once back, they heaved the line taut, soon we began to bump a bit as the rising tide lifted us, and in a few minutes we were off again.

"Thought you couldn't move to save your life," I said to Jack.

Annie chuckled. "That's a Newfoundlander for you."

He smiled but said nothing. I felt sure he had not felt that this was any crisis, for he and the Doctor had been in some really tight spots. But from voyages on sealers and trouble in storms it was part of his creed to act on the assumption that the ocean waits for nobody.

We all helped hoist sails and slipped on through the murk again. After daylight, at seven o'clock on the morning of September 5, we came into North West River. It was snowing hard and the rigging was all furry with it.

CHAPTER XII

FOR FIVE DAYS there was hardly time to get my suitcase un-packed. A woman named Mrs. Martin was in the hospital with T. B. meningitis, and it was plain her chances weren't good. Right away Doctor Paddon did a lumbar puncture with the hope of relieving her. The woman was unconscious and screeching most of the time. Then she died. She had two bright children in the school, which made it all the worse. We buried her in the little cemetery among the fir trees back of the village. There was an Indian cemetery near by too, but separate, fenced with curiously carved posts. I couldn't discover whether the Indians wouldn't be buried with the whites or vice versa. Perhaps it was a Catho-lic-Protestant affair, since the Indians were all Catholics. Mr. Martin couldn't come to his wife's funeral because he was working at a Hudson's Bay Company post 300 miles north. We sent him a letter next time a boat went down the bay. (Three years later on a canoe trip north of here he was guiding two sportsmen from New Jersey when winter caught them in the bush without food or gear, and all three per-ished.)

You wouldn't have supposed that in this woodsy, pretty harbor of snug, low houses by the river grim things could happen. But they do, everywhere. There were gay happen-ings too.

Each day a couple of little girls, an old lady, somebody, came to the hospital ostensibly to ask me for medicine. But in reality it was curiosity to see what the new nurse was like. The women admired my white uniforms with pearl buttons, and most of all my British nurse's cap with veil at the back. They had never seen such fine organdie and such pretty hemstitching. A new person, a person who was going to spend the winter, was a rarity, an object to be considered, thought about, talked about and cultivated for the sake of amusement, of wonder, of new information, and best of all for the sake of possible new tales. The motive was never personal gain. There weren't any Horse Harbor boys here.

"So you want some pills," I said.

"Yes, Miss."

"You don't have to call me *Miss*."

"No, Miss."

It seemed to be a custom I couldn't change, and they continued to call me Miss even after I had been here for three years and we had become fast friends.

An odd assortment of cultures was combined here. For instance, no road ran through the village, only paths. There was not a wheeled vehicle of any sort, no wagon, not even a wheelbarrow. The barrows were hand barrows (two poles with slats), and heavy things were carried on these by six or eight men. It had always been the custom to do things by hand here. Back in the 1880's when the Hudson's Bay Company used to raise oats on a level piece of ground that the Indians had cleared for a campsite, the plow was drawn by a long line of men heaving on a rope. Even now any extremely heavy piece of freight had to stay where it was until wintertime when it could be hauled on a dog sledge. Yet there were a number of motorboats anchored in the cove, the village contained two saw-rig engines, several radios, and the hospital had a Delco electric light system on a gasoline generator. The trapper folk who lived here reflected all this. They knew something of civilized amenities, yet still possessed primitive strengths.

Every house, whether of board or of logs, was built by the shore, since all things travelled by boat in summer and on the ice in winter. There was a beach in front of the hospital, a long sand point sticking out into the bay, and pointed spruces and firs on all the hills around. The first snow had melted, but the great seamy mountains across the bay were crowned with white and would stay so until another summer. In the village I saw gardens with ripening cabbages not yet taken in. Every house had a stovepipe sticking through the roof; only the mission and H. B. C. buildings had chimneys of imported brick.

Once I looked out the window and saw three heavily loaded canoes paddling away. A few women and children stood on shore watching them go. "Where are they bound for, Pearlie?" I asked.

Pearlie Burns was the ward maid, a jolly plump thing. "Upriver. Trapping. Gone till after New Years," she said. "Most of the men are gone already."

"Really?"

"Yes, Miss. My pa and my three brothers leave in another day or so." She must have seen my face, because she added, "But you wouldn't like it."

"I wouldn't?"

"No. 'Tis cold and wet, and they travel fast and they get short of grub and they don't wash."

I took all that with reservations. "What's up the river, Pearlie?"

"More rivers."

"Any towns?"

"No."

"What would you come to finally?"

"I dunno. Nothing, I s'pose. Nobody's been beyond Michikamau Lake much. That's a month's travel."

Apparently it was too big a subject to settle right this minute.

From the very first I had been surprised at the size of the hospital, a white, frame three-story building. In many respects it was amazingly modern, with hardwood floors, roller beds, linoleum in the kitchen. The big difficulty was that the ward was on the second floor and no bathroom was there, no sink, no water facilities of any kind. In the huge cellar was a broken hand pump, but the water wasn't good. "Do you mean to say," I asked Doctor Paddon, "that you built a $4000 hospital here, and no water?"

That was the way of it. He couldn't help it that the pump in the cellar had seemed to be good at first and then had petered out. For a hospital to have as its supply a mangey horse and dogteam, barrels on a stoneboat, an Eskimo boy (Joe) to engineer the operation, seemed pretty precarious, though.

"Don't you be running down my horse," said Jack. "Maggie's the only horse in Labrador." We were sitting in the little radio room off the front hall, where Jack had a dot-dash sending set as well as a receiving outfit which enabled us to communicate with Newfoundland. He pointed to the window. "You see way across the bay there at the base of the mountains?"

"Yes."

"That's Kenemish. That's eighteen miles. Malcolm Mc-Lean lives over there, and he's one of the old king-pins—twenty-two children, a white beard, looks like somebody out of the Bible, eighty-three years old and still going strong. Well, the McLeans had Maggie left to them by a lumber company that failed and went away. They used 'er to plow garden and haul wood till she got so balky they couldn't manage her. I said I'd manage 'er, by the Lord! So I went over a little later than this when the bay froze, and brought 'er back. Tried to ride 'er and she tossed me off twice, so I finally walked her the whole eighteen miles home across the ice."

I pictured it as a wonderful combination of incongruities —a sailor on ice with a horse.

Jack took me to see the new barn, a marvellous place with a cement floor, four cows and a bull named Rufus. These also were the only cows in all of Labrador. "It's an experiment. We have to have grain shipped in, but we get our own hay. The Montagues, Johnnie's folks, have learned how to do it and they're going to keep a cow of their own. They're building a log stable for it now. A few people are going to start in keeping goats. They say you can feed 'em on fir brush if you run out of hay in the winter, but I don't claim to be a farmer, me."

The Johnnie Montague he had mentioned was the only patient in the hospital at present. He was nineteen, short, powerfully built, with a wide smile and thick arms.

"Where did you get such wrists?" I asked him.

"Sure, Miss, I got them to Indian Harbor rowin' boats. We go down there fishin' most summers."

He was an arrested case of T. B. (a prevalent scourge in these parts, as it is in every region where Eskimos and whites or Indians and whites have been in contact). But he was chipper as a lark, and apparently strong as a horse. Nothing could have kept him in the hospital except his respect for Doctor Paddon and the fact that he had seen a number of people die of T. B. On his part Doctor Paddon thought John's condition excellent, but wanted him to have several months more of preventive build-up before the boy took up a hunter's hard and sometimes ill-fed life again. So Johnnie had the best of food, and we gave him his breakfast in bed and called him our Star Boarder. But about ten o'clock he'd sneak into his clothes and go to splitting wood or fishing or hunting or doing any chores he could get anybody to give him. Sometimes he'd take his canoe and be gone duck hunting for a couple of days. Then, having supplied the hospital with a dozen or two black ducks and three or four geese, he'd virtuously manage to stay in bed for a day or half a day. Even when he was in bed he spent most of his time knitting smelt, salmon or trout nets for the hospital to set out front in the river.

"You are the funniest patient I ever saw," I said.

"Lord Heavens! Nothing ails me, does it?"

It came out that he remembered Billy Smith very well. "You knew Miss Smith?" he said incredulously.

"Yes, I met her in Paris. She told me about this place and that's why I came."

"Well, don't that beat all! Where's Paris?"

"In France across the sea."

"Is that where Miss Smith is to now?"

"I don't know."

"Miss Smith is the prettiest girl I ever saw," he said. "She's the prettiest girl ever grew, I s'pose. All the boys here say so."

He seemed to think more of me as soon as he discovered I was a friend of Miss Smith's, and he said he was going to take me duck hunting with him if I promised not to give him any sour medicine.

He did take me with him early one frosty morning before the weather got too cold, in a green canoe with an armful of spruce boughs stowed in the bottom. We paddled down the bay to windward of a big flock of black ducks and then put the branches across the bow of the canoe as a sort of screen. Crouched behind this, we drifted down on the ducks, John paddling a little, very silently, and I kneeling in the middle, the gun crosswise in front of me. When we were quite near, he whispered, "Up gun now and give it to 'em."

Peering through the branches I could see them swimming here and there rapidly, restlessly. It was the psychological moment; in another instant they would take alarm and fly. I had never fired a shotgun, and was a little surprised to find that it had two triggers, but I picked the thing up, aimed and pulled them both at once. The recoil knocked me over backward and would have swamped the canoe but for John's quick shift of weight. The gun clattered into the bottom of the canoe, though it might just as well have fallen overboard for all of me. My shoulder received a bruise that was with me two weeks.

We were more than half a mile from shore, and the water was icy cold, so it would probably have been the end of us if we had turned bottom up. Even John was a little flustered. "I s'posed everybody knew about double-barrel shotguns," he said. "You never fired one before?"

"No."

"Well, come on, we'll try again."

The prospect didn't please me. Time and again he put me within shooting distance of companies of ducks, but my shoulder was so sore that all I could do was close my eyes and endure the gun's kick. The ducks all flew away and pitched again a mile or two off, mockingly.

"Get down low," said John, "and don't show your head. I see some big fellows." For a long time, with the utmost caution, he paddled silently toward the village. I was crouched in the bottom, seeing nothing.

At last he whispered, "They're right in front of us, great big ones and you can't miss 'em. Now!"

I rose up with the gun and found myself face to face with three of the mission cows that had come down to the shore to drink. Luckily I didn't pull the trigger that time.

John thought it was a wonderful joke. But he consoled me, saying, "Never mind. I'll learn you if it kills me. We'll go duck hunting again in the spring and you'll hit some that time, I bet."

I saw that it was well for a person here to know something of guns, so I bought myself a Winchester .22 at the post and practised with it all through the winter. I found that I couldn't shut my left eye with any effectiveness, but I could close my right. So I learned to fire left-handed, and eventually became a good enough shot to kill several hundred partridges with it. The best I ever did was to clip a ptarmigan running on the snow at twenty yards, and that's pretty good shooting with a rifle. But I was never any good with a shotgun.

I bought a pair of snowshoes too and began learning to use them as soon as the snow grew deep enough, for there was no getting around in winter without them. Everything was new and strange, with a thousand Indian and Eskimo ways to become acquainted with, but I enjoyed learning.

There were sixty children in the mission's grade school, most of them from two- and three-house settlements twenty or thirty miles away. They lived in two boarding cottages, one of which was run by Annie Baikie, the other by a Newfoundland housemother named Miss Pye. Polly from Massachusetts and a lonesome soul known as Miss Winette, from an Alberta homestead, were the teachers. Joe as chore boy, Jack as foreman, a dogteam driver and a laundress, me as nurse, Sarah Jane as cook, Pearlie wardmaid, Doctor Paddon boss, completed the staff. I was housekeeper at the hospital, where most of them lived. I managed all food stores, requisitions for next year, shortages for this, all bookkeeping, and was in charge of the clothing store, an immense proposition in the hospital attic where twelve huge cases of coats and apparel from the States sat waiting for me. Not the least of that problem was the fact that people paid for the clothing with salmon, trout, firewood, partridges, berries, moccasins, baskets, hooked rugs and labor. Are two salmon, a bearskin with some holes in it, three arctic hare skins and a hooked rug the equivalent of four sets of woollen insides (underwear)?

I walked with Doctor and Polly to the top of Sunday Hill which rose behind the village. On the way we passed the hayfield, dotted with piles of brush and stumps ready for burning. It had been the work of years to clear that field, much of which the Doctor had done himself, and he was proud of it. We went on through the woods to the hilltop where we had a view westward of rolling forests, and North West River curling back through an expansion known as Little Lake. At the far end of Little Lake was a gap through the hills, called The Rapids, where we saw water winking, and beyond that Grand Lake, thirty miles long, with huge headlands pushing out into its blue-gray depths like the muzzles of monstrous beasts. Beyond that Doctor told me were Nascopi River, Red River, Seal Lake where seals lived in a freshwater lake and never left it, Michikamau Lake, hundreds of lesser waterway chains, and a wilderness that stretched a thousand miles or so to James Bay. In the other direction, to the east and south, were other rivers which we couldn't see from here, the Hamilton or Grand, the Kenemish, the Kenemu, the Traverspine, the Goose Bay River. Indian Harbor had been the sea land, but this was the river land, linked by waterways so varied it would take a person a lifetime to know them all. North West River was a sort of hub for all the river spokes, a gateway to the fur country of half a dozen watersheds, and it was that that had made this town of 150 souls the biggest village and fur post in Labrador.

I was in the mission motorboat with Jack, skirting the beaches of the bay. Doctor Paddon had given me a day off to go with the boat to a settlement named Traverspine to pick up two little girls whose family wanted them in school. The place was a true wilderness settlement of three houses, one vacant, in clearings on the bank. As we drew in, the two little girls stood half hidden under the branches of a tree, watching us. One took the other's hand and said, "Come on, girl," and they darted away with the speed of a couple of weasels, their bare feet flying on the frozen sand, their thin cotton dresses fluttering in the wind. Their father, James Michelin, had tuberculosis and a bad cough. The family was very poor in consequence. We had tea at the house while Jack told them news of people round the bay. "What's the news?" was always the first question.

We saw nothing of the girls except an occasional glimpse of their shy wild eyes gleaming at us from around a corner. They did not want to leave home, but since they were eight and nine years old, it was time they had some schooling. After all, it was their father and mother who had sent for us. At last we coaxed them into the boat, but the trip back to the village was a silent one.

The poor little exiles were miserable and impossible to comfort in their first few days at the boarding cottage. At meal times when they thought nobody was looking, they snatched pieces of bread and hid them under their dresses. Later they ran upstairs and hid the bread under their pillows like squirrels storing nuts. Annie tried to tell them that there would be plenty of bread again tomorrow, but they were difficult to deal with because they would not speak. They cried at night, homesick for the dark river curling out of the forest.

It took them nearly a week to get over their bread-hiding ways and to start making friends. As they had practically nothing to wear, we commenced outfitting them, and it was that that really brought them 'round. I made them some warm plaited skirts of some larger ones in the clothing store, and got some village women to knit stockings out of wool brought from England. Gay sweaters of red and blue brought a sparkle to their faces, the little savages, and Effie came and said, "Miss, I likes my sweater wonderful well." She was plucking at her skirt and swinging her body from side to side with the heart-stealing coquetry of a wilderness child. I thought it awesome to see this wood-mouse tamed by bright new clothes; apparently we are all sisters under the skin.

The teachers took the motorboat up Grand Lake one weekend with Joe and a tent and a lot of school children, berry picking, hoping to get a barrelful for the winter. Everybody here picks berries like mad for about a week in autumn. When they returned, Polly had a little tale to tell. It seemed that Miss Winette was fond of trees and had a passion for transplanting them. The village itself had long ago been denuded of trees with that thoroughness woodsmen so often display. When they get to clearing, they *clear*. Miss Winette took along picks and shovels to get the boys to dig up some birches for planting in front of the school, but she found the boys were not enthusiastic. The ground was stony, and the trees resisted. The land was so full of trees it seemed absurd to dig up half a dozen. At last one little fellow threw down his pick and sat on the moss resolutely. "Miss Winette," he said, "are these trees goin to look any prettier down there than they do here?"

She couldn't get them to dig up another one.

I was surprised to learn that Jack and Doctor were going to make one or more voyage in *Yale* before the bay froze. The steamer on her last trip was bringing to Rigolet (ninety miles down the bay) some necessary last-minute freight. There were a great many food boxes to be prepared before they left, and bundles of dogfeed. Doctor would leave these at various settlements around Rigolet now for the purpose of replenishing his stock on winter dogteam trips. It was much easier to carry loads on *Yale* than it was on a komatik in winter.

Jack came and asked for a new dishcloth for *Yale* in anticipation of their trip. "I been overhauling the engine, and I guess I got grease on the dishcloth. Anyway, it seems to be a little bilge-watery."

I found him a new dishcloth and new towels too. They always travelled so hard and fast on *Yale* that mighty little housekeeping ever got done, though they had to eat and sleep just the same. Those voyages up and down the bay were always ruthless and hardy and saga-like and wholly masculine. When the wind was fair, they didn't stop for storm or sickness or cold or hunger or any mortal thing. The minute they started they seemed to sink their individualities, pool them so to speak, in the boat and the success of the trip. Ordinarily the people who happened to be running *Yale* were as comfort-loving as anybody else, but when they were voyaging, all that was changed. They were different then, sterner, and they tried to believe that it made no difference whether they were cold and wet or warm and snug. The thing was to get there before a head wind came up.

"Jack," I said, "that boat is filthy. Jane and Pearlie and I are going down this afternoon and give it the scrubbing of its life."

"Oh, no," he said. "No."

"Yes, we are."

"Well," he admitted reluctantly, "maybe you better."

We pulled out all the dishes, pots and pans, utensils, and took them up to the hospital for an overhauling, also the blankets off the bunks. We scraped and scrubbed and rubbed, removing grease and grime by the bucketful. We threw away dozens of painty, greasy rags and I don't know how many worn-out mittens and toeless socks. We filled their sugar and tea, rice, bean, flour and lard cans, we emptied out the ashes from the stove, and when Jack came and looked at it he said, "It sure is clean, but I wish't I had a new spark plug for No. 3 cylinder."

"The head thing you need," said Sarah Jane, "is a smack with a broom," and she gave it to him.

First of October was cold, stormy, and they dreaded the trip, but, having received a wireless message, they started off one gloomy morning, just Doctor and Jack and a sixteen-year-old boy for crew.

The teachers came to me that day with the sad news that they must teach singing but had just discovered neither of them could carry a tune. Could I? Yes. Would I? Well, I went and was glad I had. I came to look forward to Friday afternoons. The kids sang because they liked it. They opened their throats and poured it out. In their patched shirts and faded skirts and scuffed sealskin boots that never would stay up the way they should, they sat on rows of home-made benches and put such volume into *Funiculi Funicula* that it rattled the windows. I'd say, "What shall we sing?" and a dozen voices shouted, *Sweet and Low, God Save the King, Swanee River, When Irish Eyes, The Maple Leaf Forever, Then Blow Ye Winds Hi Oh, The Marseillaise.* They had picked up songs from everybody who ever came to the bay, but their favorite was a song about Grand River that they had made up themselves. This was a singing place, a place where people made up ballads about their work, memorized tunes from gramophone records and played duets on mouth organs that sounded like a whole symphony orchestra. The children were so crazy for storybooks and picturebooks that every afternoon at four the teachers had to push their pupils out of the school and shut the door on them.

The east wind was roaring in from the sea, the Indian Harbor wind that could blow men flat. For two days now it had been howling round the hospital, whistling by the corners, moaning at the eaves, bringing rain and coldness, making the heat of flame the only beautiful thing on earth. The bay was brim full, raised feet above its usual level by this "in-wind." Even here 200 miles from the ocean the water out on the point was salty today, though usually we could drink from a boat anywhere in the upper end of the bay and find it sweet and fresh. This was an equinoctial gale such as Doctor and Jack had feared. This was the ocean reaching for our feet and saying, "You think you live in the woods, do you? I'll tear your trees to pieces."

I sat in my cold bedroom in the late afternoon looking out the window at the torn white bay. Downstairs Sarah Jane was wailing her sad song, her rainy day song, "If you thinks I loves another, go and leave me, never mind." The bar was breaking all across the river mouth, and through the squalls of rain and spray came the long-drawn roar of surf on miles of beaches. In the fading light the wave-tops were growing whiter like teeth, and the gulfs between yawned blacker like maws. I wondered if I was really safe here. I wondered where *Yale* was this evening and what trappers in the woods did on raw wet nights like this when the rushing wind through the trees drowned even the sound of heavy rapids.

I was aroused by the sound of running feet across the floor downstairs and Johnnie Montague shouting, "The boats have gone adrift. The water's way up. They're breakin' up in the surf."

People were streaming to the shore, women in shawls, boys, old men. Most all the able-bodied chaps were away in the woods on their traplines by now. I threw on a slicker and hurried after the crowd. I found myself trotting beside a hobbling old woman who was covering the ground much faster than seemed possible. "Wunnerful dirty night, eh?" she said with a smile from under her dripping shawl. "When you comin' down to the Bight to see me?"

"Oh, soon," I said. "You're Mrs. Goudie, aren't you?"

"Aunt Suzannah Goudie, that's me."

Six motorboats, a swarm of rowboats and the mission's big green scow had been hauled up for the winter on the beach. With rollers and planks they'd been heaved well above high-water mark. But now the beach was flooded, and the boats were afloat, whole clusters of them pounding together, knocking pieces out of each other.

Joe Broomfield, the Hudson's Bay Company dog-driver, took charge. Older boys plunged in to the armpits to pull out the little boats and hold big ones apart. Broomfield produced an enormous coil of rope from the post, and with this, after the little boats had been beached, the big ones were slowly heaved out of the water. The job of setting rollers under looked dangerous to me, for if you caught your hand or foot, it would be flattened like dough on a board. But a couple of sixth graders managed that, and they knew, and were quick. As darkness came on, somebody brought lanterns; every one was drenched in the squalls. I didn't suppose that a crew of mostly women and children had the strength to move the big scow. But they set their feet in the sand and seized the rope, the song rose in the rain, the rope stretched so tight it trembled, and the heavy scow moved. The power of sixty women and children heaving together was something to make your eyes stick out.

"Now, once again, boys!" shouted Joe. They swayed on the line with rising force as the chantey rose to crescendo pitch. "Oh! here's *to* my Johnny *Po*—ker and we'll *rock* and roll 'er *ov*—er and here's *to* my Johnny *Po*—ker HEY-Y-Y-Y!" They turned their faces up to the gusts, straining on the hawser and laughing at the same time, while majestically, like a surprised dinosaur, the scow moved up the beach. Against the writhing backdrop of the dark bay the boys skipped through the icy water delighted with their own heroics, and the people sang. Sodden old Aunt Suzannah spat on her hands and danced for joy. On the tail end of the line was a little fellow forty inches high who threw one leg into the air and yanked as though he'd sail off into space with boat, rope, people and all streaming after him.

Seeing that my horsepower was neither here nor there, infected by the general levity, I passed the magic word, "a party," and ran home to put on gallons of cocoa, of which there was in the cellar not one barrel, but two, sent by some blessed cocoa manufacturer who had been touched by Sir Wilfred's tales.

We sat in the big "social room" at the back of the hospital and sipped hot cocoa and wrung out our clothes on the floor and sang. They were gay and laughing while the wind howled round the corners and moaned in the eaves. Before I knew, Broomfield was fiddling in the corner *The Girl I Left Behind*

Me, and two sets were stepping off *Soldier's Joy* with a swing that made you forget your own name. I didn't know how to do it, but they made me learn. This is the way to live, I said to myself as I rolled into bed that night.

But where was *Yale?* Days went by and she didn't return. Had she been lost in the storm, really lost this time? Mr. Lerou, the manager of the Hudson's Bay post, a formal, spare, military-looking gentleman, was kind enough to take it upon himself to worry with me. He considered trappers an inferior people, and he kept them at arm's length. "I'm no duchess myself," I warned him.

"Indeed yes, Miss Austen," he said. "You have at least lived in Paris."

"Was the storm really bad, as they go?" I asked him.

"The storm was of extraordinary severity, even for this storm-infested wasteland," he said.

He was the only person in the village who wore civilized clothes, felt hat, necktie, tweed suit, polished shoes. Sometimes he carried a thin cane. Formal, Paris-educated, he had travelled widely in the fur trade, knew Great Slave Lake, the Northwest, the Cree Indians, had been down the Mackenzie River to the Arctic Ocean. He had made such sledge and canoe journeys as would fill ten books, and once came here all the way from Newfoundland in a leaky twenty-two-foot boat with fishermen who couldn't make the engine run more than half the time. "I had to contribute my suspenders, which served in lieu of steel springs the incompetent bunglers had broken. We ran out of gas in Sandwich Bay and sailed forty miles with a tent stuck up on an oar. Extremely tiresome."

He never dirtied his hands.

We walked to the top of Sunday Hill to look for a glimpse

of *Yale*, he with a fine French telescope tucked under his arm. We could see for nearly thirty miles down the bay's long gray length, but there was no sign of any boat. She had been gone now fourteen days.

To stop myself from thinking about it, I asked him, "Why do you charge people such high prices for goods at the post? Is it possible to be frank about it?"

"My dear Miss Austen," he replied, "all is fair in love and business."

I decided we were a long way from the village. We went down the winding woodpath, he with his courtly air and his back straight as a ramrod. He was terrified lest his daughter Annette, a charming youngster, fall in love with "a native."

"She couldn't do better," I said, which put me into his black books for keeps.

The winds blew, and the coves iced over, and snow fell again. At last *Yale* came, sheathed in ice, laden deep. They tied up at the H. B. C. wharf, since ours had been washed away in their absence, and Jack and the boy stepped ashore.

"Where's Doctor Paddon?"

"He's gone."

"Gone where?"

"He almost died on the way to Rigolet of a gall-stones attack. He had to be carried aboard the steamer on a stretcher, and he's going to be operated on at St. Anthony and sent to the States for the winter. He won't be back till next July."

"No doctor?" I said helplessly.

"You're the doctor now. Give us some tea, will you? We're froze solid."

CHAPTER XIII

So INSTEAD of being the helper-nurse to a veteran doctor who had spent twenty years in this forest-rimmed trapper settlement, I suddenly became, at the beginning of our long isolated winter season, head of the station and the only medical authority on the eastern edge of this continent between Belle Isle Strait and the North Pole. I would have to make the doctor's dogteam trips. And what of surgery?

Unwilling to worry about all that, I set to work getting acquainted with the women of the village. They were a pleasant lot, neat, clean, hardworking, cheerful, and expert hands at handicraft and needlework. When they lacked milk, they fed their babies on rolled oats pap, with molasses for sweetening, and very well it worked in most cases. There was one trapper's wife who didn't like me, Mae McLean, a sister of Annie. Mae was going to have a baby, so I stopped in to see her. She was polite but firm. I could do nothing for her and I was not to suppose that I was going to take care of her when the baby came. Some former mission worker had been superior to her, and Mae had taken offense. "High people, think they are better than we are. Come here and call us *natives*. I wouldn't call on the mission if I was dying."

I begged her to remember that I was not responsible for any former slights. But to no avail. The Scotch traits certainly predominated there.

Though others were not so frank as Mae, I soon saw there

was great pride here. There was no helping people unless they felt that you were a friend. I found myself saying now and then, "Baby shouldn't sleep with mother, and for goodness sake make him stop sucking on that sugared rag all the time."

On October 29 near midnight Naomi's baby son was born, with Polly and me officiating. Polly had never seen a baby born before, so the teacher was taught something. Naomi is, I believe, of English blood both on her father's and her mother's side for as far back as any one remembers. It was Naomi's first baby, and labor was long and moderately difficult. Of all the hundreds of confinements I have attended, this was the first mother I had ever seen who did not cry out. There was no anesthetic. She did not moan; she made no sound. Now and then she asked for a drink of water. When it was over and she had rested a little, she said, "I'm glad of my baby." That was all.

CHAPTER XIV

SNOW FLEW and the gray storms rolled. Slab ice drove restlessly up and down the bay looking for a winter home, smashing and humping the frozen coves. I knew it would all really jell some day, but it was so new to me, such a strange and unbelievable phenomenon, that the thought of those miles of heaving waves locked hard and silent seemed more of a miracle than a natural change of seasons. When the shore ice had thickened till it could not be smashed, waves froze on it as they broke, building a jagged wall, cementing in big ice cakes helter-skelter and freezing them under great rounded beards of crystal. Known as *ballicaters*, these built-up ice edges wound for leagues, and would remain all winter as eight- and ten-foot barriers with unexpected hollow spots in them where you could catch a leg. No one left the village and no one arrived. This was the time when nobody travelled the bay.

One cold night when the wind fell silent, the bay caught completely over. The sun rose over the Mealy Mountains and shone on a great flat mirror where blown snow slid as homeless as the ice cakes had been. Soon more snow covered it, white and gleaming, a magic carpet twenty miles wide unrolled in front of the village, with the black river, still open, sliding under.

The sight seemed to affect Johnnie Montague too. "Winter's here," he said. "I'm going up Grand Lake on my trapline where I belong. I can't hang around the hospital no more."

He was gaining weight, strong as a horse and his cheeks were rosy. I was unable to find anything wrong with our T. B. suspect. I tested and stethoscoped and poked and sounded and pounded him, and told him, "All right, go along." He departed on the run and was gone until Christmas.

The bay was frozen and a baby was sick at Mud Lake, which combination added up to travel for Miss Austen. "The ice is teen yet, teen as glass," said Jim Pottle, the Doctor's dog-driver. He arched his heavy eyebrows, drew the corners of his wide mouth down and shook his head ominously.

"If it's thick enough for them to send a message, it's thick enough for us to go, isn't it?"

"Yes Miss, 'tis teen, but 'tis makin' all the time. We'll get there. Now about the grub. There's nothin' like mince pie, Miss. Plenty of mince pie on a trip keeps a feller goin'. You needs good nourishin' food on a trip, somethin' that don't freeze, like mince pie. That there canned hash mixed up with a can of corn, now there's a good feed too, me and Doctor always says, and the grub box can't be too full of it."

"Yeah, yeah," said Sarah Jane.

"Baked beans with plenty of pork and plenty of molasses into 'em, that sticks to yer ribs! Plenty of sweetening, so it don't freeze."

Sarah Jane had been sick in bed with quinsy sore throat which I had had to lance. I had been doing the cooking for a week. When Jim was gone, she said, "Yes, them's his favorites, that's all ails him."

But she made us a mince pie from some cherished mince

meat in tins, and she stowed lots of canned hash and corn into the grub box. She made a mess of baked beans too, spread them on a board, froze them hard as rocks, busted them into chunks with an axe and slid them into a bag. "Won't freeze, eh?" she chortled. "Men!"

We were in a boat, Jim and I, crossing the open river. For miles the ice off the river mouth, eaten by current, was bad, so rather than drive way out around, we ferried over. The hospital's ten fine sled dogs, raised and trained by Jim, sat fairly still in the boat, which was well, for we had a komatik balanced on the gunnels, and underneath it a load of sleeping bags, bearskin rugs, medicine chest, grub box, kettle, axe, gun, dog whip, dog feed, piles of dog harnesses and traces. Whenever one of the dogs whined and moved about, Jim tapped it on the head with an oar, gently, a subtle hint.

As I surveyed the gear assembled here in order that I might go on a nursing case, it seemed a long jump from the starchy uniforms and the white shoes and stockings of other days. I remembered a little travelling case that I was once very fond of, all fitted up inside with ivory toilet articles and a powder box with pink roses painted on the cover; and into my svelte little bag I used to pack my thinnest lingerie and my silk dresses and my geegaws, call a taxi and depart for a house at something-or-other Wellington Avenue.

As you looked out from North West River, you would think that this was the end of the bay, for having sailed up the Hamilton Inlet 190 miles in a southwesterly direction, you came just beyond the village to a long wooded shore barring the way. But by following that scalloped shore eastward toward the mountains for ten miles or so you came to the end of a long tip of sand, rounded it to the south and entered Goose Bay, a small imitation of the big bay, a mere twelve miles in diameter. Into the far corner of Goose Bay poured Grand River, making a sandy, tree-clad delta land of mysterious channels all around its mouth. In this region of waterways, just a mile or so up Grand River, was Mud Lake, built on the banks of a small tributary to the great stream.

Jim and I followed the bay shore toward Sandy Point, and then, instead of going way out around it, turned across its base toward Goose Bay on the most travelled portage path in the region. Here and there on both sides of the trail were blackened, much-burned stumps where hunters returning from the far reaches of Grand River, snowshoe walking, manhauling their tobaggans, always stopped to boil the kettle before the last long haul to home and North West River, which they could see beckoning far away over the ice.

The portage crossed two frozen marshes with islands of stunted trees. The sun was bright and the sky a brilliant turquoise above the forested hills. The dogs trotted easily through the glistening powder snow, and I, travelling for the first time in my life on frozen water, sitting on a bearskin aboard the komatik while we slid across the white, meadowlike marshes, decided that dog-team tripping was the nearest thing to fairyland.

On a wooded island, the one black clump in all of Goose Bay, we made a fire and had tea, reclining like a couple of solitary emperors on heaps of balsam boughs that Jim had spread beside the flames. I've always been a tea addict, and have sometimes managed twenty cups a day in time of stress, but tea by a fire in the snow, the black kettle lifted off the blaze with a stick, sugar spooned out of a canvas bag, the smell of balsam and wood smoke, and then, from the dented tin mug, the oriental fragrance rising to the frosty air of North America around a nose that never fails to be surprised —that's the best tea of all.

As we drove on, a wind sprang up and made it cold way out there on the ice. I jumped off and ran till I got a stitch in my side. I jumped aboard again and sat reflecting on the marvellous powers of hauling dogs. It was dogs like these that took Peary to the North Pole and Amundsen to the South. Hour after hour they loped for us, tails curled over their backs, trailing their tongues in the snow occasionally by way of a drink. No mugup for them on a journey. Travelling days they were fed only once, at evening when the run was over, and then their fare was a chunk of frozen, half-rotten seal meat—that was what they liked best—or some dried fish crunched up bones and all, or boiled corn meal mixed with seal oil. They can eat almost anything, snowshoes, their own harness, boots, etc., but oddly enough a good dose of salt food kills them. The Labrador fashion is to hitch them on individual traces of graduated lengths, all brought to the front of the sledge and tied to the bridle in a special kind of knot. Our leader, Daisy, a beautiful black-and-white bitch, was sixty feet out in front on the longest trace, and behind her came a team composed wholly of her sons and daughters, some of whom were sons by her sons. At any rate, the best teams have a bitch for leader, and the rest are her own pups, who follow their mother instinctively. Good leaders know *hedder, edder* and *ook, ook,* just as horses know *gee* and *haw;* they know bad ice and trails travelled long ago, and can find a way home in the thickest storm. Through the portage our team had bunched up in

single file, but on the open ice they fanned out to avoid the
rub of one another's traces, though one named Tom ran
straddling a trace more than half the time. They were fresh
and well fed, and seemed glad to run; even a skeptical
realist could not miss the fact that they liked pulling the
sledge.

As we drew in toward Grand River, we had to watch out
for thin ice, which can be particularly dangerous under new
snow. Jim went ahead testing with the axe that fine frozen
water which I noted was only two inches thick right here
beneath us. I tried to make the dogs stay a long way behind
him as he told me to, but I couldn't manage them in any
way whatever. He returned and put the drug on—a loop of
heavy walrus hide which is flicked over the prow to catch
under the runners and serve as a brake. "Say *aw-w-w*,
aw-w-w and hold them here till I sign ye to come on."

He made them lie down, and took the whip with him,
theatening them with it from time to time as he walked off
a long way on the white plain. His arm beckoned me.

"Come on, boys, *whr-r-r-t!*" I said professionally. They
stood on their hind legs and threw themselves into their
harness, but the drug was still on, and that slowed them
some. Jim held up his hand for me to stop. He was scout-
ing around; the ice was getting thinner; little pools of
water were forming in the axe cuts. I jumped off and made
the dogs drag me; I said *aw-w-w*, but they wouldn't stop.
Jim saw my difficulties, uncoiled his thirty-foot lash, let fly
one thunderous report in their direction, and they stopped.
By and by he found a way, and we got close to land, climbed
over some ballicaters and followed the thick shore ice. There
was water under the snow near the bank, which I considered

alarming. Jim paid no attention to it. "Double ice, Miss. 'Tain't nuthin'."

Things are like that on dogteam trips. Water there is dangerous, water here is not. A safe spot today may be sure death tomorrow. Conditions and places change, and are seldom twice the same. I could see it was no mere coincidence that travellers here have sharp eyes and ears; if they didn't, they wouldn't last a week.

We drove up the channel past some other houses toward Uncle Johnnie and Aunt Sally Blake's place, and they were at the door to welcome us, a fine old white-bearded man and his chipper little wife.

He was a former sea captain as well as trapper. He sat on the couch, holding his favorite cat in his arms, while I took off my boots by the stove. "Now Sally," he said, "make the nuss a cup of tea."

"Yes Johnnie, the kittle's boilin'. I see them comin', and I says I'll put the kittle on 'cause they'll be cold and want tea. Me and Johnnie always looks after the hospital folks when they comes. Doctor always sleeps here on his trips, Miss. You like an egg for your supper? I'll cook you a nice little egg. My fowls lays well all winter, yes indeed, and me and Johnnie likes eggs wonderful well."

So she chatted on, about most anything, including the fact that "Johnnie has a little money in the bank, and it's something called the interes' we uses."

Halfway through supper I made the mistake of passing the potatoes to Uncle Johnnie, thinking he might want another helping. The table was small, and he could perfectly well have reached them himself. He didn't like it to have a stranger offering him his own potatoes. His face froze.

"No," he said, "I generally takes enough to last me first go."

Aunt Sally had a funny little red pitcher with a duck's bill for a spout. She had sent away to one of the big American mail order houses for it. "Mr. Montgomery Ward sent it to me, he did, for only nineteen cents. Now wasn't that nice?" They were so kind to me that I thought everything they did and said was of the utmost charm. I gave Uncle Johnnie a bottle of mixture for his bad asthmatic cough. It seemed to help a little and he was very grateful. I had also brought a few old books and magazines from the hospital's stores, which he seized on avidly, for he was a voluminous reader and would read anything from *Alice in Wonderland* to *The Magic Mountain*, but it was Zane Grey he liked best.

The sick baby at Mrs. Ray (Nettie) Sharp's was apparently having nutritional difficulties. I had been pretty sure that might be it, so I had brought baby food with me. I made up a formula, wrote a list of what it was to have, the hours, the exact quantity, and said I would come back in the morning. I advised the mother to give it a little more fresh air, and not to keep it wrapped up tight in a hot room. I said it shouldn't sleep with mother either; shift the other children around and by all means put it in a crib by itself.

The mother was expecting another baby soon. She said she felt poorly. She had had a bad time with her last baby and was naturally apprehensive about this one. With pregnant women the nurse's job is always the same old unlovely routine: test urine, and so forth.

I couldn't find anything wrong with Mrs. Sharp except her eating habits. I read her the riot act on the subject of diet, for she had that old idea that the pregnant mother must eat twice as much as usual "to feed the baby."

I made rounds through the village then, with a fourteen-year-old girl to guide me along the snowy paths through the trees. It was bright moonlight, and as we crossed the ice of the channel and plunged into another patch of woods across the point, the moon cast a path of diamonds. I had never known that the world held anything so enchanting as this village with the ugly name, buried in sparkling silver and purple shadows. Usually an exquisite thing is small, precious, but all around me now were thousands of miles of quiet perfection spread under the moon. Visiting ten houses, doing sixteen treatments of various small kinds, I soon lost my bearings and couldn't tell for the life of me where I was among the channels and the moonlight.

At every house they welcomed me like an old friend. The father was nearly always away in the woods, the little ones tucked into homemade wooden beds in alcoves off the big square kitchen. Above was a loft where the older ones slept, and sometimes a tousselled head peered down the ladder from the blackness up there. Life revolved around a big black stove in the center of the kitchen, a stove built like a two-story oblong box. Most of these bore the name of a Quebec foundry, and had come here long ago. By the look of the homemade loaves, the stoves were good bakers.

You entered each house through a "porch," which was really a shed filled with wood and tools and dog harness. There was one grand black-haired woman whose shed had burned down soon after her husband went up the river. She and the children put out the fire and then built up a new shed. " 'Tis a mite crooked," she said, "but it keeps out the snow."

Home again at Aunt Sally's, I was given a bedroom all to myself, upstairs, warmed by the stovepipe. There was a bureau with a mirror, a china chamber pot, a hooked rug on the floor, four woolly blankets and a deep, deep featherbed.

I visited Mrs. Sharp's again early in the morning, leaving prunes for prune juice, and then we took the trail for the Groves', a two-house settlement in another corner of Goose Bay. Uncle Johnnie rode with us a few miles to visit his close-by traps, and his whiskers were soon frosted under icicles like stalactites. For a while we followed a winding channel on the other side of Grand River where rising water had frozen and made a glare-ice roadway twisting through the forest. A white-winged ptarmigan flew up ahead and sailed and lit and sailed and lit just ahead of us for miles while the dogs, mad to catch it, galloped with great leaps, making the komatik hum and career around the bends. By and by we stopped; Uncle Johnnie tied on his homemade skates, shouldered his gamebag and skated away. We waved good-bye down a long forest aisle, and were soon out on Goose Bay again in the bright morning sun.

A heart-warming welcome and baby-business again at the Groves'. Pregnant Mrs. Charles Groves was suffering from severe headaches, not drinking enough water and not eating properly. She had a bad kidney condition, usually a simple matter to remedy if caught in time, but extremely danger-ous if it is not. Both men were gone away up Goose Bay River which went winding toward the western hills like a road that I wished I could be following.

We had lunch there and set out for home. A long stretch on Goose Bay, through the portage again, out onto the big bay at dusk, and then we headed for the twinkle of North West River lights against a bitter night wind. Polly and Pearlie and Jane were so glad to see me, and I to see them, that it was a happy home-coming. They had a fine supper ready (Pearlie and Jane had caught 150 big sea trout through the ice), and after supper Polly read poetry aloud by the hospital fireplace.

Next day, Sunday, I wrote a sermon for Jack to give. Everybody in the village was coming to the service, which made him nervous as a witch. I sang a solo hymn too, "Come Ye Yourselves Apart and Rest Awhile." There was no end to the strange things I found myself doing.

In less than a week a team came from Mud Lake to say that Mrs. Sharp had been in labor for twenty-four hours and still no baby. Jim harnessed up, and we were off with a rush. The trip was infinitely colder than before, and in consequence I ran and ran on the hard-packed snow trying to keep warm. I ran so much that I was stiff as a poker next day.

The Sharps' house was crowded with neighbor women. An old girl named Aunt Gantry Blake seemed to be master of ceremonies. "God's will be done," she said. "I minds what a time her mother had borning a baby. Finally died of it, she did. Too bad. Nettie's a smart girl too."

Nettie was groaning on the bed. The stove glowed red, the windows were chinked with cotton, and it was about 102 in the shade in there.

"What are all the people for?" I asked as I unpacked the medicine chest. "Now"—with a brisk smile—"clear out, good-bye, come again some other day. All but Mrs. Hicks. You stay and help me, will you?"

The women shuffled out slowly, looking hurt and reluctant. I supposed I had been tactless, but it didn't seem a time for tact.

"Oh," moaned Mrs. Sharp, "if only I could have a drink of water."

I brought her one.

"Is it all right to drink it?" she whispered, hesitating.

"Of course."

"We always says," Mrs. Hicks spoke up, "nobody must drink when the pains are on."

"I know," I said, "but it's been found out long ago that that isn't true. Go ahead, Mrs. Sharp, it's good for you."

It's utterly dumbfounding how little the lay person everywhere knows about the common, necessary, universal phenomenon of childbirth. You'd think it was something that happened, rarely, to women on the moon. Plenty of fluids, an enema and a catheterization are certainly the simplest matters in the world, but they contributed much to the improvement of Mrs. Sharp's condition. Thousands of women have died in childbirth for the lack of them.

I listened to the baby's heartbeat. Everything was all right.

"Don't you worry now. Everything is coming fine. You won't have to wait much longer."

I took special care to teach local midwife Hicks, because an increase in her knowledge would represent a permanent improvement in conditions long after I was gone. I showed her how to sterilize. "Did you know that an obstetric doctor washes his hands in three different solutions for five minutes by the clock?" I talked with her of such emergencies as cord around the neck, blue baby that won't cry, premature births, breech deliveries, the *un*lucky aspects of "born with a caul."

The baby picked that hour that babies usually pick, somewhere around the middle of the night. Nettie was glad of her boy. "Herm says when he went away, 'Make me another boy and we'll have one for each end of the wood-saw.' "

Late the next afternoon I felt I could leave. Jim and I drove to the Groves' for the night to see how Mrs. Charles was getting on with the headaches and the kidneys. My idea was always to see the pregnant women round the bay for purposes of checking up and discovering whether they were normal. If they were healthy, I would not need to worry about them, for birth is a normal thing, and when pregnancy goes well, the birth goes well as a rule too. I wanted to know which ones needed to come to hospital for their confinements. Mrs. Charles with her albumin-urea for instance—within one week after my visit and advice, all her dangerous symptoms and headaches had vanished. Polly used to kid me and say that I just went gadding around on dogteam trips because it was such fun. But I didn't mind, since I knew that was only half true.

We slept at Mrs. Charles Groves' while a big snowstorm roared in during the night. At daylight, looking out the drifted windows, I could see no sign of the dogs. Jim gave a whistle, and little buried mounds rose up from the snow, shook themselves and were black-and-white dogs strolling about on top.

We started out with Jim ahead breaking trail on snowshoes, the dogs following, and I, on snowshoes too, walking behind the sledge to lighten the load. The dogs bunched up in line and followed the track well, since they couldn't do anything but jump from hole to hole once they left it. My thighs were in knots from running so much the day before, but it wasn't bad on the beaten track. After a number of miles down the endless whiteness of Goose Bay I took it into my head that it must be bitter hard for Jim to break trail ahead all the time. Forgetting that men are absolute masters here and unaccustomed to suggestions from women, I stopped him and said, "Let me break trail awhile."

He looked at me rather peculiarly, but answered, "If you like," sat himself on the sledge and began to fill his pipe. The dogs pulled him without any difficulty, and I decided that I might just as well have been riding all this time.

But I was breaking trail now. The snow was so deep I had to lift my racquets high at each step, which put a greater strain on my lame thighs. I still wasn't any wonder on snowshoes, for though I had practised faithfully all during October, that doesn't compare with being practically born on them. Now and then I stumbled.

Nobody could have recognized the shores we were inching by as the same land we had seen a week ago. Then they had form and line, but now the bushes were obliterated, trees plastered with drifts, points, coves, everything erased in the glaring white. Where was this gallant flying over the ice that you read about? It seemed to me Jim always bolted off with the komatik before I was half on, and much he cared whether I was on or not. It seemed to me I had walked or run more than half of every journey we'd made so far.

Step, step, lifting high, knee-deep in the stuff, I began to sweat. My collar was chafing my neck raw. I had on twice too many clothes for walking anyway. I had dressed for riding, for gallantly flying over the arctic tundra, the way they do in Siberia or somewhere in books, not here. Every time I looked back, Jim was lighting his pipe. The dogs were getting tired, their tails drooping, but all he had to do was

crack the long whip over their heads to start them hauling
in earnest. If only I could crack the whip, I'd be able to ride
myself, but I couldn't. Often I'd tried to throw out the
lash and snap it, but all it did was to curl back and wind
around me with a thwack that hurt through the heaviest
clothes. All the same, I could have sat on and yelled to
them.

But I was stubborn and wouldn't ask for a ride. Surely
Jim would suggest a change soon. I slogged on toward the
portage, not sure where it was, now that the world had
changed so completely, but I hit it after a while, only losing
about a mile because I had headed too far west. I didn't look
back; I didn't want to see him lighting his pipe again. My
thighs were aching.

We left the ice and entered the trees. In there where the
wind had not blown, the snow was many feet deeper. I
struggled for each step, winding slowly along the crooked
path between the trees. Surely Jim couldn't realize how
hard the walking was. I looked back and saw him putting
out his foot to pull the sled around a turn.

"Jim, I can't walk any farther. I'd like to ride."

Without a word he took his snowshoes and walked ahead.
In a few minutes he was out of sight. The dogs wouldn't
pull for me the way they did for him, since they knew I
couldn't use the whip. Gruffly I shouted, "Whur-rt, get on!"
They gave a half-hearted tug, the sled ran off Jim's narrow snowshoe track and sank nearly out of sight. That
stopped them dead. They looked around and leered at me
with their wild eyes.

The mission sledge was an eighteen-footer, and when I
came to lift its nose, I found it weighed something. To the

waist in snow, heaving and shouting, I got it headed straight again. A pull from the team, and we'd have been on the track again. I yanked the sled a foot ahead by myself to encourage them. Rather that made them laugh. They lay down in the snow and looked away. I kicked the sledge and whipped the bushes. Nothing would start them except an individual knock to each one, from Daisy right down the line. Perhaps they didn't know what I wanted. When I thought of Jim's quiet cluck that would have set them straining and rearing against their harness, I nearly foamed at the mouth. At any rate, we were moving again, I balancing from side to side, now pushing, now pulling, afraid we'd leave the narrow track and plow again. But the path was full of narrow turns, and I didn't heave the prow around a bend quick enough. We ran off and got hooked behind a fir tree with a jar that made it dump its load of snow on my head. The dogs lay down to admire the scenery.

The sled was too heavy for me. It was too brutally heavy to be dragged backwards and set on an even keel again. The nicest coordination between driver and team is needed to drag a heavily loaded sledge out of a soft hole, and you can't have one hauling and the other slacking at the wrong moment. Nevertheless, my team and I got under way again, and by a phenomenal display of further brute power I kept the komatik on the track from there till the trees gave way to stunted bushes and the bare poles of the big marsh in the middle of the portage. Here the wind had done some scouring, so we picked up speed. The dogs saw Jim and began to strain.

Why had I expected I could drive them, when I'd heard that even an experienced driver often has trouble with another man's team. "Jim," I said, "let me walk ahead again, eh?"

"All right, Miss." He sat on and lit his pipe.

I was done out. I had had no rest at all. Heaving the komatik through the trees was even worse than walking ahead. Jim knew all that.

The sun was going down. I staggered through to the big bay and a quarter of a mile out onto the ice before I sagged again. We could see the village now, about five miles away.

"Sit on, Miss. They smell home and they'll follow."

Jim walked it from there without a stop.

Why hadn't he explained that I couldn't manage the sled through the trees? People here don't explain anything. They think words are only for sociability. You learn by watching or you don't learn at all. And they look at things so differently that it's often impossible to know what they are thinking. Probably he sensed that I was cross all day. Probably he knew I thought it wrong of him to make me walk ahead. Perhaps he hated riding behind a woman for the first time in his life, and decided he'd show me what he thought of suggestions on dog trips. Very likely he wanted to see what I was made of, and to determine whether it was going to be possible for me to make long trips at all. I'll never know, I suppose.

At any rate, when we were unharnessing at the hospital I asked him, "Will you teach me, Jim, to crack a dogwhip?"

"Yes, Miss," he answered. "I believe I could learn ye."

But, sad to say, I was never able to get the knack of it, though he tried his best with me.

CHAPTER XV

ONE NIGHT they sent for me from Lyman Flowers' house across the river. Lyman, a strange and likeable man with an odd uncertain mind, had been wandering the shores all afternoon singing hymns. That was always a bad sign with him. When I arrived I found his prominent eyes sticking out and glaring, his black hair straggling across his face. At such times his strong religious feeling took gigantic shapes like nightmares, and he groaned and rolled on the floor asking the Lord to kill him, yet obsessed with fears of hellfire. He was a strange fellow, gentle in his usually calm moments, and Jack said that of all the men in the village Lyman was the only one who could be trusted with the mission's sawrig and the motorboats. You wouldn't ever find Lyman running an unoiled engine, no sir, but there were plenty of other chaps who, given an engine to manage, would burn out a bearing or strip a gear once a week—rather an important matter when new parts take six months to get.

Lyman refused the sedative I offered him, so he and I knelt on the kitchen floor and prayed. I prayed and prayed and prayed. I thought of every prayer I'd ever heard, and I've heard some thumping ones in my time. I blessed the King and Queen and the government right down to the local customs inspector. Then I commenced on a "We thank Thee—" which lasted for three quarters of an hour. Lyman's knees got sore maybe. Anyway, he rose right up from that one and went to bed. Next morning he was all right again.

Since then Jack claims I'm the champion long-distance pray-er on this whole coast, but I feel sure there are men who've devoted their lives to it who can outdo me. Sometimes it amazes me, though, to think that since I came here I have preached ten sermons at the Sunday chapel services we hold in "The Big Room." At such times I always find myself trying to make them see the beauty and blessedness of this country of theirs as compared with other places. That's the trouble; the main thing they are interested in is the comparisons, the other places, naturally enough, since they know all about this one. And to me this is "another place," and that's why it interests me so.

A week later, one evening when my work was done, I was bound across the river again, this time to see Mrs. Steve Burns who was pregnant and unwell. She was the mother of our wardmaid Pearlie. It was dark out on the ice, but I could see the two little lights that marked the Burns' and Flowers' houses on the far shore. Here and there along the ice were the humps that indicated an airhole, but I kept well away from those. I was thinking about the food supplies at the hospital, which were running kind of low. Not that we would starve, but most of the jam and ham and canned tidbits, as well as a few staples such as rice, were gone already. Twelve we fed at the hospital, in addition to patients, and another sixty in the boarding cottages had to eat out of mission stores. It was my job to give out all supplies, plan the actual hospital meals, and figure out how we were going to make our food do until spring. I never have liked housekeeping, and I could see that I was going to like it less from now on.

It pleased me to be going to see Mrs. Steve Burns, however. She was such a good friend. It pleased me to be snowshoeing too, for my snowshoes made me think, somehow, of Indian legends. They were an unusually fine pair, and even in this place where the Montagnais make the most beautiful snowshoes in the world, people were always admiring them.

Mrs. Burns was surprised to see me. Sitting by the lamp, her small children tucked asleep in the shadowy alcove, she was sewing as she always is. She was the one who taught me to pleat a mocassin toe and to cut out patterns for mittens, and how to stitch sealskin so it will be waterproof. She thought it strange that I should come across alone to see her, but she never thinks it strange that she should live here by herself with three small children while four more board across the river at the mission school and Steve and the three eldest boys are away in the country trapping for months at a time—away up Nascopi River in a never-never-land that nobody knows but themselves.

When she and Steve were married, she was only seventeen. Steve possessed no boat, no house, no nets, nothing much but a ragged tent, an axe and an old gun and a few traps. They had an iron pot which they used for both frying and boiling. He borrowed a boat and they went up North West River through Grand Lake to the Nascopi, and there among the rolling woods where no one lives they built a squared log house. It still stands, gray and rotting, on a high sandbank above the river, and in summer the wild raspberries are thick.

For ten years they lived there. Mrs. Burns was alone most of the time in winter while Steve was away hunting, and she had very little help bearing her numerous children. Summers they often went down the bay as far as Rigolet in a little boat for the codfishing. Then Steve would make two trips home, one with the family and one with salt cod for the winter.

"I minds one spring we was comin' down from the Nascopi house to North West River for a spell, the whole outfit of us. It was early March. We only had two dogs, 'cause that was all we could feed them days. They hauled a little sled with gear, and Steve had a toboggan for the youngsters to climb onto now and then. But mostly we all walked. We had sunshine all the four days we was on the way, and it was bright enough to knock the eyes right out of your head. Noddy was little then, and didn't amount to much. He didn't like the glare, said it made him squint too much. So he tied an old piece of a black muslin skirt of mine over his face and walked along that way. We all teased him, but he said he could see through it enough to get along all right and it suited him.

"It was so early in the spring we didn't think we'd have to worry about snowblindness yet, but sure enough, one after the other of us commenced to take it, Steve first, and then some of the children. They couldn't see nothin'. The third evening I told Steve what the shore looked like, and he told me where to go in and camp. Next day, my eyes give out. Noddy was the only one that didn't go snowblind. We all took hands the last day and he led us. Seven years old, and that little feller led us along beside the open rapid at the lower end of Grand Lake and right down to the village, as blind as stones every one of us."

On the table beside Mrs. Burns, half hidden by a pile of children's socks, overalls, sealskin scraps and darned mittens, was a little old battery radio. The Burns were the only people in the village with a radio. It would never occur to Mrs. Burns to listen to it while she was sewing. That would be unfitting insult to so great a miracle.

"How is it working," I asked her.

"Oh, it squalls and bawls on times, but last night it were wonderful fine. Maria Flowers came over, and soon's I got the children to bed we turned 'er on. 'Tis always better at night someway. First we got a feller jabberin'—French I s'pose—and then a game called hockey to Boston. A man was tellin' all about it, and they was runnin' about on skates, seemed like it. Maria told me to ask you what a *puck* is. They was always doin' somethin' with this *puck*, we couldn't make out just what. But it were wonderful risky, and they fell down and the people hollered and bawled. Halfway through, the radio began to squeal, the way it does, and I knew that were somebody tryin' to take it away from us, but I grabbed the knob quick and I slung to 'er, and bimebye they see they couldn't get it, and they give up tryin'. We got some singin' too. I don't know what Steve would have said—'tis a good thing he's off in the woods—but we sat up and listened, Maria and me, till quarter of two."

She looked at me guiltily.

"You're a couple of bad ones, aren't you?"

"Indeed we are," she answered proudly.

Then we got to business. "Your feet are swollen," I said.

"Yes, they're puffed up bad."

"You shouldn't be on them so much. Your time's short now. I want you to come over to the hospital and stay till the baby is born."

"Oh, I couldn't do that."

Finally I persuaded her. We could parcel out the small children and take care of them somehow.

"I'll send a team tomorrow about noon, eh?"

"All right. Now, when you get across the river tonight, how will I know you dodged the airholes?"

"You'll see me light the lamp in my bedroom. Good night."

"Good night."

Of all the great-hearted, capable women in the bay it seemed to me Mrs. Burns was the prize. And here she was having her twelfth child in eighteen years. At least we could fill her up with good food and cod oil these last few weeks.

She came and settled in with us, bringing mountains of sewing. "This is a kind of a cruise for me," she said. Her feet were swollen worse than ever. I knew of nothing that would do them much good, but Mrs. Burns had a firm belief in balsam. We brought in great armfuls of it, from which she plucked the fronds, making them into small loose pillows. These she had us heat in the oven and bind to her feet. It gave her comfort and at the same time filled the hospital with a delightful scent, so everybody was happy. She sat in a sunny window, making boots for her men. Each of her hunters must have three pairs for the sharp crust that wears them so badly on the spring hunt.

Now and then when times were slack, daughter Pearlie would sit down beside her mother and sew awhile. But though Pearlie was deft, she couldn't compare with her ma. So long and skillfully Mrs. Burns worked at drawing the caribou sinew thread in and out those lapped, thrice-sewn sealskin seams, that when her time came she had seven pairs of boots completed.

Mrs. Burns' labor was long. "They also serve who only stand and wait," might be a good motto for a labor ward. Many an eminent obstetrician does not wait long enough.

There is something strange about labor days, even though I've attended hundreds of births. Some one is suffering a certain amount every hour, and she is in my care. The color and feel of the day changes, the day is momentous and a little grim, yet strong and terribly alive because a great event is taking place. I feel, maybe, somewhat as the mother feels. And one of the joys is that there is no turning back. It's tremendous and it's sublime, labor day is. And sometimes it's too big for us, but it has this—it's a peak of days and no woman's life is complete without one. Sometimes I thought it a little strange that I had ushered in so many babies, and never one of my own.

So we waited and waited all day with Mrs. Burns. She was very uncomfortable, but she did not complain. And we waited and we waited some more, leaving her alone sometimes, staying with her at others.

"I got once," she said, "so's I used to have 'em that quick I hardly had time to get help. Just a few pains and there would be the baby bawlin'. But lately I've been gettin' longer someway."

It seemed to me the baby might never see the light of day, there was such a marked inertia because the mother's muscles were relaxed from having too many children too often. But late at night a little girl was born. I had the two teachers, Pauline and Miss Winette, to help me, as well as Sarah Jane and Pearlie. When it was over, they sighed with relief, not realizing that the worst was yet to come: post partum hemorrhage, also caused by uterine inertia.

Polly and Miss Winette and I took it in turns to watch and to massage without cease. I gave all the ergot and pituitrin it was safe to give, but she bled and kept bleeding till she was literally bled white. We treated for shock, we raised the foot of the bed and bandaged the lower limbs, we injected saline, and I repeated the ergot and pituitrin as soon as I dared. Twice during the night I thought she was gone in spite of anything we could do. But at daybreak she was still there. I had hold of her wrist and was trying to find her pulse, so weak it was barely distinguishable, when she looked up and said, "Don't worry about me, Miss. I always bleeds a lot these years. 'Tis my fashion."

She rested a while and added, "The last nurse said she was real glad I told her or she'd have give me up." She smiled wanly at the memory of that little joke.

The thought of that nurse warmed me, and the thought of others who had fought the same fight this very night, somewhere. And the daylight came and the hemorrhage diminished and Mrs. Burns lived and the sun was shining and all that. It was like a movie, except that it wasn't quite so sentimental as some.

In a week she was quite gay and frisky, though I wouldn't let her out of bed, of course.

Next afternoon out of a light snowstorm a man appeared. It was Murdock McLean, who had come home from up Nascopi River with an awful tooth. He stood in front of me and swayed. One cheek was hollow, as though scooped out by the winter wind; the other a swollen, convex bulge. To see anything fat about his pared-down body was grotesque and horrible. He stretched out his long ragged leggings.

He had the biggest feet in this village of small feet, and at that his were only size nine.

"I been thinkin' about you *little*. Get this tooth out for me. I can't stand it no more."

It had been nearly 150 miles from his hunting grounds, drawing his toboggan, and almost every day there had been new rimey snow.

"Twelve days the damn thing's been gnawin' at me. I couldn't hunt and I couldn't eat or sleep. So I come home."

Looking into his mouth, I found the bad one was a molar on the lower right, black and liable to break in the forceps. However, I said, "All right, Murdock, we'll have that out in no time."

I was filling my hypo with novocaine when he looked up with horror.

"Oh, Miss, I couldn't be stuck with a needle. I couldn't stand to be stuck with a needle."

Somehow, no matter how many teeth I pull, pulling teeth always gives me a queasy feeling amidships. I tried to explain to him that a shot of novocaine would deaden the nerve so that getting the tooth out wouldn't hurt. "That's what I do for everybody, Murdock," I said. "Just let me try. What's a tiny prick with a needle, compared to the pain you've put up with for over a week?"

"No, no," he said, "no needle. I can stand the yank, but I can't put up with the needle. Just haul 'er out for me and I'll hold on."

I got a grip on the molar, deep down with my forceps, and rocked it. It was in there tight, and the poor man shuddered. How I did want to tell him to go home and rest—anything to put off this moment. We both began to sweat and I thought of Mollie O'Shea. I drove the forceps down deeper into his gum to get a lower hold because I feared the crown might crumble. Thank goodness I've a good strong hand and wrist. I could somehow sense by the pull that the root was hooked in toward the back, so I pulled with a forward leverage, trying to forget Murdock's soft groans. He couldn't bear it now, what I was doing to him. But he wanted me to go on because he couldn't stand it either for me to fail. Not to get it out would be the only unforgivable thing. Why hadn't I practiced more extractions out at Indian Harbor; how could I have ever thought it hard to spare the time from my own work to learn about teeth! Murdock, with his eyes closed and his fists clenched was holding on by a superhuman effort of will. He couldn't bear it many seconds more. I hardened my heart and tried to imagine I didn't care whether I hurt him or not. And that was the kindest thing I did that day. The tooth popped out, whole and unbroken, no splinter of bone, and at the base of the root was that telltale sac that bespeaks an abscess.

We were both limp. Murdock's head began to wobble, and blood dripped down his chin. I pushed his head down low to the level of his knees and held it there to prevent his fainting. In a minute or two he began to spit quite accurately into a bowl I had ready. I rinsed his mouth with a mild disinfectant and bustled around the dispensary as though I had a thousand other important matters to attend to and thought nothing of this. It stopped my knees from shaking.

"Thanks, Miss," mumbled Murdock, giving me a crooked, blue-eyed smile. "You done a good job on me. Soon's I sell some fur——"

"Now, now, get along home and have a sleep," I said. "And here's a couple of pills to swallow if you can't sleep. Why! Mae doesn't even know you're here. She thinks you're way up Nascopi. Won't she be tickled?"

"Yes," he said, still sitting in the chair, apparently unable to move.

I sent Joe along home with him to pull his sled and pick him up in case he keeled over. But of course he wouldn't have Joe pull his sled home the last hundred yards. I looked out the window and saw him trudging through the snow with his back bent and his sled trailing behind. Then he raised his head and looked at his house. Mae came to the door and shouted.

I threw the tooth in the can. Maybe Mae wouldn't think quite so badly of the hospital now, even though some one had slighted her once upon a time.

When Murdock was recovered enough to start back to his furring grounds again, I said to Mrs. Burns, "Shall I send along a note to Steve telling him he has a new baby daughter? Or will you write it?"

"Oh no, oh no," she said, and paused for words. Quite awhile it took her to think it out, and then she said, "Men are funny, you know. They hunts a living and such. One time when Hermie was born, Steve was in the woods about twenty days' walk and I did send him a letter by somebody who was goin' in there. I told him about the new baby, and not much else, I s'pose. When Steve came home, I asked him if he got my letter.

" 'Yes,' he says. 'I wisht you'd told me some news, though —what the price of fur was and if the boys was gettin' many minks over Grand River way and if the foxes was plenty anywheres.'

"You see, Miss, he don't take much account of babies when they're little. He can't even tell their names for certain. But when they're about three years old and gets to talkin' and walkin' around, some day he'll pick one of 'em up on his knee and look at it real careful and say, 'Ma, where'd this feller come from anyways?' "

She was silent, then said with a quiet loyalty, as though she realized it is rather important for men and women to be different, "But there's nobody like Steve to teach a boy to hunt. And I guess there never will be."

CHAPTER XVI

ONE OF MY GREAT FRIENDS in the village was Hannah Montague, mother of Johnnie and four others. She was a birdlike, talkative soul, fluttering from this to that with the pert suddenness of a sparrow. And she seldom stopped talking. Hannah was a great fisherman, and now and then of a winter day when the sun was shining, and I could manage it, we'd go off to Big Brook, about four miles upstream, for a day's fishing through the ice. We took along a hand sled and a burlap bag to hold the fish, an ice chisel, an axe and a grub bag. We'd bundle up in our dickies and hoods, and slip away from the village for a lark. Usually the west wind had hardened the going so we could dispense with snowshoes. But we always took them along in case of a snowstorm.

"My, my, Miss, them pants, ain't they a wonderful riggin'," Hannah often said of my moleskin breeches. "I always says us women ought to wear pants in winter same as men, but you're the only one with sense enough to do it."

Hannah wore pants, men's pants too, and hunter's leggings and all the rest. But over the ensemble was spread an enormous ragged plaid skirt. This I encouraged her to leave off, as it impeded her progress considerably in a head wind. But she never did.

The mouth of Big Brook was a pretty cove, ringed with pointed firs. Farther out on the river where the current was slow the ice attained a thickness of three or four feet, but at the mouth of the brook the ice wasn't too thick for us to chisel a dozen fish holes.

It was a great place for sea trout, fine big silver fellows with pink flesh, ranging from three to eight pounds. We put out a lot of set hooks, and Hannah would run from one to the other, talking a blue streak whether I was within hearing or not. Then she hurried ashore to make a fire in a sheltered place among the firs, and I stood and fished, watching for the blue smoke to curl up among the trees. Hannah was a good hand with an axe, and it didn't take her long to fix a homey fireplace with plenty of balsam boughs to sit on close beside the blaze. It always made me think of an outdoor room, if such a thing were possible.

When it was cold and blowy, we'd go ashore every hour "to get a warm." We never failed on any of our trips to lunch on sea trout, fried crisp and brown. Tea and bread and crisp sea trout, there in the cove under a big fir, and we looking out across the ice and feeling snug—Hannah and I had some good days, and they rested me and made me feel strong and healthy and that I was getting what I'd come for, which was not entirely fish.

Sometimes we had the bag more than half full of trout by afternoon, and quite often we'd have another mugup of bread and tea there by our fire before starting home. "Just to pick us up," I said, and Hannah cocked her head and twinkled her bright eyes at me, knowing very well that we didn't need any picking up whatever. We always hated to leave that spot on the point by the brook mouth, she to her work and I to mine.

Going home over the ice, with the little komatik whispering behind us and the sunset at our backs, with the Mealy

Mountains dimming way across the bay ahead and a few lights showing yellow as we came round the bend, Hannah never stopped her prattle. She knew I didn't listen, and she knew she wasn't saying anything, but that made no difference. Each of us knew the other was happy, and once as we came down the lake in the twilight hush, with the west all aflame and the ice turning purple and the stars coming out, we held hands like schoolgirls, swinging our arms and stealing a sidewise glance now and then. There is something about sunset time when the cold becomes a solid presence and the land is at its grimmest and yet most beautiful.

When we dropped the fish on the floor in Hannah's kitchen, they were frozen so hard they sounded like a sack full of rocks. She took half and insisted that I take the other half, though she always caught more than I did. It pleased me to come back to the hospital with fish enough for the whole crew, and gave me an idea how a hunter feels at the end of a good day.

But then a seeming misfortune overtook Hannah. She began to have fits. And they were always in the middle of the night or very early morning. In her little house she'd begin to moan and rave. She'd tumble out of bed and squirm about on the floor. Her family was aroused, the neighbors were called, and the nurse of course.

I noticed that the symptoms were always different. Sometimes Hannah was rigid and quite still; sometimes she thrashed about in a loose-jointed manner and screamed and yelled like something hardly human. This happened twice, and at the third midnight alarm I was not very pleased.

I found a large crowd of neighbors, friends, and relatives thronging the house, all gathered around Hannah, who was prone across the seats of two chairs, stiff as a poker and groaning occasionally. They were smallish chairs, and it seemed odd to me that she could balance there. I spoke to her and from the flicker of her closed eyelids I was sure she heard me, though she didn't answer. I lifted up her eyelid a little. The pupil contracted and her bright eye twinkled at me in spite of itself.

Now, you know, a person in a true fit will just stare without a sign of life.

It came to me that cold water was one of Hannah's great dislikes. It is a perfectly natural aversion, produced by the environment. The preceding summer when I had asked a trapper if he didn't enjoy swimming in the sandy shallows of the Bight where the sun was warm, he answered, "I gets enough of cold and wet without swimmin' in the stuff."

So I said to the crowd at Hannah's, "We'll have to bring her out of this. It's dangerous to leave her in this condition. Fill a washtub with ice-cold water, and if she doesn't come round in two minutes, we'll put her in. The shock may possibly bring her to."

There were two buckets of water on the kitchen bench, but I told the men the chill would be off that, and they'd have to get some fresh. The tub was set in the alcove where Hannah might be disrobed with some vestiges of privacy, and the bucket brigade clattered down the bank to break open the water hole.

But before they were back, Hannah stirred; she threw her arms above her head, opened her eyes and said, "Where am I?" We were able to help her to her bed where she rested quite comfortably.

"Now," I said to the family, in Hannah's hearing, "if

this ever happens again, don't wait to call me. Fill a tub with ice-cold water and plunge her in. It is important to do it immediately, without waiting for anything, because the longer she stays in one of these fits, the harder it may be to get her out of it."

The family shuddered, but nodded solemn agreement.

And Hannah never had another fit.

What was it? Hysteria? The need for love and friendship? Was I not myself sometimes lonely and longing for love? A mental snarl was certainly at the bottom of it. But who can say where the border line lies between the mental and the physical? Perhaps Hannah's case faintly resembled a school girl's crush for a well-loved teacher. Sure it is that in Hannah's hard life there was a sudden welling up of need for friendliness, sympathy, attention. Though there would seem to have been nothing "physically" the matter with Hannah, though an outsider might be tempted at first glance to say that the midnight alarms were a fake and a put-up job, I believe that her attacks were at the time impossible for her to control.

In any case, it was all right with Hannah and me; we were still friends, and went fishing again many times that winter. I didn't say anything to her about the attacks she'd had. But I felt pretty sure she was all okay when one evening in March coming home from Big Brook, she put her mitten in mine and said, "Miss, I hopes I'll never have no more of them fits."

CHAPTER XVII

GIRLISH, black-haired Mrs. Stewart Michelin sent for the
nurse at 10:30 in the evening. This was her seventh baby.
She was healthy and strong and in splendid condition. Her
husband was the jolliest man in the village, the champion
snowshoe traveller of the whole bay, and he looked like a
boy. Quite an achievement for the father of seven children.
On dull days he would go out of the house, throw a tin
can into the air and see how long he could keep it up there
by well-placed blasts from his prized repeating shotgun.
"You shouldn't waste cartridges," said his careful neighbor.

"Ah, that's what they're for, b'y," said Stewart pityingly.

He loved to bait the Hudson's Bay Company manager
with taunts about the high price of goods at the post, and
he was one of the few in no need of credit who dared to
do so. He was always going on trips just for the fun of it,
often taking his family if it was summer. His fur path took
in from Grand River only about forty miles away, so he
was home now and then in the winter, and thought nothing
of snowshoeing home just for a dance, where he and his
wife were likely to be the handsomest, laughingest couple
on the floor of the cleared-out schoolhouse. Withal, he con-
sistently made one of the best hunts in the bay, and his furs
enabled him to have a motorboat and a special little fifteen-
foot canoe for duck hunting—sure sign of affluence. Stewart
had sparkling eyes and a battered hat. When he came in

off the bay on a winter afternoon, having hauled his toboggan thirty miles since sunrise, he'd come up the bank with an insouciant grin and throw you a quip that had half a dozen barbs in it.

Polly and I answered the baby call that Saturday night. We found Mrs. Stewart in bed, smiling, with labor pains well advanced.

"How long have you been having pains?"

"Oh, some hours now."

In the kitchen, strung on a line across the stove from wall to wall were innumerable pairs of deerskin moccasins, ranging from the two-inch size on up, all made by Mrs. Stewart.

"Did you wash all those?" I asked.

"Yes," she said. "I always do all their shoes after their baths on Saturday night. Then the floor is so tracked up, I mops it with the water that's left, ready for Sunday. I'm glad I got through in time."

"Yes," said Stewart, "I had to do that corner under the bench myself. Now weren't that a shame?"

The pains increased, but she smiled between pains right to the last. Polly gave her some whiffs of ether at the proper moments, and the babe was born two hours after we got there.

One small boy had awakened, and his father sat in the kitchen holding the sleepy one on his knee. As Polly passed him on her way to the stove, she said, "I guess I'll take that fellow home to the States with me when I go."

Stewart laughed. "You better take my woman instead. At this rate we'll soon have seventeen, and I don't know how I'll feed 'em."

Walking home, Polly said to me, "Birth control."

"Yes," I said, "I know. But it isn't as simple as all that. It was the first thing I thought of. I met a woman on the steamer crossing the Atlantic who said to me, 'Oh, the Grenfell Mission, I'm sick of those pitiful tales of eight children under ten years and the mother dying in childbirth. Birth control would solve the whole problem.' So I thought of it. But this territory belongs to Newfoundland, and birth control is contrary to Newfoundland law. I had it in mind that I'd break the law in cases like this on my own hook, but when I enquired in St. Anthony for birth control supplies I was given orders not to teach birth control. The mission, I was told, had troubles enough already."

"We could work to change the law."

"Let's shake on that." And we did.

The Indian head behind Indian Harbor Hospital.

North West River beside the river mouth. At far left, the Hudson's Bay Company, next the hospital, the school, boarding cottages, and dwellings. Firewood is stacked at the water's edge. Hospital vessel Maraval *at the wharf's end. Yearly supply schooner anchored in the stream.*

Murdock McLean

A Montagnais woman, wearing a traditional beaded cap.

Sir Wilfred Grenfell, little Ethel, and nurse Kate Austen. Ethel was badly burned, but after four months of intensive nursing she is shown here almost recovered.

A trapper's home in North West River.

Montagnais Indian women at their camp across the river.

"Bud" (Elliott) Merrick the winter he snowshoed 700 miles with trappers.

Montagnais Indians making canoes across the river from North West River village.

Kate Austen on one of the warm sandy beaches on Grand Lake, where nobody lived. That summer "we fished and sailed to our hearts' content, subsisting on goose and salmon as well as love."

CHAPTER XVIII

CHRISTMAS was a tremendous event, so we began to get ready for it long ahead of time. A present for every child in the bay was a tall order, but up in the attic in the clothing store our twelve big cases were full of wonders, not the least of which were three bolts of blue denim. We made denim overalls and denim shirts by the dozen in the fall for the poorer cottage children, and we became handy at making dickies of it, with trimmings of colored braid and the hood fancied up with a fox tail. To see a child's face looking out of a fur-edged hood always made me feel that the giver ought to know there wasn't anything else to put over the sweater inside, that this kid was freezing yesterday.

There were wonderful men's overcoats which we gave away as presents to women who could make children's pants and coats out of them. Out of the scraps they made mittens for the young ones. There were four barrels of newspapers and periodicals, which, after being read and reread and studied and passed on, would finally be pasted on someone's walls to keep the cold out.

The Estey Organ Company of Brattleboro, Vermont, had sent a little foot-pump organ which the village was going to go crazy over. Some Girl Guides and girls' clubs had sent boxes of dolls and dozens of jackknives. From a wholesale firm had come a barrel of odd pieces of china, enough to give one cup or saucer or plate or bowl to every woman. A needlewomen's guild from somewhere in the States had contributed dozens of cretonne sewing bags containing scissors, buttons, needles, thread, thimbles, skeins of wool, tape measures, hooks and eyes, elastic.

In the middle of one of the magic cases I found a separate box of beautiful knitted things for children. The little red sweater had cloth reinforcements down the buttonhole seam, and a pocket. The knitted cap had a beautiful tassel and some white bunches of wool tied in here and there for contrast. There were five children's sweaters, five pairs of children's wool stockings, mostly navy blue or brown. In addition the box contained three outfits of soft white baby clothes and five scarves. I could visualize almost every baby in the bay whose mother would be awe-struck by the baby things.

On one of the clothing store shelves was a piece of green homespun made on the mission looms at St. Anthony. This I sent to Mrs. Stewart so she could make her daughters skirts to go with the sweaters for a whole new Christmas outfit. I found flannel for Mrs. Burns, to go with the red cap and mitts for Dennis. When the wonderful box of knitted stuff was empty, it still had a clean smell of lavender mixed with the scent of wool. There was a card in the bottom:

Laura N. Russell
Toronto

I was hoping no call would come from some faraway sick one during the days before Christmas, because I had all I could handle. Every day I had my regular visit to a certain Mrs. Gear who was dying of T. B., the meals to arrange, and other calls around the village attending various aches and pains and sores. Somehow or other, mostly late at night,

Polly and I made new curtains for the whole hospital. I baked Christmas cakes for the Gears and for an old widow woman named Mrs. McKenzie, and while I was at it, baked eight more for other people. We were having a Christmas tree on Christmas Eve for the village, and in readiness for that we bagged up eighty packs of candy. My room was so full of packages I could hardly find room to sleep in it. Wednesday before Christmas I had the school children in to practice some songs for the Christmas tree. Quite a few letters came in from down the bay asking if I could send canvas or denim or wool of any description. Jane had a temporary illness and I did the cooking; every night we rehearsed "The Birds' Christmas Carol," which we were going to put on Christmas Eve. There was also a Santa Claus suit to make.

One day Mrs. Elizabeth Bird came in with an enormous bundle. I was glad to see her because she hadn't liked it at all that I had encouraged her son Jed to marry Naomi.

"I brought something," she said. "You know, I used to live in Newfoundland, and once when I was in the hospital in St. Johns, I had nothing for my sore head but a hard straw pillow. So I began thinking these last few years I'd make some soft pillows for here. These are a present to the hospital."

It seemed mighty decent of the dear old soul. Three or four years it must have taken Jed to shoot enough geese for all this down.

In the last days before Christmas, trappers began to arrive from the woods. Steve Burns and his boys pulled in from Grand Lake-Nascopi region, and on the way Murdock Mc-Lean and Johnnie Montague had teamed up with them. The men hadn't caught much fur in there as yet, but they were going to load up their toboggans with fresh supplies of grub and go back in a few days. Stewart Michelin came in off the bay from his Grand River path which he calls Sandy Banks. We spotted him when he was only a tiny black dot rounding Point Gibou. Jed was home too from his path which takes in on Big Brook and goes four days' walk to the southwest. These were the lucky ones with hunting grounds close to home. The other hunters were too far away to make the trip, and all we could do was think of them in their snowed-up cabins on the height-of-land by lake shores and rivers that most of us women would never see. Looking out through a little hole in the log wall at the forest and sky, they'd be thinking of us as they cooked their Christmas dinners of partridge stew.

The day of Christmas Eve a snowstorm came on about midday. Though the wind dropped at dark, snow was still falling when I saw the lights around the village begin to go out. We could hear them calling along the snowy paths. In one of the hospital windows we had three red candles which glowed on the snow outside and lit up the steps. A cluster of people were by the door laughing and joking and flapping the snow off themselves with their mittens. There were crowds of mothers and children and sleds and snowy blankets and komatik boxes packed full of little round faces. "Merry Christmas, Merry Christmas," "Hi, b'y," "Come on in," "Up you go." Babies wrapped in blankets on which the snow glistened showed nothing but the tips of their pink noses. Johnnie Montague stepped softly in, his feet shy and quiet in new beaded moccasins, his face wreathed in impudent grins. He sniffed at the balsam boughs tied on the walls with red ribbon. "Fir brush!" he scoffed. "You wouldn't think so much of them old stuffies if you'd been sleepin' on 'em for months."

Stewart came in with his rolling snowshoe gait, carrying little George done up in a canvas sled wrapper. "No, Miss, I couldn't stay away from this, you bet." He caught sight of John. "Ho, b'y, any fur up Grand Lake these days?" And they commenced on foxes and marten and otters and mink and all that.

Mrs. Burns came in with her brood from across the river. The river ice was bad with lots of dangerous air holes. "But I never mind 'em, me, if Steve's along."

"We got a good long komatik that bridges most of 'em," said Steve reassuringly. Compared to his adventures in the country a few air holes opposite the town weren't worth speaking about.

Mrs. Steve pulled the new baby's outer wrappings aside and showed me the knitted shirt from Toronto. "Fits perfect. Ribbons! Think of that now!"

"O-O-O," whispered Effie, looking at the big tree Jack had cut, and the tinsel decorations and colored paper chains and the hundreds of presents hanging on the branches and laid out underneath. Some of the girls in this town, fourteen, sixteen years old, are so pretty they'd make your heart turn over, for they have the strong sweet beauty of wild flowers, the first ones you find in the woods in the spring. They don't realize it, and that makes it even more terrific.

Little Harold Blake, about sixteen inches high, waddled in, dressed in overcoat, moccasins, mitts, cap and scarf, with just two bright eyes shining out. He was amazed at the tree too, but he wasn't going to let on. "Where's Santa Claus?" he shouted.

Dan's four girls followed next, two lovely fair-haired ones and two very dark, their cheeks red and glowing, all their eyes sparkling. When they had their outer covers off, they showed me the new bright sweaters with the caps to match, and the homespun skirts. Their mother said to me, "The mother is happy when the children are warm."

The room was jammed, and too hot. The boarding cottage kids poured in like a river going over a broken dam. Jack ran to cool off the furnace, while Polly, playing the new organ, started the school children on their song, "Jolly Old St. Nicholas," and I sneaked up the back stairs to climb into the Santa Claus suit. When the song was about over, I went down the front stairs and came around the hospital through the snow, jangling some bells. As I burst in the main room door, nobody knew the deep voice, of course. I went to the tree and called out names in the big voice and passed out the presents and candy and toys and clothing as quick as I could, because I was dying of the heat, the way Santa Clauses always are.

Jack was in a corner showing Annie a varnished clothes chest he had built for her, and she was critically fitting onto him a handmade red wool coat. Polly was down on the floor trying to make a toy train go, and boys were waving jackknives, looking for sticks to whittle. Kids were eating apples and candies, spilling bags of suckers, rolling around on kiddie cars, dragging toy sleds. My bread-stealing wood-mice from Traverspine were now the friendliest little nippers alive. They had dolls, with petticoats. The most inconsequential articles pleased the men, for it was the one gift they received a year. A cake of soap, a ten-cent bandanna, left them speechless. Stewart had a red scarf knotted around his neck like a pirate. "Look at this," he was saying. The girls were clutching their dolls, and the women waving their china pieces and comparing sewing bags. The formlessness of their gratitude almost choked them. Who could it be who had scissors and knives enough to give away?

Santa Claus went out into the snow and the cold. The stars were very bright and looked unusually low in the sky. I took the pillow out of my stomach and sat on it in the snow and looked at the yellow windows and the candles, and listened to the hum inside. It seemed to me I had never experienced a Christmas like this one. Pretty soon I was rested and freezing, so I went upstairs by the front way to get into my Mrs. Ruggles costume for the play.

A play in these parts is so literally taken, the audience so breathless and wholly lost in the doings on the stage, that, ham actors as we were, we wondered ourselves which was real, this make-believe or that everyday world we used to know. If real art produces enchantment, lifts people out of themselves and makes them forget their own names, then for the time being we were artists. The attention of the audience was so fixed, so intense and focused with concentrated power it was tangible. When the end approached, we felt sad to know the final curtain would break that solid link between us and the audience, as you might break a bar of transparent ice. We stood in front of the curtain with our wigs off. It was over. A sigh went up from the crowd as though they hadn't drawn a clear breath since the play began.

Mince pie and coffee were next on the program for everybody. The sleeping babes were laid in rows against the wall. Johnnie said we ought to auction them off to the highest bidder. "There's plenty more where they came from." Considerable impromptu harmonica music filtered through the crowded room in spite of the mince pie. I sat munching between my old pals Suzannah and Mrs. McKenzie. "The best party I ever was to," Suzannah mumbled.

The children were all so sleepy, it was time to break up. "Good night, good night," "Oh, aren't we lucky," "Look, Miss, the doll shuts her eyes," "So long, Jacko," "*Meeamee abishish.*" Caps and mitts on again, sleeping cherubs in blankets, sleds full of children, runners squeaking on snow, stars, yellow lamplight reaching out to the edge of the snowy trees. "Good night," "Merry Christmas." It was quiet, quiet as it must be by the shores of those long winding lakes in the country.

None of the hospital staff had had time for supper, and mighty little for refreshments. We decided we needed some toast and hash in front of the fireplace. We exchanged Christmas presents there, silly things that made us laugh because we were so tired: a huge coil of rope to Jack because when he went to carry some medicine across the bay last week, he took Annie with him and bounced her off the sledge; a tea bag for me; a little piece of duffel sewed to a clothespin for Miss Winette because the frost bites her nose about every time she goes anywhere; an onion for Polly because she's trying to give up cigarettes, and Jack says when you're eating a raw onion you can't think of wanting to smoke.

It was one o'clock by this time and we were due to meet one of the Hudson's Bay clerks named Symington and Johnnie Montague at the post for a little carol singing. We put on our dickies and pants, because it was nearly twenty-five below outside. We had practised carols a couple of times, and with the whole staff and Symington's bass and John's tenor, we had quite an idea of ourselves. Sarah Jane volunteered to stay and look after the house. "When I sing," she said, "folks think it's a old black crow with a sore throat."

"You can't get any sympathy out of us," said Polly. "Anybody who's had four proposals!"

It was a fact. Sarah Jane was the Unattainable Female. She had turned down four offers of marriage, some of them pretty good offers too.

The snow was very deep, so we were all on snowshoes, which creaked quite sociably in the cold. Symington and John were waiting, their breath sending up great clouds of white in the moonlight. We felt like conspirators, and so we were I suppose, about to wake up the poor tired village when it had just settled down for the night. But Christmas comes only once a year, and there are so many quiet nights.

Anyway, we filled it with song. We began on Johnnie's family at the upper end of the village with "Silent Night" and toured on down with "It Came Upon the Midnight Clear" and "Little Town of Bethlehem," singing a song at every house and carrying it away till we reached another. Jack said he had a stomach ache, and Polly had to smoke a cigarette, but we produced quite some volume nevertheless. In the frosty air with the snow glistening bright, and the woods dark out back, and the bay half alight, the songs sounded sweet and glad. Symington was magnificent, booming out the bass, and on the high tenor notes John opened up his throat and poured it out like a bird. Our trouble was that, like most amateur armies, we were all generals, and so busy harmonizing gorgeous chords there was hardly anybody left to carry the air. For some reason or other we finished up with "Sweet and Low" and "Steal Away to Jesus." The notes died away. We took a last look at the moon going down, and rolled into bed at three-thirty.

Christmas morning Jack and Polly and I went to see Mrs. McKenzie. Now, Mrs. McKenzie was very special. For a woman over seventy years old to live alone, and live by washing, is something, I call it. She was so independent the mission couldn't do much for her. She did all the washing for the H. B. C., which included the Lerou family of five, and three clerks (pronounced *clarks*). She was gray-haired and stony-looking. The stony look hid shyness and pride. Long ago her husband had gone crazy. I believe they tied his hands to iron rings in the floor, and then he went crazier than ever and soon died. The H. B. C. supplied her with sawed wood as part of her laundry pay, but she split it herself. Now and then a litle boy would come along and split some for her. I don't know why. It wasn't as though she could give him anything for it. I had hardly ever been in there when clothes weren't hanging all across her kitchen-sitting room, damp and mournful, shrouded in steam from the washboiler on the stove. And yet she was cheerful. What had she to be cheerful about? She was not an easy soul; she couldn't visit around the village and be a jolly old grandmother to everybody. That was not her way, her Scotch way. She stopped at home and bit her lip and worked.

Mrs. McKenzie had broken her axe a few days before Christmas, and she was troubled about it. She had to have lots of hot water which meant lots of wood to split, which in turn meant borrowing an axe from the Montagues, though one of her mottoes was, "Neither a borrower nor a lender be." We found her sewing by the window, a red braid bow tied in her dress for Christmas and an old stamped gold pin at her neck. Hannah Montague had brought her a wreath of balsam which hung outside by the door.

"Here you be," said Jack, and handed her a brand new axe he'd bought out of his own pay. Polly had a piece of dress goods for her, and I had a Christmas cake.

Mrs. McKenzie was excited, you could see, but it was the axe her eyes kept returning to. That was linked with her fight for independence. We "sat" for a minute and looked at her lined old face and work-worn hands. "I'm going to the Montagues," she said. "They've asked me for dinner. I'll take my new cake."

Polly indicated me with a wave of her hand. "It was made by an expert," she said. She stretched out her legs, her beautiful legs encased in new sealskin boots with beaded vamps and tied at the tops with bright blue ribbon drawstrings. She pulled up her new red plaid skirt so Jack could see her knees, and sighed soulfully. That meant she was dying for a smoke. A charming vixen, Polly is. I wondered what Mrs. McKenzie made of her.

Polly went on, "I hope we didn't wake you up with our singing last night."

Mrs. McKenzie put a withered hand to her breast. "For a little," she said, "I thought it was the angels."

We went home then, because Jack had a radio schedule for eleven o'clock with Ern Jerrett in Brigus, Newfoundland. In between hearing news of Newfoundland, which is always uniformly bad, Jack clicked off a message for Ern to forward to Doctor Paddon, now quite recovered from his gallstones operation, telling him that all was so fine with the station we were being mistaken for the angels.

Messages to the north were coming through from CKAC in Montreal, and though our radio wasn't behaving very well, we could get some of them. Many were to Hudson's Bay Company posts far north of us at Chimo, Wolstenholm, Port Burwell and Ponds Inlet. I heard one winging its way to Mr. Harlan, my acquaintance of the steamer. It seemed strange to think of those fur traders so far away, who stay five years and see but one ship a year, now sitting close to the magic box, hearing from home, but unable to reply.

There were a great many greetings to Royal Northwest Mounted Policemen in Baffin Land from their sweethearts in Canada. "Nellie sends lots of love and kisses to Sergeant Ben Marsh," and it was most interesting to hear that five or six girls from Edmonton to Quebec were sending the same. Then the messages began coming through for us. "To Miss Polly Coates, North West River. Uncle and Aunt send love and Christmas greetings. Letters and food are on the way." "To Miss Kate Austen in North West River a message from Sydney, Australia. How are you and when are you coming home if ever? We are all at dinner together thinking of you and sending greetings as warm as the Australian sun." We got no more clearly, just snatches, messages without senders' names, names without messages. "—with love from Henry and I will never forget you—Br-r, crackle, pop!" "—the mittens that were ordered—" "—on this Christmas day—" "To Miss Henrietta Winette, North West River, b-r-r, b-z-z!" The ether had given us all the magic it was going to, in spite of Jack's fiddling with knobs and wires. It was disappointing and maddening. We vowed we wouldn't listen ever again. But on New Year's Day when another such broadcast to the north was scheduled, we were all packed in the radio room again, tantalized again by more fragments and static howls.

A week passed. I had been working hard all day seeing to some impetigo cases in the school and a number of other things, so I hadn't had time to see to Mrs. Gear. Poor soul, to be dying of T. B. and to have nothing but what the mission could provide. I had often thought that she ought to be in the hospital where I could look after her better, she having been sick a year and getting worse. But every time I urged her, she said she preferred to stay home with her husband. "Jim does pretty good for me, and I'd be lonesome to the hospital."

After supper I wrapped up a bowl of creamed codfish for her (nearly every day we sent broth or any particularly appetizing or nourishing dish we might have), threw on a coat and cap and mitts, took my snowshoes off the peg and started out. Jack came to the door with me. A northwest gale was making the snow hiss with squalls of drift. We couldn't see Pottles' lighted window, though it was only a few rods away.

"I don't know as you should go," Jack said. "It's bad, and getting worse. Can't see anything."

I knew I'd be all right. All I had to do was keep the wind on one side of my face and I'd end up against some house or other. I started off across the picket fence, which was completely snowed under. Gear's little two-room cabin was only a quarter of a mile away down on the point, but I was about perished when I got there. The snow cut like a rasp, and the wind almost blew me flat. As the drifts hadn't settled, I sank almost to the knees at every step, and without snowshoes it would have been impossible to get there. Jim opened the door for me, and I fell in, snow and all. He was a grand little sawed-off Englishman, getting on in years now, but a clever carpenter and the best hand in the village at patching a stove-in boat or finding one of those mysterious leaks that nobody else can trace.

"A dirty night," he said. "You didn't get off your course?"

"Not quite. Heavens, it seems quiet in here." The little flat-wick lamp was serenely burning on the table, the stove was warm. Against the windows snow hissed savagely.

I found Linda had a high fever. Her wispy hair was all stringy and uncared for. Her bed was rumpled and wrinkled, and she wouldn't eat any creamed codfish or drink any broth. I got her to let me do her hair and I gave her a sponge bath and gently massaged her back. I lifted her too easily as I turned her onto the fresh sheet, for she weighed only sixty pounds. She did drink half a glass of water, and I stayed to visit a few minutes, hoping to cheer her up by telling her how rough it was outside, how pleasant within. "Rachael is making a new quilt," I said. "A black and yellow and pink one. Rhoda finished a hooked rug today. Donald's boy came from Mud Lake after some yeast. He says that Nettie's baby has been sick again, but is better now. They've caught a few trout off Birch Run Point. He says the snow-shoe walking is very deep. He was going to start back this afternoon and spend the night in Point Gibou tilt, but the storm is so bad he's staying. He saw a fox coming across Sandy Point portage, but he only had his shotgun, and it was too far. He's staying with Harvey at the Company kitchen. Two Indians are there too. They came from up Nascopi after tobacco. They say caribou are scarce in there this winter. Nine children in the school have impetigo, and I'm going to clean that up once and for all or bust."

Linda smiled. "What a lot of news."

"I'd better go now. I'll be down tomorrow. What about some of that broth?"

"Well, just a sip."

She took half a cup.

"Good night."

"Good night. You won't get lost?"

"Not likely."

My snowshoe track was completely blown out, and the wind was truly awe-inspiring. It blew the breath back into my body as it raced over the village and tore out across the bay with a howling roar that did not go away, but stayed out there yelling like a thousand devils. Honestly, a person couldn't live very long on the bay in a wind like that. Everything was so dim and smothered in drift that I got a little confused for a moment until I bumped into the big up-ended woodpiles which stood like ghostly tepees on the shore. I turned against the gale and made for the spot where I knew the hospital was, but I hadn't gone more than twenty steps when suddenly the snow opened and swallowed me. My snowshoes knifed off edgewise one on top of the other and I sank a good nine feet straight down, all tangled up, snow in my face and down my neck and up my sleeves. I thought I must be out on the river falling through an air hole and drowning. Then it reassured me to feel the branches of a little spruce tree under my leg. I knew that little tree. Some former nurse had planted it by the gate for a shrub, a thing of beauty. Unfortunately the bushy little tree had caught the snow, kept it from settling and left a huge hollow. I began to kick and crawl, but I only buried myself deeper. My snowshoe thong was hurting me, my face was wet and freezing. The top level of snow above me was at least four feet over my head. I remembered what a huge drift there was in front of the hospital where the wind eddied around the woodpiles, cutting the ground bare to the very ice and piling it in a long windrow beyond. I was at the bottom of that, with clouds of drift whirling in at the top of the hole and settling down on my head. I kicked and screamed and beat the snow, panic-struck as it crumbled and fell away like quicksilver under me. I rolled and shrieked, but no one heard. Maybe I would never get out, maybe the hole, already drifting in, would be filled by morning and my body would lie here till spring. So close to the hospital door! How sad and ludicrous it would seem!

Rage blinded me, rage that I wasn't snug and warm in my bed this very minute. All on account of this shrub, this beastly thing of beauty, this joy forever! My teeth began to chatter. I wasn't getting anywhere this way. Suddenly I remembered hearing Pleeman Blake say he fell in a big hollow once, where a willow bush held up the snow. What did he do? He said he took off his snowshoes and dug.

I lay on my back half buried and unwound the thongs from my feet. I stood on one racquet and dug with the other, trying to make a step a little way up at least. At first there was no place much to put the snow, but I crammed it in behind me somewhere. Digging and stepping up, I progressed until my head was at the level of the surface snow. There the wind cooled off my dripping brow. I lost one snowshoe in the bottomless fluff and had a long setback finding it, but at the end of half an hour or so I staggered out. In the hospital it was midnight. I didn't tell a soul, largely because they were all sound asleep.

In the morning I went out and had a look at my excavation. The drift had partly filled it in, but you could still have lost three horses in it. After a few days the hole covered over. Nobody had a chance to say, "Gee, it's immense!"

More hard luck hit me soon. Helping with supper next night, I knocked a boiling coffeepot off the stove onto my left leg and hand. I yelled and pulled off my stocking. In a second Polly and Jack came running, but they were so horrified they just stood looking and saying, "Oh!" and wringing their hands. The pain was great and I was so upset at what I had done to myself, that in a sudden, illogical fit of anger I said to them, "Well, do something, can't you? Get something to put on it!" I knew so well that if it had been either of them, I'd have had the dressings on by now. "Lord save us, if I were dying I'd have to treat myself. Can't somebody do something for *me* just once?"

"What shall I get?" asked Polly in a small voice.

"Oh, for Heaven's sake get picric acid."

When Polly came hurrying with the dressing, we were overwhelmed with contrition, I for having lost my temper and she for having been slow. We smiled at each other and didn't say anything.

I had to go to bed. It was quite a bad burn all down my thigh and knee and calf. My left hand was burned even more deeply, and in the night water blisters rose on it two inches high. Jack slept on the floor beside my bed in case I wanted anything. He said it was a good chance to try out his new sleeping bag. I simply lay there in great misery, unable to sleep, thinking what a fool I was and wondering what would happen if a sick call came from far away. I went over in my mind all the coming babies, and I couldn't think of any due yet awhile, which was a blessing.

In the morning Polly had to cut and dress my blisters while I told her what to do. She did quite a nice job too, and was pleased, because she had never supposed she could chop people.

In the afternoon Mrs. Elizabeth Bird came to see me, bringing another pillow, a little one this time, "to rest your hand on." I thought it was very kind of her. "Goodness, where do you get all the down?" I asked. "That's four pillows you've given us."

"My boy is a good hunter," she said. "He brings home lots of geese." She seemed very proud of Jed, and of Naomi too.

Next day I felt a little better. Sarah Jane and Pearlie couldn't do enough for me. It seemed odd to sit still and watch other people working, but, as the pain lessened, the time did not go too slowly. Then too, a number of people came to sit with me. Aunt Suzannah came hobbling up from the Bight with a huge bundle in her arms. It was a potted freesia plant, wrapped in a blanket so it wouldn't freeze on the way.

"I heerd about your burn," she said, "and I wants you to have this."

It had a beautifully fragrant smell like a hyacinth. I feasted my eyes upon it, for such a bloom is a rare treasure here in the middle of winter. It was Suzannah's only blossoming plant at the time, although she had others coming on, geraniums, begonias, and even tulips. Every night, I knew, she carefully placed all her plants on a rocking chair in the center of the room, near the stove, as far as possible from the frosty windows and the cold that comes creeping, and there she tenderly wrapped them in a blanket and a quilt. Her flowers and her hens were Aunt Suzannah's chief concern, and now she was giving me the firstling of her flock.

Mrs. Jim Pottle came in to sit, a smallish, very busy, gray-haired woman of about fifty. She did the hospital laundry, and hardly a day went by that I didn't see her trudging about on snowshoes behind the house, hanging out the clothes, no matter what the weather.

She can't read, she hasn't any small talk, she knows no news except the news of the village which I know too. She sits and rocks with me, to help me pass the time. We converse in a wordless way, with long pauses.

"Got your washing done, Mrs. Pottle?"

"Yes, Miss, all done. 'Tweren't very big this week. Wunnerful fine weather for washin' we've had."

"How's the ironing?"

"Fine, Miss."

"Children well?"

"Yes, Miss."

We sit and rock for twenty minutes, and I sense that she feels she should leave.

"Well, I suppose you must be getting back?"

"Yes, Miss, and I hopes you'll soon be well again."

She departs. It is as simple as that. What does it matter if she has no small talk? I think how often I have seen her wrestling in the wind with a union suit frozen hard as a board. The thing is as unmanageable as a sun-stiffened, un-cured cowhide. She has a pitcher pump in the kitchen, she heats all her water on the stove, she irons with flatirons. Since she and Jim both work for the mission, they are fairly comfortable. Much of their pay they take in clothing and good food. They do not think it right to live in the midst of this plenty without sharing it, so, being childless, they have adopted three orphans whom they love as their own.

I was laid up a week, and the last few days were very quiet and painless and strangely sweet. One so seldom has time to simply *be*, and to cultivate one's self. I think a little sickness is a pleasure in every life. I played my beloved records by the hour on Polly's portable Vic, and in my Beethoven and Brahms I heard messages and mysteries I had not known before. I read my dear old *Golden Treasury*, and I remembered concerts in Sydney that I had scrimped for months to go to—Melba, Kreisler, Paderewski. Somehow in a faraway place like this with the snow and cold pressing in at the window, and at night the icy stars and the killing winds, one's cherished books and songs become doubly dear. There are so few material possessions, there is so little art here, one's feelers become supersensitive to lovely things as they used to be in childhood.

During my last few days of precious leisure I went over the list of donors who had made our Christmas possible. I wrote to the Estey Organ Company and the ladies' club that had sent us the sewing bags, and the man who sent the barrels of papers. I wrote the china contributor, the denim company, the doll people, the jackknife Santa Claus and the toy givers. Many of the clothing-store blessings had come anonymously, but I wrote to those who had sent their names. I told them it seemed wrong that we should have all the joy of giving out the things they had sent. I just felt in the mood for it, and I tried to make them see the individual tears of joy. Particularly I wrote to the woman in Toronto who had sent the knitted goods. I told her about Mrs. Dan, and Effie that beautiful child, and Cyril with the sparkling eyes, and Mrs. Burns. I told her how a man had snowshoed twenty miles to bring a note of thanks his wife had written. For once I wanted this illogical old world to be logical, and this Canadian woman to see how much happiness and warmth she had created.

To finish this story I have to jump temporarily eight months to the following August. Here is the letter that came for me aboard the August mail steamer. It was from the woman in Toronto.

Dear Miss Austen,

Your letter made me happy. I did not expect such a full return. I am eighty years old, and I am blind. There is little I can do except knit, and that is why I make so many caps and sweaters and scarves. Of course I cannot write this, so my daughter-in-law is doing it for me. She also sewed the seams and made the buttonholes for the knitted things.

I know something of the work you are doing. At the age of nineteen I married a man who was going to China to be a missionary. For forty years, with an occasional year at home in America, we worked in China, and during that time two sons and a daughter were born to us, of whom only one son survives. After forty years, my husband's health began to fail. We returned to the States where he took charge of a settlement house in Brooklyn, New York. A surprising number of the problems we faced there were similar to problems we had met in China. When my husband died, I came to Toronto to live with my son and daughter-in-law. They are very good to me, and I pride myself that I am little trouble to them (THIS IS TRUE), though it is hard for a blind old lady to be sure of anything.

What I most wanted to say, my dear, is this. For sixty years I have been making up missionary packages of such clothing or food or medicine or books as I could collect. In various parts of the world and to various parts of the world I have sent them. Sometimes I have received a printed slip of acknowledgement from the head-quarters depot or mission board, sometimes nothing. Occasionally I have been informed that my contribution was destined for Syria or Armenia or the upper Yangtze. But never before in all that time have I had a personal letter picturing the village and telling me who is wearing the clothing and what they said. I did not suppose that ever in my lifetime I should receive a letter like that. May God bless you.

Sincerely yours,

Laura N. Russell.

CHAPTER XIX

A FACTOR in our lives was the outdoor W. C. back of the hospital. A neat little oblong building, a two-seater with a wooden partition between the lady and the gentleman, it was set quite a long way off among the trees, in the Spartan manner of the English. With freezing fingers, numbed anatomy, and buttons half buttoned, we ran to and fro through the snow like orphans of the storm. In the fall had been the worst time when gales blew through the whole structure, for the thing was built up on skids, Jack's idea, and a Newfoundland custom, he claimed. The scientific principle was that from time to time you could dig new holes and slide the house over them. The principal result we noticed, however, was a fine sweep for the wind, and a ghostly way the paper had of rising in the draft.

After snow had banked around our "Little Hell," as it was familiarly known, high as the roof by February, the cold was merely of the still, bone-paralyzing variety. In our trips to and fro we avoided one another with an unspoken, guarded sort of caution, but on occasions when each side became occupied by an opposite gender, the partition seemed very thin. The feminine strategy was to maintain an absolute silence so as to fool the unknown gentleman into believing that no one was freezing a foot away. Men have neither the fortitude nor the stupidity to follow such devious courses, which was fortunate or we would all have died of frost bite ere long. "Playing possum," Polly called this diversion.

It was a business to put on one's boots and furs and tramp out there. No one, of course, ever shovels a path in this country; keeping it shovelled would be too hopeless a proposition. Consequently an added trial was that after a snowstorm the first fellow out in the morning had to break trail on snowshoes, which meant that, as well as buttons and other impedimenta to freeze his fingers, he had snowshoes to take off and put on again. By March our tramped path was high, high as the top of the door. You slid down into our patent freezer as into a cave. The door, jammed with ice, would open only slightly, and hardly close at all. Some weeks later, it wouldn't move either way. Playing possum became a difficult art. They say that Eskimos, when their hands are freezing, lay them upon their stomachs to warm them up again. Many times I have done the same, and I can vouch for the fact that the stomach is often warm when the rest of one is not.

Whatever else may be said for our tribulation, which we all minded much worse than taking baths in one washtub with the feet in another, it certainly hardened us to the cold. By the time spring came and the mercury crept up to ten or twenty above zero, we ran in and out without coats or hats, and thought it was balmy.

In the eight months between October and June we received three dogteam mails. Now that New Year's was past, we expected one of those mails most any day. From Blanc Sablon on the Gulf of St. Lawrence it would have travelled up the coast some 700 miles or more on the irregular course the sledges had to follow, each relay being carried from fifty to a hundred miles by a local mailman, crossing wide bays if the sea ice was strong enough, scaling steep trails through the coast hills if it wasn't. To stay on the level sea ice, each local mail driver was willing to take big chances. Consequently it was not at all unusual in bad ice for a bag or two of mail to get lost, and sometimes even a mailman. Weight being at such a premium, they carried no packages or magazines, just letters. A dozen clever teamsters had had a hand in forwarding our mail to us, but the only one we saw was stubby, blue-eyed Little Jarge.

One sunny afternoon in the middle of January he came. A boy had spotted him with a telescope and spread the news an hour before the team pulled in. Polly was almost crazy with suspense to know who was President of the United States. Every one in the village, except me, ran to the Company store, which served also as post office. I couldn't leave the hospital, but through a window I could watch Jarge, a diminutive thing less than five feet tall, in a huge fur hood, crack the dogwhip and stage a spectacular sprint with his beautiful fourteen-dog team on the full gallop, the loaded komatik swaying straight through the village on the main path, and he giving never an answer to all the calls, "Hi Jarge! Hi Jarge! What's the news, Jarge?" When he reached the steps in front of the post, he conveyed with considerable artistic skill the illusion that he could hardly bring his team to a stop.

Pretty soon the hospital mailbags came over. We moved the chairs back to the walls in the living room and dumped out the flood of letters in the center of the floor, a magic cascade from far away. We could hardly wait, each one of us, to clutch our own and huddle into some corner where we might devour these words from our friends. It did not matter that they were months old, that my Australian letters were five or six weeks older than the rest. That made them all the more valuable.

Since Jarge would be staying only a day or so, I soon had to get busy with replies to the scrawly letters written in pencil from places around the lower bay. It was *Dear Nurse, Henry's sick with awful backaches going on three weeks and we hopes you'll call in when you can;* requests for bandages, medicine, a few cans of milk, a coat for Sammy, canvas for a dickie. Some of them were addressed to Doctor Paddon by people who still didn't know that he had had to go south months ago. Somebody had an axe cut that wouldn't heal; a little girl had a bad cough; some one wanted yarn or underwear or salve or mustard plasters. Some one was figuring on a baby "along in April sometime maybe. Do you think I'll be all right after the last time?" It was a little cross-section of the hopes and needs from down the bay. And every one who wrote for supplies would appear in the summer, come boat-transportation time, with produce, firewood, etc., and a profound desire to pay.

We worked till late that night filling prescriptions and clothing-store requests, answering notes and giving advice. I decided that before long I'd go down the bay myself and see to those cuts and babies.

Jarge dropped in several times to sit in the social room and listen to the music box. It was a super music box that wound up. I was secretly and unsympathetically in hope that the spring would break some day, but it never did. This durable contraption spun a metal disc punched full of holes, which caused to come tripping out of a painted door an unvarying selection of tinkling Swiss, dancing-in-the-shade, spun-gold, long-ago-and-far-away tunes that were famous the length and breadth of the bay. With that what-might-have-been quality Swiss music-box airs specialize in, they were wistful and fay, delicate as cobweb, and implacable as death. I liked them at first; they made me feel pleasantly sad. But enough is enough. Day in, day out, this infernal machine ground out the same collection of pretty, irresponsible tunes as different from the hard life of winter here as day is different from night. Perhaps that was what people liked about them. Frostbitten trappers closed their eyes and listened to them hour after hour, over and over again. And Jarge had no intention of going back down the bay without hearing them a good five times.

"What's the news, Jarge?" I asked him as he sat on a bench staring at the whirling disc.

"No news, Miss. I dunno nuthin', me."

That was the unvarying formula. People everywhere pestered him so for news, and he was so shy that he had invented this reply, as stereotyped as the endless repetition of the music box. Only by the most assiduous cultivation could intimate friends glean a few facts from Jarge, and then he let them slip as though by accident. Truly a strange messenger and go-between was Jarge, in a land where little bits of information come so rarely and last so long.

As I watched him soaking up our Swiss tunes, I saw that Jarge was humming them, remembering them, salting them away. And I felt sure that some night, caught out on the barrens in a blizzard, half frozen in his sleeping bag in a precarious shelter of canvas and snow and the turned-up komatik, Jarge would remember our *tra-la-la-lalala* and smile while the wind screamed and buried him deeper. The wind, the high-pitched *Ai-ee!* of the gale that was roaring over his head like a pack of demons mad for prey—that was a commonplace. But *tralala*—how did it go?—now there was something strange, oh wunnerful strange.

On lonely winter afternoons when the snow was blowing and dusk came early, the insidious nostalgia of the music box finally became too much for me. I hit on a wonderful plan, though. I said to Sarah Jane and Pearlie, "Every one loves the music box so—it does seem selfish for us to keep it to ourselves. Don't you think the generous thing to do would be for us to lend it round the village? Let each house keep it a few weeks and then pass it on?"

They thought it was a fine idea. And, glory be, the thing didn't come back for a whole year.

CHAPTER XX

By EARLY FEBRUARY my dogteam midwifery had netted fifteen new babies. There were baby seasons, occurring nine months after the trappers' midwinter return from the woods and nine months after they came back in March from the spring hunt.

"Well, Miss," the mother would say about the second day, "you and me have borned him, now what'll we call him? I likes a strange name, like Arminius or Rhonora."

One of the strangest was Noti, given to a boy born when there was *no tea* in the house. I liked simple names myself, so I suggested Kate for girls and Austen for boys until I began to fear that a whole generation of duplicates would hate me for an egotist. Then I started in on the names of my Australian brothers and sisters.

I was trying to remember the middle names of my in-laws one snowy day when a ten-year-old boy arrived with a message, having made the 22-mile trip on snowshoes in the most intense cold—forty-two below zero all day. It was not a baby case this time; rather, dysentery at Traverspine.

Crossing Goose Bay the woods seemed to whisper about us, while distant scene-shifters folded the points together, and a mirage lifted the trees off the ice and hung them in crooked strata along the edges of the sky.

"Looks fine and warm, eh?" said Jim, crooking his mitten thumb at the blue smoke of houses in Mud Lake. He pulled his fur hood closer around him, and, giving the long lash a little throw, sent it cracking lazily above the dogs.

Three houses of logs and boards high on a sandbank; behind the houses a rolling ocean of trees; that was Traverspine. One house was empty, and one belonged to James Michelin, a consumptive whose family were so poor they could hardly have existed without help from brother Robert who lived in the third. Robert's wife, Matilda, a smallish brown-haired woman in her early thirties, looked haggard and sleepless.

"Are you sick, Matilda?"

"No."

"You look it."

I went into the kitchen, glancing about for the children, one of whom was screaming. It was Louis, an emaciated little seven-year-old in a tiny shirt, standing up to the end rail of a bed. The child was half delirious, crazy with pain and weakness. In a room off the kitchen a little girl who was trying to get out of bed had toppled onto the floor. She was lying there crying softly with little flutterings in her throat. I went to her and picked her up, but she howled with fright to find herself in the arms of a stranger, so I gave her to Matilda.

Two more little girls were in a big homemade bed in one corner of the kitchen. The eldest, Sevilla, was asleep with one hand under her cheek, and seemed not too seriously ill. The other, three-year-old Olive, was unconscious, collapsed.

Matilda rattled on, "I've done everything, but no matter what, they don't get no better. I don't know what to do. It's no odds what I try, they just get worse. They won't eat. If they do, it just goes right through 'em. They get worse and worse. Will I give you a cup of tea?"

"No," I said. "I'll try to fix them up first. Louis looks bad. Olive seems to be worse."

One of the most important steps was to get some nourishment into them. They had been sick five days already and were literally starving to death. Jim brought in the box which I had packed with frozen milk, eggs and special food because I knew there wouldn't be much invalid fare on tap.

It was plain this was the same virulent scourge of dysentery that Mrs. Burns had told me about. Years ago it struck them in winter when they lived up Nascopi, weakened her so she could hardly crawl, and killed two of the children. It is terribly infectious, very dangerous to small children, and no one ever seems to know where it comes from or how to cure it. For instance, here at Traverspine, isolated, in the middle of winter, no other soul in the bay infected, the germ blazed up as though by spontaneous combustion. I had seen from the hospital books that winter after winter the same thing happened in odd places. Certainly it didn't come in this case from the Traverspine River drinking water, for there was not a soul upriver from here, no trapper, no Indian, nobody. Several years previous, two Rockefeller research technicians had been stationed at North West River to try to find out about influenza in the North. I wished they had studied this bug and found a cure for it.

Suddenly I remembered the ten-months-old nursing baby. "Where's Bruce?" I asked.

"Oh, he's upstairs. He's not sick. He's asleep."

It seemed to me that above all we had to keep him from getting it. I suggested that we divide duties from now on. "Suppose you tend the baby, keep the place clean and cook the food. I'll take care of the sick ones, and don't you touch them. All right?"

"Suits me," Matilda said.

Right away I washed Louis up and changed his bed and gave him a hypodermic sedative. He went off for his first sleep in days. Olive (named for Miss Olive Nelson, a grand nurse who was here before me and whose special skills, kindnesses and sayings were told to me on a thousand occasions) I wrapped in a hot blanket and dosed with a few drops of brandy and water, for a start. To the other two I gave a dose of castor oil. To be sure, castor oil is not considered the panacea it used to be, and some doctors feel it has no use under any circumstances. Nevertheless, I have seen it used with good results in dysentery cases in Australia. Something must be given to clear this condition up immediately, and I had nothing else, so I held noses, and down the stuff went. When Louis woke, I gave him castor oil too. Matilda was horrified. "I'd think most anything would be better than that," she said.

Jim split and carried wood for us, and toted water up the steep bank. He was badly needed with the team back at the hospital to haul in firewood, but I couldn't let him go just yet. Before dark he spent an hour hunting partridges and setting rabbit snares.

There was washing enough to make a blanchisseuse blanch, all very infectious too, but I kept a bowl of carbolic water handy and rinsed my hands in the solution every time I thought of it. The children groaned and called out as they twisted in their beds. Matilda was edgy from strain and overwork. "If only Rob was home," she said, "everything would be all right. Suppose I get sick myself?"

"Yes," I said to cheer her up, "suppose we're all dead when he gets home and wolves have eaten everything but the buttons?"

Robert was in the woods on what was known as his Black Rock path. He was a hundred miles or so off in the ocean of trees, and in the normal course of events wouldn't be home for ten days.

There was never a moment all afternoon when one of the children didn't require attention. They tossed and yelled, frantic with pain. In that one busy afternoon I became familiar with every crack and cranny of the little house: the knots in the floor boards; the rows of clothes lines around the stove; the pretty white birch firewood chunks we kept carrying in from the porch; the tiny cellar under the kitchen floor; the rag in the broken window; the chipped slop jar and the chamber pot with the bent handle. It was all poor and bare, I suppose, and a great many things were lacking. Yet it was neat, homey, buried in snow to the windows, its glass panes frosted with incongruously tropical flowers.

Robert was a good hunter and a good father. You could see kicking around under the beds the toys he'd whittled, the little softwood canoe, the miniature sleds, the dog that looked like a cow.

"If only Rob was here," Matilda said again with that worried way she had of straining her hair through her fingers. "If only Rob was here, he'd shoot meat, he'd bring home partridges. Why! Louis can eat a whole partridge by himself, Louis can. Louis needs meat, that's what Louis needs sure enough and I know it."

I was trying to feed Louis milk and white of egg. Meat or meat broth was quite unsuitable for a child as sick as

Louis, so I thought. Anyway, there wasn't any meat. On the other hand, neither Louis nor the girls were accustomed to milk or gruel. They didn't like it, they vomited it, they let it dribble unceremoniously out the corners of their mouths and down their chins, reverting to infancy in their blind, sick rebellion against the cruelty of fate. Sometimes when they could hold their eyes open I saw them looking out the window at the snow, puzzled, wondering why they were in bed by day, what had struck them. Why were they some one else now, not Louis nor Olive nor Sevilla nor Maria? They turned a head to see if it was so with Ma too, and saw it was not, and their mouths puckered to think she inhabited one world now and they another. "Maa, I wish't I had some 'lassy bread. Maa, I wish't I could eat partridge. It's startin' in again, Maa! Oh, can't you stop it, stop it! Maa!"

I can hardly detail the treatment of four children with dysentery, it is so inelegant. They were constantly wracked with spasms. There was no rest for them or for any one else, day or night. They vomited too. They had to be fed frequently if their strength was to be kept up. Some one must be at the washtub almost constantly. Everything in the house in the way of cloth was in use, and all the washing that was hung out froze immediately. To put the washing out and take it in, I needed snowshoes, for the snow was more than waist-deep behind the house. We could not wait for the wash to freeze dry, so I brought the stiff cloths in after a little airing outdoors and hung them on the lines above the stove.

Mrs. James Michelin came over from next door to say hello, bringing a baby and three little girls with her, but I would not let them in for fear of infection.

Night came, and Matilda climbed to the cold upstairs to try to get some rest. Jim was asleep in his bag on the kitchen floor. I tended the children, and mostly they kept me busy going from one to the other hour after hour. After a long time I got a chance to put some more wood into the stove and to sit in a rocking chair by its warmth. Outside, some of the dogs had burrowed into the snowdrift against the house wall for warmth, and I could hear one of them stir near the east window. An owl had come out of the woods and perched himself on top of the woodpile where he kept hooting and hooting across the miles of loneliness. The funereal sound annoyed me. I took the .22 rifle and went out into the bright moonlight and shot him. I'd ask Jim in the morning if the thing was good to eat. For a long time again the children were moaning and twisting about with flurries of pain. I fixed and bathed and tried to feed the ones who were awake. I could see how it was going to be here, with one person busy every minute on the children, with wood to carry, water to lug for the daily washing, food to be cooked, and Matilda nearly done out herself.

In the morning Jim told me the owl was good to eat, so we put it on to boil for dinner. I asked Jim if he would drive the six miles to Mud Lake and see if he could bring my new-found friend, midwife Mrs. Hicks, to help us. As Jim was hitching up, Matilda said, "Bring Alvin back if you can, eh? He knows Black Rock. We might send him in the path to bring Rob home."

I thought it was a good idea too, for if some of the children died, as seemed quite likely, it would be better to have Robert home.

In the afternoon he was back with Mrs. Hicks and Alvin

too. Alvin was a thin trapper lad with a freckled face and ragged clothes. He wouldn't stay. He would make it eight miles more up Grand River to one of Robert's tilts this evening.

"Oh, you are good," Matilda said. "We needs Rob, or we wouldn't ask it. Take this loaf of 'lasses bread. 'Twill save you bakin'."

He tucked it in his pack, saying, "Thank you," gravely.

"Take this can of milk too," I urged him.

"No Miss, 'tis too heavy. When I come back, eh?"

He struck off into the snow, and we ushered Mrs. Hicks in. We joshed her as she peeled off a shawl, a scarf, a robe, a parka, a coat, an extra skirt, a sweater and about forty other layers.

"Good thing you didn't have to run," said Matilda.

"If you had fallen off, you would have bounced," I added.

"Little you know about it," said she. "People who live beside warm stoves shouldn't throw coals of fire on anybody's head." At this point she removed two under-petticoats of flannel.

Mighty glad I was to see this little person with her small quick hands and her small sharp nose and her unparalleled love of gossip. She began immediately. "Henry Mester is home from the river. Already, mind you. Only been away less than a month too. That Dorcus—he went to see her the first evening he was home. Dorcus's mother said, 'Go on home and wash your neck,' and she done just right too. The idea!"

Midwife Hicks, with generosity to a rival that is unusual in the medical profession, had sung my praises up and down the bay, bringing women to me for prenatal care who had never known before that there was such a thing. Unfortunately she had brought her ten-year-old daughter Elly along this trip, though Elly could perfectly well have been left at home. I felt like lecturing her on that matter.

In forty-eight hours Elly was down with the sickness, also Mrs. James Michelin and two of her children. We brought the two James children over to Robert's, which gave us seven young ones to manage now. Three small heads in one double bed made it look like a plague spot for fair.

We worked like Trojans, and the worry and strain were terrific. I was so busy that the days and nights ran together till I lost track of them. Injections of saline were all that were keeping Louis and Olive alive. Louis was so exhausted and nearly dead that he never even noticed the needle prick when I gave the subcutaneous saline. At first they had all objected strenuously to me because I was a stranger, and to the rectal irrigation treatment which was stranger still, but now in their exhaustion they seemed to realize that a short respite came afterward. Morphia suppositories relieved the awful tenesmus for a little while, and during that brief time I hurried, trying to get them to take some food and have a little sleep. No sooner were the rounds done than one of them would double up in pain again, and it was time to start over. Day and night with no sign of improvement and no sign of let-up this continued.

After awhile I developed a chronic state of sleepiness. Whenever one of us went upstairs and tried to sleep, there was a commotion going on down below: children crying, pans banging, something. Once a day I religiously went up there and took a bath in a pint of water, standing near the stovepipe for warmth. I thought, "Now I'll sleep."

Instead, I lay awake and wondered whether I was going to pull them through, and tried to think of something more that I could do to bring them round. The roof up there was low and close to the bed. Try as I would to keep my eyes off the roof boards and the rafters above me, which were all papered over with long-forgotten copies of the Montreal *Family Herald and Weekly Star,* I could not do it. Doubtless my resistance was low. The headlines jumped out at me: FISH MERCHANTS PROTEST DROP IN PRICES; AT MURRAY BAY FOR HOLIDAY FETES, and line-cuts of Buicks that looked like castles in Spain, and others of women's bust-and-hip fashions. The papers were pasted on at different angles, all lapped crazily, and often an item was cut off halfway through, or sliced diagonally so the lines grew shorter and shorter, leaving more and more to the imagination. It was a fascinating and exasperating game. I did not want to read that accursedly newsy wallpaper, but I found myself once more following the career of Mrs. Pierre Edouard Bouchier, of Ste. Anne de Beaupré. She had been married, and very happily, for sixty-five years. Mrs. Bouchier was once caught—here Mrs. Bouchier's affairs were terminated by an account of a cold wave in Winnipeg which caused policemen's toes to freeze even in fur-lined boots. But I kept thinking about Mrs. Bouchier and wondering what she was caught at. Robbing a bank? Infanticide? Maybe she was caught by the hair and dragged through a blackberry patch. I wished I had never heard of the woman. Squirming sidewise on the featherbed and screwing my neck, I was able to follow a Montreal murder of 1911 up over a rafter and down the other side, right to the bitter end, and very gruesome it was. I turned on my face and squeezed my eyes tight and thought maybe I ought to give Louis some more castor oil, and maybe I ought not. After a few days I got so tired I could go upstairs in odd daytime hours off watch and doze a bit and read the papers and wake and doze again in spite of the noise. It was not wholly satisfactory as a rest, but it kept me going.

Poor Mrs. Hicks couldn't snatch sleep that way. She couldn't turn the world upside down by working at night and sleeping by day, and she didn't intend to. One morning after we had had a particularly busy night ministering to our seven, I said to her, "Go on upstairs now for awhile and catch yourself a nap."

She didn't want to go to bed in the daytime in spite of the fact that she was groggy with sleepiness. But at last she disappeared up the stairs, her stiff back, her stiff knees, and finally her stiff ankles mutely protesting. An hour and a half later I went up, and a sight met my eyes. There she was, fully dressed, with pillows packed behind her, bolt upright in bed, staring at me. I was flabbergasted; it seemed such a crime to waste good resting time that way. As usual I spoke without thinking. "If you only had a hat on, I'd think you were in church."

She was hurt and angry immediately. "I can't sleep in the daytime," she said.

"Well then, slide out of there and I'll sleep," I said.

So she did, and I dozed and read the rafters again for a spell. But she had been hurt by my bald remarks, and the rest of the day she would not speak to me. I was sorry, as I always am when my tongue slips.

There were plenty of potatoes in the house, some salt fish, flour, sugar, tea and a few beans. Matilda baked the bread, and mighty good bread it was. By putting a bit of the dough aside to freeze each time, she made one yeast cake last all winter. On the whole the diet for us well ones was none too nourishing. Twice a day we usually ate bread and tea, and for supper we added potatoes and gravy. Occasionally there was codfish, fried salt pork, or beans.

Louis kept saying he wanted partridge, partridge. I kept trying to get milk and whites of eggs into him, but with very little success. Olive had not improved either, and, all in all, I did not see how they continued to live. Sevilla and Maria were better about taking their food, probably because they had not been so exceedingly weak when I arrived. I felt that they, though grotesquely emaciated, were picking up a faint shade each day. Ellie and the two James Michelin children were miserable enough, and needed frequent feedings and attention, but I had dosed them immediately and kept up their strength, so they were not desperately ill.

The work at the washtub required lots of hot water. We kept a big iron potful heating on the top of the stove all the time. We shoved in so many hundreds of those white birch chunks that I said to Matilda, "Robert will be shocked to see how the wood is going."

"No odds," she replied with a smile. "The men always say we burn wood faster than they can cut it, no matter what."

The washing equipment consisted simply of a tub, buckets, a soap dish, a scrubbing board. Emptying out the tub was a nuisance. I did think there ought to be a simple way of letting the water run out a pipe onto the ground, and it made me mad to carry the dirty water out after having once carried it in. Aside from that I stood it very well, though it was the hardest kind of brute toil. I wrung the sheets between my two fists with a kind of fierce joy and in the process acquired the beginnings of a "weeping sinew" in the left wrist, an affliction common among stevedores and weight-lifters, which is with me yet. All the same, I was glad to be there doing the work. I'd been all through the supercivilized tendency toward softer beds and hotter heat and comforts piled on top of conveniences in abnormal quantities, and I had come out on the other side. I was happier to wrestle wet blankets for this family than I have been to tell the house-keeper in certain other homes to tell the first maid to bring a boiled egg. These Michelins were my kind and they were worth keeping alive.

As I scrubbed at Traverspine, whacking the clothes around the steaming tub and slamming them into a bucket, I was happy. I have a funny streak in me, I expect, of masculinity or something. I like to be useful and I felt that these were among the finest days of my life.

Of course, I was low sometimes. There was so little chance to sleep. When I felt worst, late in the night, my watch, and the rest asleep, I'd step outside the door and feel the stars and snow, and see the river winding, and think it was magic that I was here in a place called Traverspine in the winter woods so far from my born home. When I was a girl I used to think it was only rich people who could wander the globe, and that poor ones had to be mice. Now I was overturning that idea, just simple me, Kate Austen, satisfying my need to burrow into the heart of strange places. For Traverspine was that—a far, strange place full of secrets, and I was right in the middle of it.

Another heretical pleasure was the water carrying. There was a cask that I filled with water from the river once a day. I'd put on my outdoor clothes and my moleskin breeches and make a session of it. I felt suddenly alive in the cold air. There was no need to stand around and wait for orders from a surgeon, no pussyfooting, no shillyshallying, no restraints. There were steps cut in the icy path down to the river. I found it easier and more fun to sit and slide, letting the buckets roll down ahead of me. The waterhole did not ice up very thickly, because every day when we were through we kicked snow into it. Climbing the steps with a bucket of blue, sparkling water in each hand, I felt so happy I had to sing. It's strange what will make people happy, is it not? Matilda thought that carrying water was a frightful chore, naturally enough, since she'd had too much of it all her life. But I thought as I slid down to the river on my slick slide that I'd never had enough. Here was no sickness and no steamy washtub; just the trees and the pure snow and the white river winding out of sight. Maybe some day the children would get well, and I could sneak off for a whole day up the river with a packet of grub for my nooning and a chance to look around the bends and see what was what. Climbing the steps again, I really saw the house in true perspective, a snug little home in the snow, with smoke drifting out of the stovepipe. I could imagine how a man would look at it and feel it was a home worth working for, that pretty, low, graceful little house on the riverbank.

Matilda smiled and said, "You've got a smooth place like an otter rub," and she told me how the otters play on a bank, sliding on their stomachs, climbing up and sliding down again, pa, ma, and the children.

Outside in the dark we heard a frozen rope creak. It was Robert unlashing his toboggan. Matilda picked up a lamp and carried it out into the quiet, frost-locked night.

"Hello," she said.

"Hello, how are they?"

"Louis and Olive are bad."

Robert straightened up, putting his hands to his hips to lever himself erect. His face, all frosted around the cap and eyebrows and beard, glared white in the lamplight. "It's damn cold out here," he said, and picking up the hauling line, dragged the sled clattering in over the doorsill to the middle of the kitchen floor. He pulled a bench up so he could sit, and methodically began removing gun and axe, folding back the frozen canvas wrapper and unloading tent and tin stove, blanket, kettle, fur-bag.

"Where's Alvin?" asked Matilda as she stirred the fire, moved the kettle, laid out cups, put on the beans to heat and opened a can of condensed milk.

"He'll be along."

"They been working you, little, I s'pose," he said to me with a half smile.

"Not so hard as they've been working you." The sight of his frayed moccasins, his knees patched and repatched from the wear of kneeling at traps, the blackened hole burnt in his sleeve from a campfire, the cloth of his jacket shoulder rubbed threadbare by the hauling line, the little stick sewed on in place of a button, the empty flour sack and the plump fur-bag told more than he ever would. The hunter-Indian smell of wood smoke, grease, sweat and balsam beds pervaded the house, wild and sharp and disturbing.

He looked around and saw three children in one bed, two

in another, Louis and Olive in separate ones. "You've got a houseful by the looks," he said.

He went to Olive's bed and stood looking down at her. Then he moved over to Louis. Louis was his favorite, Louis was going to be his helper and hunting partner soon. He had taught Louis already to shoot and row and paddle. Louis had snared fifty rabbits and shot thirty-six partridges the winter before when he was only six. In the porch was a tiny komatik that Robert had made for him to hitch a couple of dogs to and drive along the river shores hunting. Its runners were shod with thin strips of steel which Robert had garnered from the edges of a broken bedspring. The boy was asleep for once, exhausted, transparent-looking, thin nose pointing straight up, eye sockets great purple hollows, breath sucking in and out noisily. The hand outside the covers was a claw.

Robert shook his head. "Slink! My Lord, like a weasel!"

"We can't get him to eat, Robert. Yesterday I thought he was picking up, but today he's worse."

"He wants a good meal of meat," said Robert. "There's a *pinu* in the bag I brought. I'll get more tomorrow. I'll get plenty."

"He can eat a whole partridge, Louis can, when he's well," Matilda said for the fiftieth time.

I didn't say anything. We might as well try him on meat if he liked it so much. We weren't getting anywhere as it was. Nothing could be worse than it was. I remembered how it had been with my sister's baby whom I nursed once in an epidemic during an Australian heat spell when the thermometer never went below 100 for eight nights and was always over 110 in the day. The child had a high fever, to lessen which we laid dampened sheets over him every half hour. He wouldn't eat either. Finally in desperation I phoned the doctor and said, "I can't get any nourishment into him. He says he wants crackers and marmite all the time."

"Give it to him," said the doctor. "We've nothing to lose now." So we did, and that unsuitable mixture brought him round.

While we were discussing Louis, Alvin came in with a pack on his back. Wearily he swung it to the ground and staggered to a bench. Matilda poured the tea, which Alvin sucked up gratefully. After three cups of tea and four slices of bread he was able to smile weakly. "We been drivin' 'er, Rob and me."

His manner of lifting the teacup showed that every muscle ached. He'd lost at least ten pounds since he left here.

"All last night comin' out of the woods, all day today drivin' 'er down Grand River," he said. "We come three days' walk since yest'dy." He took off his moccasins and crooked his toes lovingly.

"We'll have a big feed in the morning, b'y," said Rob. "Eat some more now."

"No," said Alvin. His eyes were closing. He was untying his blanket, which Rob had been carrying for him on the toboggan. He was asleep on the floor in the corner before he could get his pants off.

Robert drowsed on the bench. "Why don't you get your clothes off and go to bed?" I said.

"I will if she will," he said, indicating Matilda. He spread his socks under the warm stove and climbed the steep stairs.

"There's oil in the lamp, there's wood and I guess everything is all right," Matilda said, looking around.

"Yes, Matilda, everything is all right."

She went upstairs, and I heard the buttons click as her dress dropped on the floor.

I sat by the stove and thought about Robert. One thing that made him unusual was that he had been outside, outside to the World War of 1914–18. About all he brought home from the trenches of France was a limp, result of a leg wound. Invalided back to Newfoundland just before the war ended, it was autumn when he reached there. No vessels were running north till spring. He'd have to spend the winter convalescing. He would eh? Instead, he got a motorboat to Battle Harbor at the southern tip of his own Labrador, gathered together makeshift gear, patched snowshoes, army rifle, toboggan hewed and whittled by himself, and started home cross country. Four hundred miles or more through the hills and woods and lakes it is, nobody knows how far. No map, no Indian portage route, nothing. Day after day threading the long lakes, plodding through thick, dark woods, emerging on streams. By and by he struck the headwaters of the Traverspine. I wish I could have seen him the day he rounded the last bend and stood on the ice out here, stood with feet apart and hood pushed back to let his head sweat, home from France with a game leg, home, looking at his house. I think it must have been one of those moments. I'll bet Matilda came out, and he said, "Hello, Mat," and she said "Hello Rob," and then she pushed the kettle over and took the teacups down. But don't suppose her hand didn't tremble as she took the teacups down. And don't suppose they didn't melt together like the completion of a puzzle, like the waking from a nightmare, like the sleeping after pain. Words are not much, and so there is no room for them sometimes. Perhaps it was a little like this night. Perhaps, perhaps.

In the morning we tried Louis on partridge broth. He lapped it up and asked for more. We took a double flyer and gave some to Olive too. Don't ask me why, but from then on the children began to gain. It was a good thing too, for next day Matilda took the sickness, the following day Mrs. Hicks was laid low, and the third day it was my turn. For thirty hours I was out of the picture, not caring what happened to anybody. Shrivelled and cold, thirsty and vomiting as soon as I drank, so weak I couldn't stand, wracked with cramps of unbelievable intensity, I wondered how those children had stood the pain so long.

But Robert was there tending fires, feeding children, hunting, lugging wood and water. Robert was like a rock. I hadn't realized what a relief it would be to have some sure person to unload responsibility onto. We had been three women all to pieces at the end of the world, but that was changed now. Robert walked around and saw to things. Robert laughed and said everything would be all right if we left it to him. He took a hammer and axe, and knocked together two new bedsteads so more children could lie alone. When I went to sleep upstairs, I knew that if the house caught fire Robert would put it out. The roaring in the stovepipe sounded kindly instead of dangerous.

Jim Pottle had come with the team, and it was time for me to go back to North West River. All the patients were picking up, even Louis. Robert laughed. "M-m, now you've got 'em to the cranky stage, you're going to run, eh?"

When all was loaded on the sledge, Robert took from

his fur-bag a glossy, big, sleek cross fox skin that was black with a silvery ruff down the back and across the shoulders. Tanned and lined with silk and made into a neckpiece, it would retail for close to $175. At the post here it would fetch about sixty.

"I want you to have this," said Robert.

When I would not take it, he hung it over my shoulder.

"Thank you, Robert, a thousand times, but I work for the mission. If you want to pay somebody, pay the mission."

"I know," said Robert. "I'll give the mission something. But you're the one that did the work. Take this."

"I couldn't. It wouldn't be right."

All the way out to the sled we handed the beautiful skin back and forth. Matilda tried to get me to take it, and Robert looked so sad and baffled I was sorry. I wanted to accept for his sake. I knew how he felt and how he hated to be under obligation to any one.

"Take it, now. Lord sakes, my kids are worth a fox skin to me, aren't they?"

"You don't understand. I work for the mission. This wouldn't be honest." I gave the fox skin back to him one last time. "Don't worry, Robert. You know me, I know you."

"All right," he said. "But some day I'll work for you." He looked at me so straight and level with his blue eyes that it was like a vow.

Jim couldn't hold the dogs any longer. I climbed aboard, and they soared away, past the Jameses and the waving hands in the windows, down a dip to the river ice. I looked back and saw Rob, the fox skin trailing from one hand, the other raised. Once again I had come to the end of a case, something won, something lost. I had a feeling for that family and their home. Robert had said that he would help me if I ever needed help. It was a comfortable feeling, like money in the bank, for if he said it, he meant it. I had not met many men like Robert. There aren't many, I suppose.

The komatik slipped along slow and softly, in a great feathery curtain of snow that was sticking to the trees beside Grand River and piling onto Jim's cap like a white pancake.

"Brung 'em all around, did you?" Jim said.

"Yes, Jim, we were lucky."

"I hauled in a thousand turns of wood since I saw you last."

"That was good work, all right."

We pointed out across Goose Bay, steering by compass, and while the sled crawled on and on I dozed in a caribou robe. It was all unreal, the nothingness of falling curtain round us, the world, the sledge, the dogs, Jim and myself. We did not know where we were going in the moving circle of snow. We were nowhere and did not care and it was pleasant in this land of quiet weariness, this cool, free, bodiless, day-after-sickness land where snow was falling and I could sleep.

The couch in front of the fireplace, the big, shiny hospital kitchen, the vast amounts of provisions, my own bedroom, the gramophone, the faces—North West River after three weeks in Traverspine was like a great metropolis full of luxuries and unexpected excitements. Polly had sworn off smoking three times since I left. Symington had come to call every other evening. She was wondering what it would be like to be a Hudson's Bay Company factor's wife.

"He might be sent anywhere, Baffin Land or anywhere.

Picture me stopping on the trail to have a baby behind a bush."

"Some parts of Baffin Land have no bushes," I reminded her.

The well at one of the cottages had gone dry. Buttercup had a new calf. Aunt Suzannah's fifteen hens were laying fourteen eggs a day. No urgent cases had arrived at the hospital, but our T. B. chronic, Willie Shippan, had grown noticeably weaker as the inevitable end approached. He could no longer turn himself in bed, and since he was restless and uncomfortable, some one had to see to him. Jack and Polly and Henrietta Winette had been taking turns sleeping in the ward to turn him. That gave them a broken rest one night in three, for he would wake at least every hour and ask to be shifted. "Turn me over to the logs," he said when he wanted rolling toward the wall.

At the end of a week I drove back to Traverspine with Jim to check up on any possible relapses. We started very early in order to make the round trip in one day. I found them all well except for the James Michelins' two-year-old baby girl. She had caught it since I left, and was now very sick indeed, a handsome, wild, dark little thing, as charming as the two wood-mice sisters who were at North West River school. We carried her, tucked in a caribou sleeping bag, back to the hospital.

Little Indian eyes, dark and shy as deer's eyes in the big ward bed, she took to me, we took to each other. She was very sensible for two years old. She had bronze cheeks and straight black hair. She always wanted to be held in my arms. She put out her hands and begged, "Carry me, carry me." But I couldn't always be doing that.

I had to ask her, "Wait until my work is done and then I'll hold you and rock you." She nodded her head and waited patiently. But sometimes it was a long wait. She was so patient and so weak. I tried hard to build her up, and every day as I held her in my arms, so trustful, so wild and primitive and sweet, she became dearer to me. I suppose it was having her there all to myself, knowing her utter dependence, feeling her curl close to me for warmth, that woke maternal hungers. There were times when I honestly forgot that she was not my very own.

She did not progress. I cured her of the dysentery, but I couldn't seem to get strength back into her. She did not pick up from her dreadful nervous exhaustion. Things happened to her. She bit the inside of her cheeks. It was the irritability and exhaustion that made her do it, and it was her weakened condition that made the injury become infected. Night and day I treated her now, irrigating her mouth every hour. Her face was horribly swollen, but she could still smile. Her eyes still followed me, dark and tender and wonderfully wise. The infection spread to her throat, she could not swallow, I fed her with a tube, I did everything I knew. Poor small one, on a night two weeks after coming here, she died. I had thought I could save her. I had grown to love her so. Now she was dead, inanimate, a thing in the bed. As I sat there alone, late in the night, I heard a step. It was Polly coming to take her night turn with Willie.

"I loved her so," I sobbed.

"She is all right," Polly said. "Don't cry, don't cry. You can't always win."

CHAPTER XXI

T. B. WAS the greatest source of trouble in the bay. I've never seen it worse or more deadly anywhere. We nearly always had a tuberculosis patient in the hospital, suffering not from infected lungs but more often from a general infection that would appear in bones or anywhere, who was, to put it baldly, dying. At this time our two chronics were Willie Shippan and Devotion Pardy, a single woman, twenty-five years old, from Tarney's River down the bay. She had been badly neglected for years, not that it was any one's fault particularly, but she had insisted on being about the house when she was so weak she could hardly move. I had been pretty sure it was really of no use for her to come to the hospital; however, I had asked her to because I knew it was better than infecting the rest of the settlement. As often happens, rest, good food, stimulants, weeks in bed, gave her a temporary improvement. She filled out a little, became cheerful and took on a faintly healthy look. But it was only fate playing cat-and-mouse. Soon a relapse came, and now she was going downhill again, which was all the sadder because she had begun to hope.

Owen Martin, a little boy in Annie's boarding cottage whom she had been trying for months to build up, developed acute appendicitis. He looked terribly motherless in the big hospital bed, as indeed he was, being a child of the woman who had had meningitis when I arrived here. For twenty-four hours, treating him with ice bags, I had him "under observation," which is to say I looked at him about every five minutes until I was afraid I'd scare him to death. To do or not to do, that was the question. I had assisted at so many appendectomies in times past that I felt sure I could do one. I paced the floor and pulled my hair. If, while I hesitated, the appendix ruptured, I would never forgive myself. For half the night I drilled Polly and Jack in a rehearsal operation performed upon two sofa pillows. Polly was the anesthetist. Every instrument and implement was laid out so Jack might learn exactly when to hand me each, and what to do in any possible eventuality. In the morning we advanced upon Owen with our courage screwed to the sticking point. Lo and behold, his fever was down, and he was beginning to subside. The risk of an operation was not justified. It was a most curious anticlimax, to have done nothing, and to feel so exhausted. "A gyp, I call it," said Polly gratefully. For my part, I was never so pleasantly cheated in my life.

Time rolled along, and snow fell almost every day. Once a week all the women of the village came to the hospital for "Club Night" and we sewed and had a good old gab fest like other women. Now and then we also had a meeting of the "Association Against Consumption," a simple and therefore very fine public-health project which Doctor Paddon had started. The "entertainment" consisted of a speech from me on the subject of separate cups and spoons, open windows, green vegetables. The refreshments consisted of whole-wheat bread and cod oil. People here had seen too many relatives afflicted to take all this as lightly as one might suppose. I was constantly running into examples of the wonderful work Doctor and Mrs. Paddon had done here in their twenty years of service. They loved this bay, and it was their true home. Mrs. Paddon had raised four sons of her own here, and women were always telling me that they had learned more about feeding and caring for their children by imitating her than in any other way. If she made her babies sleep alone, opened their windows in winter, tacked up old curtains in summer when she lacked screens, they decided they could do the same.

The snows shut us in and enveloped us and made us cosy and sealed our houses from the wind. It seemed to me I had never enjoyed my life so much, never found it so sweet and vital. I was always conscious of the wonder of the world outside, the raging drift, the constant change, the mountains shining in the sun, the savage cold at night, the northern lights stealing above the bay and bursting into all the colors of the rainbow. It seemed remarkable that we could have warmth and comfort and plenty of food in the midst of such cold. I never sat down to a meal without thinking it was blessed.

If it was possible I sometimes took an hour in the afternoon to go snowshoeing with one of the school boys who was making the rounds of his rabbit snares. We stood on top of Sunday Hill and saw dusk tinting the bay all violet, and lights coming out in the town. There was supper and a fire in the fireplace, and then I'd sit and read and play Victrola records and write twenty-page letters to people I hadn't seen in years, and all the time I was thinking that every breath I drew was the purest happiness. And all the time in the ward, Devotion was getting closer to the end of all this, and Willie, too.

One morning during a snowstorm, a tall thin Indian man came with the news that children at an Indian camp forty miles away near the head of Grand Lake were sick and bloated like bladders. Two were dead already. He made us understand that the wind was sweeping down the lake with hurricane force, pressed in on either side by hills that were like the sides of a funnel.

"We'll have to wait till the storm lunns down," said Jim. "The dogs wouldn't face it, nobody could face it. Swasheem, he tol' me the weend to the foot of the lake come within a inch of blowin' him into the rapid, and he couldn't see nothin'."

Well, that was all right with me. The storm was roaring, and if we couldn't go, we couldn't go. I spent the day getting ready.

But next day, though the wind had dropped a little, Jim still wouldn't set out. It was now more than thirty-six hours since the first call had come from the Indians. I didn't know what to do. It seemed to me we ought to go if it was humanly possible. They might be dying by the dozens. Another thing, suppose this should be the same contagious infection as the outbreak at Traverspine. Suppose, since I wouldn't come to them, the Indians came to the village and started an epidemic in our school. There'd simply be no coping with it.

I put on my duds and walked around in the snow on the river. Drift was flying high, visibility was very limited, and the bite of snow was kind of smothering. Still, it seemed to me we could get along a little way at least. It seemed to me we wouldn't perish, and that we ought to try. Twice on trips lately Jim had said, "The dogs are done out. We'll have to lay up a day." It seemed to me he was beginning to say that too often. All last week he had been on the point of going deer hunting, but it was always too soft or too t'ick or too hard or too something. He was the best driver in the bay, but the mission life wasn't agreeing with him. Or maybe the trouble was, once again, that I was a woman and not a man.

I went in and told him, "I'm going. I don't think the Indian children can wait any longer."

He said, "The dogs would be done out in two hours and we'd have to turn back. I don't like to turn back from nowhere's, me."

"Well, I'm going."

He refused to go, and that was that. Jack was much concerned about all this. "Ye'd go to certain death," he said, and it was wonderfully dramatic the way he put it.

Nevertheless, I sent for Johnnie Montague, who was home from the woods. "Will you try it, John?"

His face wrinkled up in the cocky grin I knew so well. He wasn't quite as tall as I was. "Try it? You bet! I know that ol' lake like the paam a my hand, and it's never blowed me off my feet yet."

The wind that wiped out a footprint in two minutes had drifted the village path deep. Nevertheless, we followed the place where the path was, more from habit than anything else. I was snowshoeing ahead to break trail while John managed the team. Hard as the walking was, that was better for me than trying to drive the dogs. It was true they did not want to go; they tried to run off sidewise and go back. With me as driver they would certainly have bolted and gone home, which would have been an unusually sad spectacle under the circumstances. But John kept the whip cracking now on the left, now on the right, and they preferred facing the storm to facing that.

So far I found it exhilarating, plowing through the deep, deep snow in a cloudy sort of gloom that made everything unrecognizable. I was a little afraid that I was doing a Florence Nightingale sister-of-mercy act, but that was better than sitting down and doing nothing. As we passed close in front of houses, hugging the walls where eddies of wind had scooped out the drifts, people waved. We saw their hands move dimly at the frosted panes. Mr. Lerou had heard the whip, and was looking out the window at the post too, but he did not wave. It was, I suppose, his way of saying that he did not approve either. I confess to a moment's pride as the drift from our passing whisked high over the roof of the post and Johnnie screamed, "You don't catch *him* walkin' ahead of the dogs."

When we came out above the village onto the ice of Little Lake, I had to stop. The wind blew the breath back into my body, and I was really frightened by the piercing, inescapable cold. I knew how the lake should look, but there was no seeing anything, and I felt lost already. I went back to John. The wind tore at us and rocked us where we stood, freezing the frost on our hoods to hard, scratchy masks.

"The wind," he shouted, "the wind is your pointer. Keep it about two points off the starboard bow, right there. Go like that for a while, then we'll head off to strike the shore. I don't want to get into the bad ice to the foot of the rapid. You all right?"

"Yes, I'm fine. I won't lose you, will I, John?"

"You might. Here, hitch yourself to Daisy's harness." He produced a piece of codline from his pocket, and looped one end around my waist. "Then we'll know where we're to. I can't see you more'n half the time."

I followed up along the line of dogs to Daisy and tied myself to her, but taking off my mittens to tie the knot nearly froze my fingers. I found the wind so strong that I had to bend nearly double to get ahead. Daisy kept coming steadily, however, and did not jerk me. To look back and see her now and then was reassuring, since I rarely caught a glimpse of the sledge. If only we hadn't been forced to buck the storm head on, things would have been much easier. I kept my big hood pulled well over my face, and held my mittens up too, leaving a slit about an inch wide through which I could squint, first with one eye and then with the other. Without this protection, I could feel my face begin to freeze in less than a minute. The flying snow that drifted across my feet was as unvarying as a compass needle.

After a long time John stopped the dogs, which stopped me too. I unfastened my string and went back.

"Keep your eye peeled now for black water," he said. "Here, take the axe and make a chop now and then. If it goes through, stop. Head off more to the right till we strike the shore. We'll follow it up through the rapids to Grand Lake and then I'll take a turn ahead. The dogs'll get better the farther we go from home."

So we started off again, the two females still in the lead. I was feeling fresh and strong yet, but a little worried by the slowness of our journey. However, we had a tent and stove lashed on, and I supposed that if we couldn't get anywhere on Grand Lake, we could camp somewhere deep in the trees in a gully. Daisy was following me well, and I wondered if our common femaleness was any bond between us; a silly thought, but you have to think of something as you walk along. In a storm sometimes, you feel very much alone. It is kind of like swimming under water.

There was shelter among the trees beside the rapid, but above it the wind thundered down the long lake. The gale came from the northwest, so we followed the north shore to get in the lee, heading into a deep cove, then out around a point and into a cove again on tacks that were miles long. Such a course made the way much longer, but it was the only thing to do, and in the lee of the longest points both of us were able to ride and get a rest. Each of these points had a name, Five Mile Point, Seven Mile Point, and so forth, marking its distance from the village. Hundreds of times for men like John this lake had been the road to home.

In a deep cove where there was slight shelter we stopped once and sat in the lee of the sledge with our backs to the wind, chewing raisins and drinking coffee out of a thermos flask. A long time after, John caught sight of a couple of bent trees on the end of a point, and stopped again. "I'll go ahead for a spell while you drive. So! Daisy! Up, you Spot!"

I thumped on the komatik with the whip butt, and the traces tightened again and the runners began to whisper in the snow. But it was too cold for anybody to sit on very long. I walked behind and didn't seem to feel very tired. I was mostly glad to be out fighting it. I was a little surprised and triumphant too that we were still alive and able to blink our eyes and flap our arms much as usual in the middle of this enveloping hostility that seemed bent on smothering and burying and shattering us. I was beginning to sweat inside my hood, inside my little house that I carried on my back, and it seemed reassuring that I could sweat in the face of a blizzard; it made my portable house, without which I would have died in a minute, seem secure and well-built. Maybe we were invulnerable, maybe John, lost and reappearing up there like a shadow dancing, was a medicine man who could put storms into a bag or go straight through them the way a ghost goes through a wall.

I was sorry, though, that John had frozen one cheek already; it seemed as though I should have been the one to freeze. I kept my mittens up to my face as much as possible, hoping to avoid frost-bite, for it leaves a sore that heals with difficulty, like a burn.

We were heading for Wattie's tilt, a tiny cabin about half way up the lake, built on the shore underneath a mountain. Late in the afternoon the dogs began to speed up. "Somebody's there," John said. "They smell smoke."

Soon he smelt it too. But I didn't smell anything; I was beginning to feel cold and weary in the gloom that was deepening fast. The wind was tiresome, and my fine sweat that I had been so proud of was giving me the clammy shivers. If I hadn't had great faith in John and seen him doing wonders all day, I could easily have thought he was inventing the whole business to encourage me.

The snow deepened, the trees ashore jumped out of the obscurity like a dark blur, then I smelled smoke too, we were up the bank and John was shouting, "Hello-o the tilt."

The low door opened to let out two boys, fifteen and seventeen years old, who hopped about in the snow in their stocking feet, so surprised and delighted to see somebody they could hardly speak. They were Gordon and Roy Mc-Lean, who had been up the lake hunting partridges, now snugged away here until the gale blew itself out. We were even more delighted than they, for the fire was going in the little tin stove, the candle was lit, the corner was piled with split wood and the tilt smelled of fresh balsam they had laid for a floor. But it's always so in this country; people are never-failingly delighted to see one another, because, I suppose, people are scarce and precious.

It was quite dark now at 4:30 in the afternoon. We had done twenty miles in seven-and-a-half hours. The kettle was boiling, so we ate bread and drank tea, such delicious tea, then set to preparing the fit end for any trip, "a real scoff, b'y," of partridge stew to which we contributed potatoes, frozen sweet, a can of corn, and for dessert a pie. Meanwhile John was out in the cold, building a fire in the snow, boiling the corn meal, adding the evil-smelling seal fat, cooling it off, pouring out supper for the ravenous dogs. That chore comes hard at the end of a long day, but I never saw a Labradorman omit it.

The tilt was only six by eight inside, with a glass-less window into which a gamebag was crammed. But, sitting on the brush floor with our legs curled out of the way, intoxicated by the warmth after cold, food after hunger, we heaped our plates with stew and thought the place was perfection.

On the lake the gale still roared, though we could scarcely hear it in the deeply buried tilt. Having lit their pipes, the boys lost their shyness and began asking me questions about "outside." What is a lamb chop, how big is a kangaroo, how many wheels has a bicycle? But I was too sleepy.

They insisted that I have the log bunk which, in the night when the fire goes low, is slightly warmer because it is raised a foot or so above the floor. I laid my sleeping bag there and crawled in, removing my heavy moleskin breeches and not much else. I sank into the bliss that comes after a hard day, while the fire crackled and shadows moved on the rafters and the boys talked in soft sentences that ended with a musical little questioning *eh? m-m-m-m-m-eh? m-m-m-m-m-m-eh?*

Sound as the logs around me I slept, waking only once to stretch and ache gratefully in the warm, sweet darkness. Johnnie, whose business is travelling, had a quick breakfast of bread and tea into me, our gear collected, the komatik loaded, the dogs harnessed, almost before I could get my eyes open. Long before sunrise we were out on the lake. The wind had dropped utterly, stars were out, the lake a deep blue, the cold like a knife. The blow had hardened the lake and fluted it in pointed patterns which streamed for thirty-five miles between the great bold headlands, now touched with gold. As we flew along, both riding, the shadows of the hills retreated like purple pools that shrink in droughts, and then the sun was up, gleaming on a plain of gold and silver crystals. In the magic of the sunrise I wondered, not that I was there, but that I had never been there before to see it. Where had I been all my life, and what could I have been busy about?

We saw black specks far ahead, which turned out to be two Indian men, each hauling a toboggan that carried the bodies of dead children. John knew the men by name, and talked with them, interpreting for me when he thought of it. One of the bundles was much smaller than the other. A ten-year-old girl had been sick many days, but a small baby had died in the night without their knowing it was sick. They were bound for the Indian burial ground at North

West River, and said that many more were sick at the camp where Nascopi River empties into the lake.

Their clothes were of the best, not tattered as Indians' often are. All of new, smoked, dressed caribou skin, their outer coats and pants and leggings and moccasins were soft as velvet, a light faun-color, absolutely windproof. The stuff is more like chamois than anything I know. Coming cross-country lately, their band had killed many caribou and was now camped preparing skins, *babische*, sinew, and eating up the meat.

"When they get plenty of meat," said John, as we drew away from them, "you ought to see them eat. Sometimes they camp near my furring grounds up Red River and I visit with 'em half the winter."

I was sad to think we had not been in time to help those two. But Johnnie seemed unimpressed by the sacrifice of two lives to what was probably pure ignorance. "Some years there's whole families starve because they can't find caribou. Then there's years when they get plenty and stuff themselves till they die of that too."

"You've diagnosed them already, eh?" I said.

He didn't know what diagnosed meant, but he thought it was a fine-sounding word anyway.

The team scented the camp on a white plateau above the shore, and, breaking into a gallop, dashed up the slanting path and into the middle of the tents with the bit in their teeth. Daisy in the lead grabbed a bag of fish that was hanging from a tree, and slit it wide open in one slash. Pandemonium broke loose, with screaming women, howling Indian dogs, and people running. The center of the Indian camp was a wild tangle of fur, fish, snarling jaws, tangled traces, and John, wading into the middle of it with the whip. When it was all over, the fish had completely disappeared, and a few quiet, innocent-looking dogs with soulful eyes sat on their haunches licking their chops. The Indian owner of the fish generously shrugged his shoulders.

In the little dome-shaped *meetchwops* made of canvas and skins tied over a frame of bent willows most every one was poorly, but the children were worst off, as usually happens. Five of them were very sick with tremendous pot bellies, great distension, high fever. Their rolling black eyes and shiny faces made them very pathetic. Some of them were too young to have any idea what *toganish squish* (doctor girl) meant, or who I was or where I came from, but even the smallest knew I was a stranger of a strange race.

Here was evidently one of those epidemics of enteritis that comes with an abundance of fresh meat and fat after near starvation. I knelt on the balsam brush floor by a fire treating a child, while its mother held it, and John, filling his pipe nearby, interpreted for me. Soon the child was much relieved and lay still as though the pain had gone away; so I went on and treated the other four similarly. To the adults who complained I gave doses of castor oil or rhubarb and soda, depending on how sick each seemed, but the rhubarb and soda was much the more popular.

Every tent was neat, with blankets rolled against the outer edge, a fire built on rocks in the center, a log in the doorway for a threshold. The most prized cooking utensil was very often an iron dutch oven which did for baking or stewing or frying. Men had been making birch axe-helves, leaving heaps of curled shavings where they fell from their curious, one-handed drawknives. Everywhere were piles of caribou skins. The five sick children were all sleeping already. I went the rounds for nearly two hours, talking to mothers by sign and gesture, looking at sore fingers and seeing to coughs. Usually the women and I could understand one another quite well even without John, who liked best to talk to the men about hunting affairs and lakes far away. Often, to tell me how old a child was, the Indian mother would pull out a treasured French calendar of saints' days and masses, point to the birthday and hold up fingers to represent the number of years. They spoke very softly, and smiled a good deal. The young ones were very pretty, with big liquid eyes and beautifully beaded moccasins, but many of the old ones were fat and dowdy, as happens in the best of families. I saw a number of bones that were now knit crooked because they had been broken and improperly set. There were also a few decayed teeth and small deformities. I did what I could for a dozen odd ailments, and wished I could do more. But they are nomads, with a diet consisting of what they can get, and it is often impossible for them to follow civilized remedies. They live much as they have always lived, the strong surviving, the weak dying. I saw two who were plainly of the doomed unfit, and I immediately started figuring how I could help to prolong their sufferings, as is my wont.

Our five sick children were still improving, with temperatures rapidly falling, so John and I decided to push on and get ourselves some food. We had put off eating anywhere near the tents for fear the complaint was something infectious, though I was fairly sure it was not.

After a mugup several miles away on the lake shore, we went on another ten miles to Susan's Brook at the head of the lake on a "social call" to the Willie and Freeman

Baikie's. In the snowy cove at the mouth of Susan's Brook, smoke curled up as quiet as mist from their two tin funnels. In this lonely place where they had so little expectation of a visitor, it was great fun for us to jog in silently and see how close we could get before they spotted us. But we were still fifty yards away when Mrs. Willie came to the door and shaded her eyes. Then she ran toward us over the snow, holding out her arms and beaming as she recognized our team.

"Oh my, Miss Austen, to think of you comin' all the ways up Grand Lake," she said. "You're a proper trapper for travellin', now ain't you! Hello John, come in, b'y, you done well to come here."

Mrs. Freeman heard the commotion and came running too with her children. These two women, each alone with her brood while the husbands were away furring, hadn't seen a stranger in four months. The only time I had ever seen them before was at Snooks Cove on the trip up the bay in the fall, but they seemed like old, loved friends now.

We scampered back and forth on the path between the two houses while the two women amicably squabbled as to which should put us up for the night. Because Mrs. Willie's house seemed biggest, we finally settled in there to an early supper of such crisp fried partridge as I had never tasted.

Johnnie wasn't very happy in the midst of so much women's chatter, and no man to hobnob with. He ate in silence, went out to see to the dogs and took a long time about it, then silently unrolled his blankets in a corner and went to bed with the hopeless air of a man whose fate is hard.

I decided there must have been some truth in Willie's tales of everything being thick here, for in the porch, skinned and hung up, were twenty frozen rabbits, and fifteen frozen partridges, a fine supply of meat—a supply no home in North West River could boast.

"Ah, we make a better living here," said Mrs. Willie. "People's thick down there, but here it's game."

The faraway people, the outbackers, did they do better than the people of the village where dogs and boys and men and women and girls were ceaselessly hunting the woods for miles around? That was one of the perennial controversies at North West River. As we dried the dishes, I looked at Mrs. Willie; she was one of the faraways, and no controversy about that, a primitive with primitive strength for killing her meat and managing her home and carrying her wood and water, as well as children. She preferred living half way out in the bush so that her husband could trap closer to home and get home more often. Looking at her lined face, her fine eyes and good jaw, I decided that women are by nature primitive, and that I had never seen a happier one than this. Looking at her I knew she did not envy me, did not wish to be as I was, would not care to know what I know.

She knows other things, I decided. She is herself, I am myself. We look at each other and smile. She does not gloat over her supply of meat or of children. It would not occur to her to apologize because there aren't enough chairs to go round and one hinge of the door is broken. She is interested in me primarily as something for her mind to take hold of and work on. I will be something to remember when I am gone, days when the snow is just white and shadowless, sunless days when the snow is the epitome of nothingness, clogging the future, "a footless sock without any leg."

And I, what do I see in her? I see strength such as I or few of my friends have ever acquired.

She does not think it is anything remarkable that she should keep the fort alone week after week way off here while the wind whines around the eaves and her man is away. Neither does she really think it remarkable for me to drive up here in midwinter, she who has walked the lake from end to end in her time.

"I hear you been fishin' with Hannah Montague. I hear Laurie Blake had a bad time. Naomi got a boy, eh?"

Women's talk, the ageless talk of women everywhere, about babies and births and children. Not very smart maybe, but if it weren't for the subject talked of, there soon wouldn't be any men to think it dull. Gabble, gabble, babble, and before we knew it, eleven o'clock had passed.

In the cold of early morning I bundled up in my heaviest dickie with a scarf tight around the hood and another round the waist to keep in every particle of heat. I took special pains with my triple moccasins and my double mitts, for I knew we would be riding and riding fast. Bumping and squeaking and dipping over the shell-like patterns of the hard lake, I felt sure all would be well with the Indians. And so· we found it. The five sickest children had grown quite handsome since their bloated yesterdays. What I had done for them in ridding them of their poison, an elementary as well as alimentary two-hours' work, seemed simple to me. Yet it was something the Indian mothers could not. do,. something that made the difference to those five between living and dying. Looking at the pairs of black eyes no longer filled with pain, I felt that the risks and controversies of our trip had been justified. It is, of course, wonderful fun to set off on a heroic winter trip, but when you can do a bit of honest good besides, your cup runneth over.

"Who was Wattie?" I asked John as we drove away from the Indian camp toward Wattey's tilt.

He didn't know, but he did know that a sick trapper man, too weak to travel, died in his tent right there on that point. And Susan's Brook, why it was up Susan's Brook that Dillon Wallace and Leonidas Hubbard and their guide Ellson went in the early 1900's, looking for Michikamau Lake. And they couldn't find it; Susan's Brook was too rough a stream for travelling, and they ran short of grub, fall came on with snow and cold, and Hubbard died not thirty miles from the spot where Willie's and Freeman's houses stand.

We came to the ballicater that straggled crooked and high across the middle of the lake from shore to shore. John said the ice wall formed there most every year, on account of the upper lake's freezing early and the lower lake's freezing late. "The fall wind churns the lower lake so it can't freeze. B'y, I seen it open from here down, even in December. I mind once I was comin' home for Christmas with Steve Burns, and we was drivin' 'er in the night to get there. When we got about this far, we found the lake wide open and had to take to the hills. In the night, pitch black, we come to a clifty place way up in the draw between them two hills. We let our sleds down on ropes, and ourselves after 'em, and next we crawled through willows till we damn near died. I got home for Christmas, but it done me no good. I fell asleep and slept all day."

"Don't you know any cheery tales?" I said as we climbed over the ballicater.

"I know I could do with something to eat," he said. So we opened the food box and had a mugup in the lee of the ice humps far out on the lake, both miserable with cold.

But there was no wood for a fire, and with no fire there was no tea. I wished with all my heart we had a Primus stove for times like this, but there wasn't a Primus in the whole of Hamilton Inlet.

As we sledged on eastward toward Wattie's, the sun brightened and warmed us a bit. To pass the time, John said, "Tell me about Australia."

It did seem far away from this afternoon of dipping over the rough snow waves, but only geographically. I hugged my caribou robe tight around me. "When I was a kid at home," I said, "there were twelve of us children. That made fourteen with my mother and father. Mother was a great hand to cook, and my brothers were hearty, no mistake. Even my younger brothers, little, fat, broad-chested dumplings, would stow away roast mutton and potatoes like men. When they passed their plates for a third helping, Mother shook her head and said, 'Your eyes are bigger than your stomach.' One of my sisters was engaged to a violinist, a grand young chap, but not like our tribe when it came to eating. He was thin, you know, and thought a lot. Myra asked him to Sunday dinner once. Mother spent the whole morning cooking, as she always did on Sunday, and then we drew in our fifteen chairs. She heaped up Myra's beau's plate like the rest, and soon urged him to have some more, as all the other men were doing.

" 'Oh, my goodness no,' he said. He couldn't eat half what he had already.

"When he had gone away, the boys teased Myra. 'The first thing you'll have to teach that man of yours,' they said, 'is to eat.'

"It made her mad, of course. She said they were all

gluttons and she was glad she wouldn't have to watch them stuff themselves much longer."

"Tell me some more," said John.

"Well, we had grapes and oranges and plums and peaches and nectarines and a lot of odd fruit trees in our backyard. My father was a great gardener. He had one tree he had grafted just for the fun of it with seven different kinds of fruit on seven different branches. One of his favorite tricks as the children grew up was to come in from the garden with his hands behind his back and say, 'Who wants a nice juicy nectarine?'

" 'I do.'

"Then he'd pull a bucket out from behind him and say, 'Go and water the tree then.' "

"It sure would be good to grow fruits," said John. "Some day I'd like to eat all the bananas and apples I could hold. I'd like to go to Australia and pick oranges off a tree."

"Maybe you will some day," I said. "It wouldn't be any stranger for you to go there than for me to come here. I think I'll drop behind a bit now, John."

That was our signal for the other one to go on without looking back. Way out on the ice, exposed to the four winds of heaven, visible five miles away, there were no flowers to pick, no bushes to pop into, no Approved Rest Rooms, nor any railway stations to drop into "to set my watch." A turning away of the head, a gentleman's agreement, a house not built with hands—that was all, and I think John minded the pitiless publicity of the ice more than I did.

At Wattey's that night we found the boys still camped. It was eight o'clock by the time we had the dogs fed and our supper of baked beans put away. I chose the brush floor that night, since I had discovered it was much softer than a log bunk. In the tilt there was most always a kettle of ice on the stove to melt, but at bedtime when we all stretched out near it, they had a rigid rule the kettle must be removed. This was on account of a trapper who once bumped the stove legs in his sleep and scalded himself.

The boys made the coffee and toast in the morning, and said I could stay "in bed" for breakfast, so I just sat up in my sleeping bag and nibbled like a lady.

With a fine day for travel, we were back at the hospital early in the afternoon safe and sound. They were all glad to see us, and made us tell about the storm, even Jim, who said he had been wondering about us. He examined Johnnie's frozen cheek and looked at me in a way that was plainly forgiving. I was glad, for I had been afraid he might be offended, but I was wrong.

CHAPTER XXII

IT WAS NOT EVEN DAYLIGHT when I heard the stovelid clang and spruce kindling begin to crackle. That was Sarah Jane. My room was so far below zero that when I jumped out of bed the pillow came with me, stuck to my hair by the frost from my breathing. Outside, along the tops of the Mealy Mountains the day was baring its teeth in a sanguine glare. The wind on the bay looked so cruel as it stirred the blue shadows with drift that it didn't seem possible we could stand the cold out there. But that's the way with lots of jobs early in the morning. I put on my woollens and my sealskin travelling pants, my socks and duffel slippers and leggings and moccasins, my sweaters too. I packed my clothes bag with spare socks and mittens in case we should get wet, and I took my sealskin boots on the chance of a thaw. You never know what will happen on a trip.

Down in the hall was a pile of gear; sleeping bag tied up with rope, the medicine chest, the grub box stuffed full. No matter how full the grub box was, it was always empty when we got back, for the houses where we stopped never failed to be short of something. Sarah Jane and Pearlie had baked some 'lasses bread which was particularly delicious on trips. While I ate my porridge, I could hear Jim squeaking up and down outside, harnessing the team.

"Some more coffee, Miss?" said Sarah Jane.

"Try some redberry jam?" said Pearlie.

The girls were so good to me, it made me almost embarrassed. Odd that we three with such different backgrounds should be closer than most sisters. I told them what to do for the patients in the ward, and left.

Outside, the air was fiendish. It made me almost ill with anguish to see Jim take off his mittens and barehanded bind all our gear to the sledge with those clever hitches he is so proud of. There was frost in our eyelashes, and in the dogs' eyelashes. We covered our noses and cheeks with our mittens as we felt them freezing.

We were off, down the bank with a lurch and a yell, the dogs glad to run and get warm. Then the bitter wind began to creep between our mittens and our cuffs, began to make our feet ache already. Once beyond the point and headed down the bay, Daisy knew she should make for Green Island, blue and far away, she had been so often before.

Jim and I turned our backs and faced astern, pulling our fur hoods close about us while we watched the bay catch alight with silver diamonds and the sky melt from pale robin's-egg to the deep, lovely turquoise of a perfect winter's day. We were oddly silent on trips. Sometimes we went for hours without saying anything.

As the sun rose higher, it tempered the frost, the sledge runners didn't squeak so much, and the team picked up speed. After Green Island had been left behind, our noses didn't hurt when we stuck them out into the breeze. Jim slowed the dogs so we could have a run on the crunching snow. I trotted behind, and it didn't matter about me, how slow I ran, or whether I fell. But Jim ran beside the forward end of the komatik where he could hop on at a moment's notice if the dogs began a spurt as they often do when they smell a seal hole. They will leave a fellow, like as not, if they get a chance, and Heaven knows where they'll go, wrecking the sledge and scattering the gear and ruining their harness on the way.

We hopped on again, tingling and excited, and all of a sudden a great joy flooded me. It had been impossible to start, it was so cold and grim and miserable. But here we were, miles from home already in the sunshine. Already the hills of home were blue behind us, the sun warm, the dogs galloping, the komatik surging. The daily miracle had engulfed us again and I was ashamed that only an hour ago existence had been a burden and oblivion in my bed the only joy.

Kneeling on the furs at the head of the sledge, Jim lit his pipe, which was always a sign of something, either good or bad.

The silver blue and wild sweetness of the bay on sunny winter mornings is more like paradise than earth. Twenty miles wide here, stretching ahead 190 miles to the sea, it was a great white highway of dreams. But I never knew anything that could flatten dreams quicker than a winter gale on Hamilton Inlet.

Hour after hour, sometimes five miles from land, we made a bee line down the bay from point to point. Just before noon we boiled the kettle on one of them. The dogs lay licking themselves. The kettle began to jump on its hanging stick, and Jim rubbed his hands before the blaze.

When the shadows of the land were creeping, and the cold was getting fierce again, we swung in. We were there, at Sabasquasho, a little river-mouth settlement of two houses, one deserted. The river and the shores were drifted deep in whiteness that was violet now.

The inside of Mrs. Edward Michelin's house was a mess. Nobody came to greet us. We just walked in. And there was Mrs. Michelin, her face a mass of sores, one shoulder and arm swollen and helpless, obviously hardly able to bear her pain, sitting up in bed telling Effie, aged seven, how to get tea for us. All that Effie was doing was to muddle with a heap of dirty dishes. It didn't take me a minute to discover that Mrs. Michelin had a bad case of septicemia.

Marjorie, a sweet little girl of eleven who might have been a great help to her mother, was sitting on the couch nursing a scalded leg. I had heard about that leg a month before, and had sent down dressings and directions. I'd supposed it was well by now, but no. From ankle to knee it was infected. Marjorie smiled sadly. She was rocking the squalling, starved-looking new baby that had laid Mrs. Michelin so low. The baby reminded me of a sparrow before its feathers come—all eyes and mouth, the latter wide open. "I ain't much good," said Marjorie, "and he's worse." There was also a small boy of eight, thin and dirty.

Jim had a look around, and went out to feed the dogs. Then we could hear him splitting wood.

Where to start. It was hard to know in this upside-down place. I wanted first of all to get the baby quiet, so I washed him and treated his sore buttocks and discharging umbilicus. He had been having watery condensed milk every hour, they said, but by the look of the bottle he had been sucking at it continuously for days. I made up a Klim milk formula and asked Marjorie to feed it to him while I fixed a basket to serve as his crib. (He had been sleeping with his mother.) Harold was seven days old and a living proof if ever I saw one of the durability of the newborn infant.

Now that he was fed, I put him into the basket and threatened to deal drastically with any of the children who picked him up or rocked him. Having been fed and rocked ever since his birth, Harold found the new idea hard to accept, but we persisted, and soon he was asleep.

Blessed quiet! Now for Mrs. Michelin. In addition to her other sufferings, she had swollen and inflamed eyes. Her bed in the little room just off the kitchen faced an uncurtained window. The glare from the whiteness outside must have been awful on sunny days, and I had no doubt she was suffering from snowblindness. I bathed her eyes, covered them with a black handkerchief, turned the bed around and shaded the window with a dark coat ready for tomorrow. She had a high fever, no appetite, and what seemed like a bad case of septicemia. After sponging her and making her bed up fresh, I started in with the time-honored treatment of long hot douches, and felt a mental sag and a premature backache as I looked forward to a vista of these laborious treatments continued every four hours for Heaven knows how long.

"Where did you get this strained shoulder," I asked her, for I couldn't figure that out. But she wasn't able to help me, she didn't know. Feeling a little more comfortable then, she took a little nourishment and I set her to drinking water, which she had been denying herself.

Next it was supper. They had nothing in the house except bread, tea, sugar and oatmeal. The children hadn't been able to get any rabbits or partridges, and the corn meal and bean supply had run out. I opened a few cans of vegetables from the grub box and made soup for every one. Hungry as the children were, they ate with a certain diffidence. It was partly that they were shy and partly that cycles of starvation and plenty were no novelty to them. The molasses bread seemed to them too good to be true, but they could hardly be prevailed upon to take a second slice. Figgy cake, they called it, because it had raisins in it.

Then the dishes needed washing, and Marjorie's leg had to be dressed. A permanent part of my kit was a bundle of old sheets. Some of these I cut up to make diapers for Harold, as he had no others. I gave Mrs. Michelin another irrigation treatment, tucked the children in, and crept into my sleeping bag on the floor at twelve o'clock, setting the alarm for four. Jim kept the fire going at intervals all night, which was a blessing, as the cold was intense enough to cover nailheads on the inner wall with deep frost and make the timbers give a loud crack every little while. I only heard the loudest ones. Harold, for the first time in his life, slept all night.

Next morning it was warmer, but snowing. Jim said he could find his way all right, so, since the team was needed at the hospital and I'd be here awhile, I told him to go back and come again in five days. I wasn't worried about him, because Jim could find his way through anything.

There's something cosy about a snowy day. It just shut us in and left us to ourselves to get things running smoothly here. While bathing her poor swollen face and cracked lips, I asked Mrs. Michelin, "Where do you suppose you picked up this infection anyway?"

She didn't seem to know and didn't care and couldn't talk much, but Marjorie, who was putting on some coffee from the good old komatik box, piped up, "Mrs. Huntley come from Mulligans to take care of Ma, 'count of Harold, 'n' she had a sore finger."

"She did, eh?"

"Yes, 'n' it got so bad she had to go home after a couple of days."

Probably that was it, I decided, and made a mental note to stop at Mulligans and see Mrs. Huntley, who had quite a reputation as a midwife. I wanted her to know, for future reference, what trouble she had caused here.

"Now, children." I said, "we're going to work hard at cleaning up the house, and then we'll have a party. We'll have some tomatoes and raisin cookies out of the komatik box, what do you say?"

The famous, fabulous komatik box! That met with a response. Wesley, the eight-year-old, filled the woodbox and set to splitting for a while until Effie should have time to saw with him on the two-handled crosscut. Marjorie's leg was a little better and she wanted to do something, so I gave her a pair of Wesley's pants to patch. She did a very good job on them, and at the same time kept her leg quiet. Wesley chopped open the water hole for us, and I carried up most of the water. They had a pretty good little kitchen range, old but still sound. The wood was green spruce and no great shakes to burn, but we could manage as long as we kept the firebox stuffed, and the oven filled with drying chunks.

I showed Marjorie how to bathe and change Harold, impressing her with the necessity for regular three-hourly feedings, as it seemed to me she would be a big factor in carrying on when I left. I spent a long time treating Mrs. Michelin, bathing her, changing the bed again, rubbing her back, greasing her lips, combing the tangles from her hair and oiling the knots that would not come out—all this over a period of time, letting her rest in between because she was so weak. She accepted a little broth I had had simmering, and then, as she seemed refreshed and comfortable, I closed the door, telling her to sleep while I took care of things.

Since it was now two o'clock, the children and I were starving. Early in the morning we had put on a fine big stew of canned meat and vegetables with rice and stale breadcrumbs and anything else we could find. How we did enjoy it, and then the raisin cookies and tomatoes. Tomatoes are called fruit here, the rarest of treats. It seemed we had accomplished wonders already. The children were glad to have a leader once more, and eager to get to work again because they were proud to do things for the nurse.

Wesley said he was pretty sure he knew a place where he could catch some trout, and he caught four good big ones which we fried for supper.

Mrs. Michelin had had such a good sleep, and more to eat. By evening she talked and seemed a lot better. I was encouraged by the drop in her temperature. The trout was good, the house was clean, floor newly scrubbed, Effie and Wesley had sawed "a monster heap, look and see, Miss," the woodbox was full, the water bucket on the bench was full too, and Harold slept quietly between feeds, accustomed to the cruel new regime already.

"We was skeered of you, little, at first," said Wesley, coming and standing by my chair after supper.

"Nonsense, I wouldn't hurt a flea. Suppose I cut your hair now, and then you can all have a bath." They looked like different beings after this beautifying process, and I said, "Come on, I'll show you a game here on the table. You can play too, Effie. You take a lot of matches and make a square with four of them like this. Then another four on top, and you see how tall a tower you can make."

They thought it was wonderful. I was overhauling some of their buttons and rips while I talked to Marjorie. "Where is your father's hunting place?" I asked her.

"Oh, up Grand River somewheres."

"You don't know where, how far?"

"Somewheres near Horseshoe Rapids, he says."

"Do you know where that is?"

"No, Miss."

"We women ought to know about the country the way the men do," I said. "The bays and harbors and islands and shoals, and the rivers. It's lots of fun we miss, just doing dishes and mending socks. Have you ever been down the bay?"

"Oh yes, once. I been to North West River too."

"Let's draw a map, eh? You draw me a map of Sabasquasho River from here up as far as you know it. Here's a pencil and paper."

We had lots of fun. She showed me camping places and berry banks and fishing spots as much as six miles up the Sabasquasho. I drew for her the shore from here to North West River, with Long Point, Big Bight, Butter and Snow, Fred Rich's, Green Island. The maps were crude and sketchy, but they were the sort of thing one should know around here to make life interesting.

It was a pleasant evening, and they went happily off to their little wooden beds, clean and well fed for the first time since their mother had been laid up. I tucked them in, gave them each a hug, and then went back to the kitchen and sat by the stove awhile. It did seem strange, the only one awake in somebody's household, to think how many families I had entered into and been part of at various times. Many of the things you do you don't get paid for. Of course you don't do them for the pay. I decided you do them because they need doing and there's nobody else who can or will. For a time you are the mother, and then you go away and are the mother somewhere else. Sitting there alone I realized that I was beginning to get a little uncertain about the roaming life. To hurt oneself always with the wonder of the world— was that well, forever? What was I roaming for? If only I could get inside of life, not just see it and touch it, but be it. I had seen enough mothers to know that what I wanted most was children of my own. I was on the outside, looking in, on the outside travelling round the edges of experience. It did not matter that some tied-down mothers envied me and my freedom and my travels. I envied them; that was what mattered. I thought of the days when I used to say to other nurses, "No, sir, no family for mine. Footloose and fancy free, that's me." But now I wished I could burrow in to the heart of life and just live there contentedly, not aching. Maybe it was that I had served my apprenticeship at last. For me it was strange to be uncertain, not to be hot on some new job, some new place, some new exciting life. That night by the fire I half made up my mind that when I went away from Labrador I'd adopt a girl like Marjorie maybe, and try to pretend she was my own.

I took a bath then, because it rests me. The height of glory here, as in many other parts of the world, is for a woman to say, "It was a terrible time. I never had my clothes off for eight days and nights!" I myself prefer a change and my two-pint bath of warm water in a pan by the stove because it rests me. After my scrub I curled up in my sleeping bag between the woodbox and the stove where I could handily put on a chunk each time I woke. The snow had stopped and it was growing colder.

So the days passed, each one showing an improvement. Mrs. Michelin had in three days picked up enough to be out of danger, but it would be weeks before she was strong enough to run the house. Evidently my diagnosis had been a little pessimistic, and the infection must have been more localized than I at first thought. Mrs. Michelin was worried that she had no milk, but now that her temperature had fallen and she was so much better, I began to re-establish the diminished milk supply, knowing its value to Harold's chances of survival. We are taught in Australia that in certain matters man has not been able to improve on nature, and that there is nothing quite so fine as a breast-fed baby— all baby-food manufacturers to the contrary. Consequently breast feeding is a religion to Australian nurses and mothers. After unremitting work, lactation began, greatly to Mrs. Michelin's surprise. Harold was stronger now, and vigorous sucking would do the rest.

At the end of five days when Jim came, I sent him to Mulligans for a relative of Mrs. Michelin's, a competent lass who soon caught on to the details of treatment. Marjorie's leg was so nearly clean and healed that in a day or so she would be out around, able to help Wesley with fishing and setting snares and hunting partridges. Harold was gaining steadily, and Mrs. Michelin was pleased with the flow of milk, which she somehow attributed to my arrival.

Early in the morning as usual, Jim was hitched up again, the empty komatik box, the medicine chest, the bags and caribou robes lashed on. " 'Tis a mild we've got," he said.

Sure enough, the eaves were dripping, and we were in for one of those freakish thaws that sometimes gum up winter travel. Mrs. Michelin had cried a little bit. "Nonsense," I told her, "you're as good as well again."

"I know it," she said. "I feel so glad, but sad you're leavin'."

"Send a letter if some one passes by," I said, "and tell me how you are, how you really are. Don't tell me about the weather."

I left her smiling on the pillow. The children raised their little hands and looked so lonesome, standing in the doorway.

For a few miles the snow bore up our runners, and at sunrise, a beauty with oceans of colored cloud fields, we were a long way out on the bay. A blue haze crept over all the shores. The dogs began to sink, the runners stuck and great clogging lumps formed on the front of the sledge. It crunched slowly from length to length like an inch-worm measuring itself. We had to walk to lighten the load, and the walking was terrific with snowshoes on, and impossible without. When we left our first boil-up place, we each took with us a stick for knocking our snowshoes, but even so, they were heavy. Lifting that extra weight stretches a muscle in the thigh and gives one what the voyageurs used to call *mal de raquette*. Nobody knows how small a person seems and how big the bay, when the team crawls and the walking is heavy. You might as well set out walking to the moon as toward the next point. It was slow and we were sweating. We wished it were twenty below again so we could travel fast and be dry and comfortable. Three times we stopped for bread and tea, and each time the breeze seemed cold, our backs shivery, our feet clammy, our mittens soggy. At dusk the point of North West River was still four miles away. I walked it thinking of a warm bath and dry clothes and some tea, and maybe Jane would make me some cinnamon toast, and I'd pretend I was civilized, in slippers and a dressing gown, with a pillow for my head. Maybe another mail had come up the bay and there'd be letters. It seemed too much to hope.

We were crossing the beach, we were going through the portage path. The back of the hospital was in sight, we were seeing the yellow windows, the Cheery Lights of Home.

I opened the door, and stood aghast. The big room was full of people waiting to see me. A baby was screaming. Murdock McLean got up from a bench and said, "I got a wonderful sick boy to home, Miss. We'd like it fine for you to come right now."

I looked around at the others. "How long has Clarence been sick, Murdock?"

"Two days now, and he has a fever, and pains all over."

Pearlie came running down the stairs. "Oh Miss, oh Miss, I got an Indian girl in bed up there that's dyin', I s'pose. Shakin' all over and don't wake up at all. She came in a hour ago and gets worse and worse all the time."

"All right, Pearlie. What ails the baby there that's crying so?"

It was Stuart Michelin's eighteen-months' boy, with, of all things, a bean up his nose. The nose was swollen, the bean was swollen, and it looked as though fourteen people had been experimenting with the situation. Beside the baby sat a boy named George Monroe from across the bay. His swollen eyes were streaming and he kept them tight shut even when he spoke. Snowblindness again.

The Indian girl sounded most pressing. I ran upstairs and found her quite unconscious, having convulsions. We'd have to hurry. I called Sarah Jane, Pearlie, Polly. "Bring up all the hot water you can. We'll put her in a hot pack." Three Indians stood by the bed. I moved them into a corner out of the way. My mind flew to an old textbook page that I could see as plain as day: an illustration of a nice white porcelain bathtub with faucets that ran hot or cold (imagine it!), and the words, "Convulsions—immerse patient in hot bath, cold pack on head, give enema at once."

"Get a history, Pearlie. Talk to them. What can they tell you? Do they know what ails her?" While they were speaking Indian, I decided it looked like a case of poison, so I gave the child a complete washout anyway. Then Polly and I rigged a bed with waterproof sheeting, fixed a blanket in a drawsheet and plunged it in the water.

"He says," said Pearlie, "that they've ate some bad deer meat and all been sick. But this is the sickest."

"I hope so," said Polly. She took an end, and together we wrung the blanket as dry as possible. Inside it we quickly wrapped the girl, covered her with more waterproofing and blankets, and packed hot-water bags around her. Then we put some bags of snow on her head. It's very easy to freeze or burn a patient in this process, so I took care of that. Gradually we began to get results. The convulsions grew less till they ceased, the eyes which had been squinting set straight, the child appeared to stir and then to sleep. Soon she opened her eyes and looked around. The three Indians came closer, to look at her. They glanced sidewise at me, serious as judges, making me feel spooky. They were wondering about my hot water and snow magic maybe.

All this took about half an hour, but it must have seemed a long time to Murdock. I put on my dickie and mitts, and got aboard my snowshoes again. While we walked the short distance to his house he told me some more about Clarence. Murdock's wife, Mae, received me cordially, for we were good friends now. A quick examination, the swollen, reddened joints, the high temperature, convinced me it was rheumatic fever. Clarence was indeed very sick, and I wanted to take him back to the hospital right then, but they wouldn't consent. As long as there was nothing they couldn't do, they would keep him. Knowing so well how little there was to do, how little, but how important it was to keep him lying perfectly still, on a milk diet for weeks and weeks, I wondered if they could possibly manage it. It's when there is little to do that the care is hardest of all. Probably I didn't have the strength at the moment, or I should have insisted. So I went back to the hospital after promising to send fresh milk daily and such articles of diet as would help. For the hundredth time I blessed the mission cows. He'd have very little chance on bread and tea with a bit of pork and gravy.

At the hospital the Indian girl was almost normal, so I sent her pals away. When Pearlie brought Mrs. Stuart up with the boy, we flipped the mask over his face and gave him a few spots of ether to keep him quiet. The poor child, having suffered for over twenty-four hours, was almost exhausted from crying. I found the bean had softened, and that I could extract it piecemeal with forceps—a few minutes' work. He came to just long enough for opening his coal-black eyes, and then dropped his head on his mother's shoulder and fell asleep. We wrapped a blanket around him, and out into the night they went.

The last patient had fallen asleep too on his bench in the corner of the big room. We took him up to treat his swollen eyes. They were so bad I decided to keep him overnight at least. First an irrigation of boracic solution, then alternate hot and cold packs on the eyelids for an hour, some soothing oil drops, and finally George was more comfortable with a black bandage to exclude all light. We tucked him in and said good night.

It was an hour after midnight.

"My, Miss," said Sarah Jane, "you ain't even had a cup of tea yet. The kittle must a boiled dry long ago."

I seemed to remember something about cinnamon toast. "Make me some cinnamon toast, would you, Sarah Jane?"

"And look at you," said Pearlie. "You ain't even got off your wet travellin' pants."

"Maybe you didn't know," Polly said, "that the mail's in."

So I had my bath and my moment of luxury at last, dressing gown, cinnamon toast, five cups of tea, letters and all. I was so sleepy I read only one. It was summertime in Australia now, and the Jacaranda trees were in flower. My dear Aunt Myrna wanted to know, "How ever do you pass the time in that godforsaken place?"

CHAPTER XXIII

SPRING and the grass and beaches and blueness! Northern seasons make you change too, shake you and make you a different being with different work and play and clothes, different ways of travel and even different dreams. I couldn't get used to the river so wild and free after the level whiteness of winter. Swollen way up its banks, it slid slick and fast with high waves past the town and out into the bay. Hundreds of trees, torn loose by the flood, bobbed past, rolling their bare, smashed limbs that had been battered by rapids and ice-jams on the journey from the inner lakes. Even yet an occasional ice-pan swirled by, gray-white, half submerged, like the back of a polar bear.

The boys, the youngsters who always see things, claimed they had seen in an eddy above the town the clear mark of a big bear's paw printed in an ice-pan. " 'Tis like his handwriting, eh, Miss? He was sending us a letter from up Nascopi somewheres. Oh, he was little big, I know, that old feller was. And if I seen him and I had a gun—Bang!" And the little boy dances and capers and staggers backward with the recoil of his imaginary gun and his blue eyes grow big as quarters.

One afternoon the boys began to shout and gallop for the shore. "Indians, look, there they come." I ran to the window and watched. Around the western point eighteen canoes slid into view, loaded with gear, little hunting dogs perched amidships on the loads. Through the Doctor's field glasses I studied them. All the black heads were low, for they paddle kneeling, sitting on their feet. They use paddles that have short handles and long, narrow blades. There were three canoes manned wholly by children who looked less than fifteen years old. The flotilla hugged the farther shore a long way off from us, keeping in the quiet water well out of the midstream rapid. They are cautious canoe men, Murdock tells me, dislike fast water and will sometimes portage all day long to avoid running a moderate rapid. Who can blame them, since their wives and babies, traps and guns and blankets, winter's fur and everything they own is in the canoes? That is what they were coming here for—to trade their furs at the post for new axes and needles, cartridges, matches, lard, twine, blankets, cloth, and if they had had very good luck, even a new gun. No one knew where they had been all winter, way off on the inland lakes, trapping and hunting and moving on and on.

The fleet landed in a sandy cove just below Steve Burns' house where there was room to unload their gear. A steady stream of them filed from the beach to the edge of the trees, carrying loads, and soon the tents were up, the sound of chopping came across the rolling river, and we saw smoke curling.

They would camp there all summer near Steve's house. He was great friends with them and in their own Montagnais language advised them and joked with them as if he were an Indian himself. It was to him and his Mrs. that they would entrust their two little hand sewing machines and the priceless gramophone when they struck camp to take up again the roving life where such things can't be carried.

It must be that the Indian women looked forward to getting back to their sewing machines and their gramophone. I wondered if they enjoyed staying in one place for two whole months.

"They'll be over tomorrow," Jack said at suppertime. "You should see them shy off from the cows. They're scared of them. They call them 'the big deer' because they haven't any name in their language for critters like that."

Sure enough, next morning three canoes poked up along the farther shore. They went nearly half a mile upstream, and then swung out into the tide and began to dig for this shore. Drifting fast and sinking nearly out of sight in the rollers, they edged across and landed at our beach. It was a good thing they went way upstream or they'd have been swept out into the bay.

Two men helped a woman up to the bank, and behind her trailed some more men, three women, some children and a baby. The crippled woman in the lead could only step on one leg, so I was pretty sure they'd want me. They all trooped into the downstairs hall where they stood murmuring to themselves and looking around. They weren't very far from the good old-fashioned idea that a hospital is a place to die in.

One Indian never comes to the hospital alone. The sick one invariably needs the moral support of the entire family. It had taken the hospital such a long time to overcome the Indians' suspicions, win their confidence and get them to accept treatment, that we now did everything possible to make them feel at home. I asked four of them to come upstairs to the ward with the crippled woman, brought Pearlie along as interpreter, and we set to work. They laid the tightly wrapped baby boy on a bed, where he seemed quite contented. He was used to being set here or there, or stuck-up in the snow while they made camp.

Mrs. Nepishish had a knee the size of a cabbage. She told Pearlie that a week ago, carrying a load, she had fallen on a portage path. "Now it gets bigger every day."

As I uncovered the knee, her husband shook his head and began to gabble. His hair was very long, reaching to his shoulders at the sides and in back. On his bronze chin he had precisely five short wispy hairs which waggled up and down as he talked. Each of the Indians had an Asiatic look that made me think of camera portraits of Mongolian herdsmen. They brought with them the woods wild smell of balsam and campfires.

The red infection, whitish at its point, covered a large area, and was headed up ready to be opened. Pearlie told the Indians, as I directed her, that there was something in there that must come out, and that I was going to put Mrs. Nepishish to sleep so it wouldn't hurt her while I opened it. They crowded around the foot of the bed closer than ever, looking worried. Mrs. Nepishish didn't seem to mind when Pearlie held the ether mask over her nose. As the Indian woman began to fade, I took a scalpel and, before the audience knew what was up, I made three, quick, deepish incisions in the knee. Matter and water gushed out of it, and before our eyes the swelling began to shrink.

One of the Indians fingered the big brass cross that hung around his neck on a deerskin thong. They seemed impressed that Mrs. Nepishish stayed asleep through all this. They all nodded their heads and began to gabble, and looked at the woman and then at me.

"What do they say, Pearlie?"

"They say it is a miracle."

I put in three drains and applied a dressing just as Mrs. Nepishish opened her eyes and smiled. She seemed to feel no pain.

"Tell them to come back tomorrow," I said. "Mrs. Nepishish will be here for about a week probably."

Meeamee Abishish, the Indians said. Then they all pattered out, and somehow you could tell by the cautious sound of their moccasins as they went down sidewise that they weren't used to stairs.

Pearlie and I had a look at the baby. He was a fine fat fellow about nine months old, breast-fed of course. He hadn't been getting enough to eat on account of his mother's illness, so the first thing we did was mix him up a bit of condensed milk formula. He was wrapped in a whole small deerskin, the way the Indian babies nearly always are, with the head of the skin made into a hood for him and the front laced up and the legs of the deerhide wrapped around and tied in back. The skin was tanned to a soft, velvety texture, and for keeping out the winter wind no cloth can compare with it. It is also washable. Inside, he was done up in a number of odd shirts and pants all very neat and handmade, even though one small sleeve was made of blue flannel and another of green plaid. Cloth material always seems to be scarce for Indian mothers, and I noticed in the clothing store that when they came for a skirt they invariably chose the great big, full, long, old-fashioned ones the trappers' wives avoided. What the Indian woman wants is plenty of material, and the garment that has the most is the best.

We discovered the boy's name was Payuk, so we took off

Payuk's variegated shirts and the caribou-moss pads that served for diapers, and gave Payuk a bath. He had never had a soak before, and I thought he might holler and dislike it, but instead he kicked and chortled in the warm water like an old timer. You might think that, never having had a bath, Payuk wouldn't be clean. But he was, and had a beautiful smooth skin. Pearlie said Indian women rub their babies over with oil and that is how they keep them so clean.

"What kind of oil?" I wanted to know.

"Oh, goose grease, beaver fat, most any kind they have. Bear fat too."

Dressed up in fine fresh white hospital clothes, Payuk looked pretty civilized. I took him in to see his mother, wondering how she'd like it.

She put her head back on the pillow and clapped her hands and laughed with glee. It was such a fetching look, it made me think of many a white woman in a fancy hospital.

"What does she say, Pearlie?"

"She says he looks like a king."

I thought about that for a while. This woods wanderer, this Indian primitive, what did she know about kings? Or Pearlie either?

"What do you suppose she means by a king, Pearlie?"

Pearlie cogitated. "Like Jesus, Miss, I s'pose."

Mrs. Nepishish stayed a week, and improved steadily all the time. She spent her days diligently plying a needle. And every day about sixteen Indians came to see her.

I became very fond of her and Payuk. Along toward the third day she pulled a pipe and a chunk of plug out of her prog bag and indicated that she wanted to smoke. There were no other patients in the ward at the time, so I broke all rules and nodded my head. I don't think I'll ever get used to the sight of an Indian woman nursing her baby and puffing contentedly on a big curve-stem pipe.

One day as she was talking to Pearlie she ran her hand over the sheets and blankets, gave herself a little jounce on the springs and said, "I've never been in a bed before."

She made moccasins and mittens of caribou skin for her husband that week, and beautiful work she did too. She also made a little coat for Payuk. But the principal thing she worked on was a beaded Indian woman's cap. They are longish, shaped sort of like an old-fashioned nightcap. But they are made of triangles of red and black broadcloth which taper off to a point at the crown, and when the Indian women wear them, they pull the crown down flat over one ear. The band at the base of this red and black cone was stiff with hundreds of rows of tiny red and blue and white glass beads which she spent days embroidering. I used to get her to try it on, and then I'd show her in a mirror how pretty it was. She got me to try it on too.

When she was well again, I was sorry to see her go. Often that summer I went across the river and visited her tent. She was usually baking bread over a fire in an iron Dutch oven, or sewing clothes or knitting snowshoes, and she always patted her knee and kicked it around and said, "Good, m-m-m! Good."

In late August, end of summer when the tents came down and the Indians paddled away upstream and disappeared around the bend, I wasn't sure I'd ever see Mrs. Nepishish again. And I never have. But the next spring when the Indians came downriver and camped here once more, there was a handsome slender young girl who came across. She was a sister of Mrs. Nepishish, and I remembered having seen her among the group who came to visit. She made me understand that Mrs. Nepishish had gone this summer to Seven Islands on the Gulf, down the rough Romaine River with Payuk and her husband. She gave me a package sewn up in thin birch bark. She bent her knee and patted it, and said "Good" and pointed off to the wooded southwest. Inside the packet was a beaded Indian woman's cap.

CHAPTER XXIV

As spring came on, dear, lovable, plump Pearlie began to pine. She had always been clumsy and thoughtless, pounding the floor harder than anybody else when she walked, dropping trays and pitchers in the ward, hollering before she thought. But now it was more so. In their rooms just before they went to bed the girls would often sing, sing good and loud as though they meant it, the way people sing here. Mostly it was hymns or the old favorites that are well known all over the English-speaking world. One of their specialties was "My Old Kentucky Home," and the fact that they had no idea what or where Kentucky was, made not the slightest difference; they had an idyllic vision of their own. There was something mournfully beautiful about Sarah Jane's quavering soprano rolling out "Jesus, Lover of My Soul" in the dark of a windy night. It made you think of castaways who scan the ocean; it made you think of her five rejected suitors. But the girls did not sing any more. Pearlie was waspish, Pearlie was snappish. "Oh, stow it," she exclaimed whenever Sarah Jane began the bedtime song.

The sunshine of Pearlie's disposition turned to vinegar, the reason being that Pearlie was thickening more so around the middle, Pearlie was pregnant. There was no chance that the father might step forward, because he was far away in Canada or somewhere. He was one of the company of fourteen professional prospectors who had made a trip from here last summer and had been on the point of departing for the outside when I arrived. She told me about it one day and cried. She seemed a bit dazed. Up to this point she had not really believed that what was happening to her could really happen to Pearlie Burns. But now the baby was kicking, and there was certainly no denying its existence. Very lively it felt in there.

I was particularly sorry, since, in my capacity as Chief Keeper of Morals, I was to a certain extent responsible for Pearlie. "What shall I do, what shall I do?" she wept.

"You'll be all right," I told her. "I'll take care of you and you'll be all right."

Pearlie cried easily, Pearlie's nature took things easily, and so would Pearlie's frame. I felt sorrier for Pearlie's mother, my friend Mrs. Burns, who would experience a twinge of shame, than I did for Pearlie, whose twinges were mostly exasperation. It was not so bad, however, as it might have been elsewhere, for here in this natural place, though illegitimates are rare, when they appear they are looked upon, like storms or deaths or a good haul of seals, as simply a proof of nature's might, to be accepted. The elders feel a bit sad; they have so long ago been convinced of nature's almighty power that this proof seems a trifle unnecessary. On the other hand, a child is always a valuable addition. A child grows up to hunt or make sealskin boots.

Sex *mores* are so different here that it is hard to make them clear. There are no divorces, and no desertions. Once they have made the decision to live together in the same house, Labrador men and women do indeed cleave together for better for worse, for richer for poorer, in sickness and in health. They have a code which is more to them than a formal marriage ceremony. Some of the older couples in the bay had three or four children before a travelling minister appeared to bless their union. Such informal old ways lend a different tone to present-day lapses; they make for more tolerance. The affair is considered understandable and unfortunate, but not a crime. Nobody looks down his nose, and nobody has ever heard of a "delinquent girl." I myself attended a marriage here which was also attended by the bride's two-year-old daughter. When somebody offhand asked the groom, "Is that your little girl?" he said, "I dunno. Hope so. Pretty, ain't she?" It would be unjust to give the idea that Hamilton Inlet morals are lax. On the contrary, there is less promiscuity than in urban centers.

I didn't ask Pearlie which one of those prospectors was the father, because, after all, what was the use? He wasn't coming back. It is natural enough for a man to leave an illegitimate or two in his wake. Hasn't the American army and navy left some 18,000 in the Philippines? The sad part of it is that it is not natural or satisfactory for a woman to be left with a child and no man.

But Pearlie told me which one it was anyhow, a virile chap, plainly a rebel from office jobs, an expert geologist with a rain-soaked felt hat, who could handle canoes with the best of them. When they returned from the 800-mile swing through the back-country lakes where Steve Burns had guided them, he was one of the ones who reported that his canoe had run Gull Island Rapid, though the trappers usually lower it on a line. He was one of those who came to dinner at the hospital and told us tales of his trip. They had had to wait here ten days for the mail steamer, and it was those ten days when the steamer was delayed by fog and storm that changed Pearlie's life. Having been two months in the bush, they were wild for gaiety and sociability. Every night they gave a party in their bunkhouse for anybody who wanted to dance to their portable Victrola, and Pearlie went quite often. I remembered telling her to behave herself and be sedate, but you know where that road leads to that is paved with good intentions.

Pearlie, jolly, plump, easy-going Pearlie, lost her sunny good humor when she thought of a prospector far away. And of course she thought of him a good part of the time.

Pearlie's was an easy birth. She seemed to be more herself in a few days, though still slightly dazed. "What'll I do now?" she wanted to know. And she was apprehensive too, for every childless family in the bay wanted to adopt her baby boy, children being here the surest helpmates in life's battle. She did not want to let him go. "They wants to take you, b'y," she'd say as she lay nursing him. And though it is hard to believe, she looked almost beautiful at such moments. Steve was put out with her and wouldn't have her live at home with her child. I told her she could work on at the hospital the same as always, but that was not going to work out well permanently, and she seemed to sense it.

Then along came Davis Hicks, black-haired, intelligent nineteen-year-old son of Mrs. Hicks, the shyest boy in the bay by far, but one of those grand products of a poor home who early decides he's had enough of being poor. If this were a conventional love story, I'd be able to say that Davis Hicks had long been Pearlie's childhood sweetheart, that sadly, in the background, with mournful eyes, he had watched Pearlie dancing and carrying on with the prospectors. But the fact is that young Hicks had never courted

Pearlie, and to the best of my knowledge had never evinced the slightest interest in her until the baby was born. If he had only been her childhood sweetheart, he might have forgiven her with such touching magnanimity, but that wasn't the way of it. Polly, in her light-hearted way, said to me, "I do believe he's fallen in love with the baby."

At any rate, ever since the news of Pearlie's trouble had spread abroad, he had been poking around the bay shores picking up materials with which to build a pretty cabin at Mud Lake. Principally the materials consisted of railroad ties, cut and hewed and stacked by the shore several summers before in a money-earning project that dozens of men had worked at. Unfortunately, the steamer from Newfoundland that was to load the ties never arrived, a big autumn tide rolled in, scattered them all over the bay, and the whole plan was a failure.

The only one to benefit was Davis Hicks. It reminded me a little of Victor Hugo's *Toilers of the Sea*, to think of that slight figure, wet to the skin, wrestling alone with the heavy squared-down timbers that were soaking in backwater eddies and bleaching behind islands high above tide mark in driftwood tangles among the trees. All he had for a craft was a rotten old borrowed rowboat. He could do nothing unless the wind was fair, and then, towing a boom, he would sail, very slowly. Now and then we'd see, way off toward Sandy Run, the point of a sail that hardly moved. If it grew rough, the ties hopped over and under the boom logs and were lost. Sometimes when it was calm, he'd put a notched tie across the gunnels to keep the boat from being broken wide open, then load her with ties laid on crosswise. In a small space amidships he sat and rowed, with an inch or two of freeboard, a mile an hour, hour after hour, humming happily to himself. It was one man against forces a thousand times more powerful than himself. It was a labor of love like Gilliatt's in the Hugo story, but with a vastly different dénouement.

"He wants to marry me," Pearlie cried, "baby and all. Shall I do it?"

"Do you like him, Pearlie?"

"Sure Miss, I do. True as true I do, not just because——"

"Why don't you go ahead then?"

"Oh Miss!" She gave me a hug, she and her shining eyes.

They were married at North West River, and were to go away to their new home that afternoon in a white skiff that Davis Hicks had been half the spring building. Pearlie seemed to have trouble getting organized after the ceremony, what with her boundless capacity for being flustered and all, so that it was nearly sunset when they were at last packed in. Davis was at the oars, and in the bow was stowed a tent, a bag of Pearlie's clothes, a few dishes, some pots and pans, and the inevitable axe. Pearlie sat with her child in the stern, all smiles and confusion. The sky grew pink above the mountains, and silver ran along the water whenever a ripple stirred. As two men waded in to shove the skiff off, the whole village, gathered on the beach, set up a cheer. And so Pearlie floated away, with her man and her baby, and (Oh, Miss Austen, ain't they beauties!) the loveliest new pair of brown sneakers with red rubber soles.

CHAPTER XXV

THE ROBERT MICHELINS had temporarily moved to North West River from Traverspine in expectation of Matilda's baby, she had had such a bad time with some of the others. Early one morning somebody knocked, and it was Robert saying, "Matilda's time has come."

By all reckonings this was about two weeks ahead of time. "Is she in labor?" I asked.

"Yes," he answered.

"It's a little soon, isn't it, Robert?"

"I s'pose, but she's awful worried."

I remembered she had told me that her first two babies were born dead. The last five had lived, however. "Is she bleeding?"

"Yes, that's it."

I got the big obstetric bag and handed it to him. "Go along and I'll be with you soon," I said.

As I hurriedly dressed, I was looking out the window at the river and the bay. It was three o'clock in the morning, but the sun was blazing warm and the sky was blue as midday. The bay was calm, so still the shadow of the blue mountains showed in the water; a mile off the river mouth toward the pointed firs of Point Gibou a company of ducks was fluttering and squawking, stirring up a pool of ripples which glinted in the low sun. There was no smoke from the Indian tents on the far side of the river; for once I was up before them, which took some doing. I could smell the wet sand of the river bar growing warm, and green grass growing brighter and brighter green, and the balsamy tang of the huge forests around us. My Iceland poppies would probably put on a full inch in this one day. I looked off down the bay, wondering if a boat would come from somewhere. It was good to be called to work like this on a morning like this. Matilda's condition sounded bad, though.

It's strange how seldom a person feels the way she's supposed to. I couldn't help being happy as I lugged another big bag full of emergency supplies up along the river path past the garden picket fence and the rows of little cabbage plants. The river chuckled in and out among the stones. At the end of the Hudson's Bay Company wharf a skiff slowly bumped the piles and stretched its painter and bumped again, as though begging endlessly for some one to let it go. It was a day to go all right, to go anywhere in the sunshiny brightness, to go anywhere as long as it was somewhere.

The stovepipe at Montague's, where Robert and his family had settled in to await Matilda's confinement, was belching smoke. Montagues were down the bay fishing at Indian Harbor. Their place was a nice little old low white house right at the first river bend with one eye on the bay and the other looking round the corner toward Grand Lake and the western hills. It was all blue and green and dreamy off there, but Matilda couldn't wait.

The five children and the helping girl were still asleep. Matilda lay in the big box bed looking thin and peaked and washed out. Her brown hair was tied in a tight knot on her head in a sort of clearing-the-decks-for-action manner. She essayed a smile.

"Good morning."

"Hello, Matilda."

"I got a few things ready. The basket is the baby clothes. The box is my things."

Examination confirmed my worst fears. Placenta prævia, one of the most dreaded complications of labor, was causing this ante-partum hemorrhage. I was frightened, for a good obstetrician with every aid at hand can't always manage placenta prævia successfully. All sorts of things can happen.

"Plenty of hot water?" I said to Robert.

"Yes, Miss," he answered, and started out for more wood.

I knew he'd split twice the wood and carry from the river twice the water we needed, but even so he was less to be pitied than the men who wait in anterooms outside maternity wards and bite their nails and have no part. Now I sent him to get neighboring Mrs. Dan Michelin, who was a good hand at this business, having had so many children of her own. I wished Matilda were in hospital, but it would take so long to send for the stretcher and then to have it carried back along the rocky path that I decided to see the case through here. Her condition was bad, but there were some favorable aspects. Fortunately, she was in strong labor and not yet showing signs of collapse from loss of blood.

Dilation was proceeding normally, and the baby was in a breech position. Had the presentation been any other way, it might well have resisted any attempt at external manipulation, and I don't know what I should have done then. Quickly placing everything in readiness, I faced what I knew I must do—something I had never attempted alone. Thoughts of cities and hospitals and doctors went round in my head, and I longed for a phone and a quick ambulance, a team of competent doctors and nurses, and all that goes with it.

Well, I was here and this was my job. When I was ready, dressed in sterilized gown and gloves, everything set, Mrs. Dan and Robert standing by, I ruptured the membranes and after a little difficulty brought down a leg, the idea being that slight traction on the infant foot will cause compression of the bleeding vessels and so check the hemorrhage. I must confess I was nervous, though I tried to conceal the fact.

The treatment succeeded. Bleeding stopped. I hurried to wrap the tiny foot and leg immediately in hot cloths, for, as most people probably know, contact with the cool air would cause premature attempts on the part of the infant to breathe before the head was born, and so result in suffocation. I listened with the stethoscope and heard the baby's heart beating strong and regularly.

Now for the long wait, keeping the foot warm, exerting slight tension on it between pains, watching and cheering Matilda, who was a very good patient, and mentally going through a routine of delivering the breech, which would be the next step. I had Mrs. Dan get the kitchen table ready, as this low featherbed was hardly suitable. Robert and I carried Matilda out. That made things better, and I felt more confident now we had got so far and the baby was still alive, as well as Matilda. My back was about broken from bending over the low bed, so it was a relief to stand up straight. I was sorry I couldn't give Matilda an anesthetic for the worst of it, but I had all I could manage without having to watch that too, and this was Matilda's eighth and she'd never had an anesthetic before, so—well——

Louis and Olive appeared at this moment, rubbing the

sleepiness out of their eyes. Robert and the girl dressed all
the children and sent them somewhere to somebody's. A
great many hours passed. The atmosphere was grim, op-
pressive, quiet, do what we would. And then things began
to happen. The baby was born, a boy who saluted the world
with a lusty yell. It was lucky I didn't have to waste time
bringing him to, for I was very busy with Matilda. I
handed the babe to Mrs. Dan, and heard Robert laughing
with relief as he looked at his son and said, "You're the
spit 'n' image of your grandpa. Hi, Joe!"

Matilda began to show signs of exhaustion, as well she
might. But the third stage gave no trouble, and she re-
sponded to stimulants. After I had worked over her a long
time, she was able to take that tried and true remedy for
all ills, a good hot cup of tea, before she fell into the
fathomless, deep sleep which comes to mothers who are no
longer expectant. Of course I had a cup of tea too, since it
was noon by this time. Relaxation now, Matilda lost to the
world but picking up every hour, the baby sleeping peacefully.

I left instructions with Mrs. Dan to call me immediately
if there was any sign of hemorrhage, and went back along
the path toward the hospital in the afternoon sunshine. The
skiff at the wharf was still tugging, but it wasn't tugging at
me any more. The morning had been bright, but the afternoon was brighter. I felt as though my morning longings
had been realized, and I had been on an adventurous journey. No one, only I, would know the struggle and the wonder. Matilda had no idea how near a thing it was. I remembered my young brother's remark when I first received my
nurse's certificate and became a registered member of the

Australian Trained Nurses Association. He looked at the initials A. T. N. A. on the gold-and-enamel pin and said, "Able To Nurse Anything, eh?"

Well, I answered him across the oceans and the years, *I did it this time anyway.*

CHAPTER XXVI

I stood knee-deep in the river, with cool water rippling past my legs. It was eleven o'clock at night and the sun was going down. Every one seemed to be asleep except me and a couple of gulls whose wings shone yellow in the long horizontal light that was gilding the Mealies too. Walking barefoot on sand was so pleasant that the two buckets didn't feel heavy as I carried them up to my flower garden. The red-and-white Iceland poppies had just come out, and the sweet peas were a riot of color. The hardy little nasturtiums were doing pretty well, and the blue lupine and pink larkspur. I had a tin can punched with holes for spraying water on my little calendulas and the French marigolds. The zinnias were only an inch high as yet, and the delphiniums might not flower this year, but my garden meant the world to me. The seeds had come from Sutton's in England the autumn before, and I had started a lot of them in window boxes in March. Such care those little plants had needed, such turning to the sun and moving away from cold windows at night, such watering and arranging to get them into warm sunny exposures. They were worse than premature babies for needing attention. But now in the long days of northern summer they were shooting up even faster than plants do in the temperate zone.

Tramping the rows, scattering the precious drops, I knew each plant individually, and associated my flowers with all the happiest times I had ever known. My mother loved her flowers too, and when she was worn out with all the work of that big family of ours, she would turn to gardening. "Why don't you rest?" we asked her. And she would pull up a handful of weeds and say, "My flowers rest me."

Now I remembered how it had been with her, and it was the same with me. My flowers were the perfect centerpiece for these evening distances, the bay lapping, the spruces against the sky, the cool sand under my toes, and memories, memories focusing on petals just beginning to close in the night-time chill. Watering the vegetables was a duty, but watering the flowers was a joy.

I went back to the beach and lay with my head on my arm. Tomorrow I must ask Jack for the fifth time to fix those gates in the fence around the garden. They were half broken and hard to close, so that nobody bothered except me. Only today I'd hunted Rufus the bull out of the lettuce, and a couple of village dogs out of the zinnias. People ought to keep their dogs penned in summer and not let them be such a nuisance, killing hens and spoiling gardens. We needed those vegetables, and Heaven knows, I needed my flowers after nine months without any.

Pretty soon I'd carry a couple more buckets, but not yet; this was too fine. I thought of tomorrow and the laundry and the meals, and the milk safe in the cellar that I must finish tacking screens onto, and half a dozen windows too. The new crew of summer wops had already put on a dozen screens and today rigged weights and pulleys so the screen doors closed themselves, which was a grand help. These four American college chaps were so cooperative and friendly that Jack, who was usually standoffish toward strangers, was fond of them already. We missed them nights like this when they were away camped up Grand Lake with the motorboat, working on a boom of firewood they'd tow home tomorrow. Fine evenings like this they had a way of wandering around with an accordion, singing glee-club quartets with really professional polish. They had taught me "Lord Jeffrey Amherst," "Far Above Cayuga's Waters," and I already kenned "John Peele." They watered the vegetables, they asked me for jobs, they wanted to help, and for several weeks they had been taking three-hour turns at night in the ward to relieve me. That was the biggest help of all. We had three sick girls now: Mary, who was seriously ill with a paralysis that I was unable to diagnose, very uncomfortable and wanting her position changed day and night; two-year-old Ethel Shepherd, recovering from almost fatal burns; little Martha Wolfrey, dying of T. B., bleeding from the lungs for three weeks, and little we could do except give her sips of water and ice to suck. Hers would be the fourth tuberculosis death, including Willie Shippan's and Devotion's, that I had been helpless to prevent in the past eight months. Her condition terrified the boys. They had never in their gay, carefree lives had to watch some one die. But they stuck to their night watches manfully just the same, wondering, as every one does, *Suppose it were me instead of little Martha.*

I lay on the beach and thought about the day. We were a big family here now, and the housekeeping and nursing responsibilities weren't light. Doctor Paddon was out at Indian Harbor again this summer, and I was still in charge here. We had fourteen in the staff to be fed, including a new cowboy who didn't always wash his hands at meals. Eskimo Joe Kullinuk's clothes seemed to need daily attention. Oh the little things, the little things, the requisitions and the bookkeeping and the letters and the buttons and the dust under the beds.

This morning one of the cows had a swollen udder, and I looked at that because, Heavens on earth, what's the use of being a *toganish squish* if you can't be a veterinary as well? One of the calves was also sick nigh unto death, thanks to Joe who had been dusting cabbages and left some Paris green where the silly thing could lap it up; so I gave the calf a stomach washout while I was about it, and hoped for the best.

After my morning visit to Mrs. Robert Michelin, a session in the ward and lunch, I was sorting clothes in the clothing store. Though it was still early summer, I had already sold $1000 worth of clothing and taken in quantities of produce as well as $250 worth of beaded moccasins and craftwork to be sold in the Grenfell shops in Canada, the United States and England. I pretty well knew the families of the bay now, and their sizes and needs, and could put aside a coat and say this will be just the thing for Liza and this for Lem. Dutifully I tried to remember that "Woman is the lesser man . . . as moonlight unto sunlight, and as water unto wine—" especially when it came to clothes, for the man had to go away to the woods, but never mind the woman. If she had nothing to wear, she could presumably stay in bed —though I never saw one that did.

About then eight Indian women had come up to the attic clothing store with a lot of caribou skins to exchange for woolen goods. Equally they came to marvel over our small heap of party bags and evening dresses and feather boas and picture hats that had come sandwiched in with truly useful apparel. Not that much junk escapes the eagle eye of the office that packs and sends clothes. Manufacturers make outright gifts of thousands of brand new winter garments, and people everywhere send beautiful woolens and wraps and life-saving warm things. But that only makes the occasional stomacher or tiara that kicks around the clothing store, unwanted year after year, seem doubly outlandish. The Indian women were in no hurry. What is time to them?—they have forever. *Tee hee hee, look at these high-heeled pumps with the rhinestone buckles.* One of them tries them on, and the rest collapse with mirth to see her wobble. All the Indians are convinced that white people are absolutely loony to spend never-ending labor maintaining gardens and houses and innumerable possessions, but they like to verify the certainty now and then by actually seeing in the life a collapsible opera hat, a rubber corset, a pair of lace drawers. And yet, they're not immune. I've seen them wearing eyeglass frames without lenses.

They stayed all afternoon long, finally ending up with bundles of woolen stockings, sweaters, jackets, and overcoats, whose material they had carefully fingered and weighed. No Indian would be caught dead in an overcoat, but they intended making children's garments and men's breeches of this stout cloth. They collected a half-dozen felt hats too, which shed rain nicely. When they were going out, Sarah Jane gave them the customary "Good-bye for a little while, *meeami abashish*," and I couldn't help asking her, "Don't you know how to say good-bye forever?"

In the evening, having sponged Martha Wolfrey and Ethel and Mary, fixed them up for the night, and asked Sarah Jane to sit with them for a while, I ran around the village paths on my regular evening call to Mrs. Gear, who was still hanging by a thread, to Mrs. Michelin to treat her and see how the new baby was doing, and to several others.

I loved the little village paths that seemed so smooth and free now the snow was gone. They just grew, they just wound along, following the spots that had first gone bare in the spring, now close to the river, now between a few houses, now skirting the woods among worn, polished roots. To skim along the little paths, unencumbered by snowshoes or mittens, picking up a bit of gossip here, a greeting there, seemed the purest pleasure. It was always, "Good night, Miss, good night," for *Good evening* was unknown here; and men sitting smoking, or hoeing potatoes, or painting boats, and women with the dishes done, sitting in the grass and sewing, surrounded by children. The bay was glassy, and the gulls were calling on the sandbar. Pleeman Blake was up along the bank, with a great following of small fry as usual, hurling stones clear across the river with a leather sling, the same kind of sling that David used on Goliath.

And then at last there was a little corner of the day for my beloved flowers. . . .

Goodness! I had been dozing here on the beach. Well, it was late now, and I must have a glance at my patients, make sure the watches were arranged, and to bed. I got up from the cool sand and carried two more bucketfuls on my way in. The sun had gone down, practically in the north, but its glow still showed above the hills, a glow that never went out these clear nights. In less than two hours the sun would peek over the rim of our world again. We weren't quite in the land of the midnight sun, but as I studied the northern hills I decided we had only missed it by about two inches.

"Oh, Miss Austen, Miss Austen, fire! fire!" one of the girls screamed. I smelled smoke, and ran for the kitchen.

Some stockings and a pair of trousers (Joe's, of course) had fallen off a line that stretched above the stove, and were now ablaze, with flames licking up the corner wall beside the stove. Ira, the cowboy, was just coming in the back door with the morning pails of milk. He threw a pail of milk all over the stove and wall, and that was that, but my three helpless ones in the ward above needed calming.

About eleven o'clock that morning, a beautiful red flannel shirt that was the pride of Jack's heart was brought in from the outdoor clothesline in shreds. The mission puppies and a couple of big dogs were racing round and round the hospital, up into the woods and down alongshore tearing and shaking and fighting over the last few bits of the red flannel shirt.

"Get those dogs penned up in the stockade," I said. "Go and get Jim right away and don't waste a minute."

While they were finding out that Jim was away wood-cutting, as I should have remembered, came another scream, "Miss Austen, Miss Austen!" Somebody had left the cellar door open, and the dogs, who were on an absolute rampage, had broken into my newly screened milk and meat safe, slashed the netting to ribbons and stolen a ham, a whole, irreplaceable, monumental, twelve-pound ham, such a delicacy as we hadn't set tooth on for months, a pearl without price, carefully treasured against the festive day when Doctor Paddon or Sir Wilfred should arrive—now torn to pieces and being dragged through the sand. You might as well chase the wind.

"Miss Austen! Miss Austen! The dogs are in the flowers!"

My heart turned over. In a panic I sprang through the door and down the steps. Desolation! Torn earth, great holes

like some pock-marked no man's land. Why did the sense-
less brutes dig up my flowers? they couldn't eat them. My
flowers, my flowers, for whom I carried manure from the
barn and water from the river in the nights when other
people slept. My only pleasure, my only joy, wantonly
rooted up and ruined. I sat and sobbed for my lovely, bright-
eyed flowers, killed with no reason whatever—just as people
die—struck down by the blindest chance—like little Martha
in the ward—and no one to help—you do what you can—and
it isn't good enough.

I wept for every injustice and indignity I had ever known,
and tears kept coming and coming, and I couldn't see any
use in stopping them or trying to go on. I lay in the grass
and buried my head.

After a bit I saw out of the corner of my eye that a few
plants were only buried, and could be revived. My grief
turned to rage. Nobody cared about the garden but me.
Nobody ever closed the gate except me. Other people, lacking the intelligence of the stupidest peasant on a whole
continent, left them open. I went and hunted up Jack, and
I was red in the face and out for blood. "If you don't fix
those gates right now, I'll rip *all* your shirts to pieces (poor
Jack, so rushed with work, and always doing a kindness for
someone). And you can tell Jim for me that I'll shoot the
next dog that gets in my garden, I'll keep my gun loaded,
and I'll shoot him through the head."

His face flushed shockingly, and I wished I could recall
the words.

I went straight to the H. B. C. post and bought a roll of
chicken wire out of my own money. Knowing perfectly well
that no power on earth could keep those puppies penned

all summer, I was tacking my wire around the bottom of the fence, and Jack was whacking methodically at the gate, when the Edward Michelins came into the river in their rowboat and landed. I determined not to speak to them. I was in no mood for it. But Mrs. Edward came right up from the shore to proudly exhibit four-months' Harold. Plump and blue-eyed, it was hard to believe that this was Little Sparrow-mouth of Sabasquasho. Holding that lusty little bundle in my arms, I wondered what today's frenzy had been all about. "Here's one flower that didn't get rooted up anyway, eh, Jack?" I said.

He wasn't very keen on babies. "Humph!" he grunted, and I knew that he was justified in being still angry with me.

CHAPTER XXVII

Jack was going in the scow to Mud Lake and then to Kenemich for a load of hay. As it was a good chance for me to return Hugh Best to his mother at Mud Lake, I went along too. Not that Hugh was sorely in need of my companionship, or Jack either, but it was one of those rare and delicious chances to exchange carbolic smell for the bay wind breezing off the ripples. My penchant for trips may have been as blameworthy as Polly pretended to claim; nevertheless, to be chained to bookkeeping, housekeeping, dying chronics, slop pails and routine duties fourteen hours a day —chained right in the middle of silver waterways and white, lonely beaches and forests full of twinflowers—was sometimes more than I could bear or want to be able to bear. Privately I dubbed such a travelling spree as this, "pay day."

Hugh was a four-year-old who had taken sick in a summer scare of dysentery that was now subsiding at Mud Lake. It was exactly the same as the Traverspine variety, its origins equally mysterious. When I had answered the call to Mud Lake a week before, I found most of the children improving except Hugh. He was lying on a cushion on the kitchen floor, half dead and hardly able to speak, with eyes dropping shut from weakness—that familiar symptom. His mother kept saying, "Don't you want to go to the hospital with the nice nurse, Hughie?"

"No," said Hugh, and began to cry.

Though I pled with the frantic mother to let me take him regardless, this went on for quite a while. In fact, since the kidnapping of children is frowned upon by even the most lenient watchdogs of medical ethics, I was about to leave without Hugh, when that forthright old gal, Aunt Gantry Blake, who was aunt to most everybody in the settlement, descended on the scene like a whirlwind.

"Here, here, what's the matter!" said she. "Don't want to go, eh? Do you think he knows what he wants—four years old and so sick he can't stand?" She picked him up from the floor, wrapped the blanket around him and stowed him in the boat. "Now get started," she said. "He's better off to the hospital, and never mind what he wants."

My opinion of Aunt Gantry Blake soared. Medical ethics don't apply when the patient's aunt does the kidnapping. We cranked up and left immediately, before the mother, who was wringing her hands on the beach, had time to change her mind.

Now Hugh was practically well again, though the mother didn't know it, since no boats had been to or from Mud Lake.

As the big green scow plowed up the Mud Lake channel, tossing in her wake the rowboats moored in front of houses, Hugh's mother came to the water's edge and stood shading her eyes. Her strained attitude said plainly, "Is he—? Is he——?"

For answer I held the child up with the sun shining on his gold hair.

She saw, and her hands came down from her eyes and clasped in front of her in an instinctive gesture of thanksgiving.

The boat had hardly touched the sand when she had him in her arms. "Hugh, b'y," she said, devouring him, "you looks good to me." But in spite of her emotion she didn't forget the obligations of hospitality. "Now, Miss, come up and have a cup of tea."

"A fine idea," I said. "Why didn't we think of that before?"

Jack chugged on up the channel on some business with Uncle Johnnie Blake, and was soon back tooting on his tin foghorn for me to come a-running and not be *all* day chatterboxing about nothing.

We ran down Grand River, across Goose Bay, out through Sandy Run and headed east toward the Mealies. Kenemich was a rivermouth place like all the rest. It was straight across the bay from North West River, but so far off it wasn't visible.

At Kenemich they were just finishing the haying. They were short on scythes for their mowing, they said, having ground some of them down so thin they were no longer serviceable. They gave Jack an order for a half dozen new ones to be sent from Newfoundland in time for next year's haying. They had hand-made wooden rakes, and all the hay was carried on hand barrows by pairs of men. Some of their hay forks were of the manufactured variety, but some had been hand-forged in their own little shop and fitted with birch handles. One boy had a fork that was carved entirely of wood, tines and all. I had never seen haying done on such a hand-labor scale.

Old Scotsman Malcolm McLean, taciturn and hawk-eyed, his square white beard waving in the wind, supervised the loading, and wasted no words about it. He showed us where to tie up, and directed the laying of a gangplank. Sons as well as grandsons obeyed a mere nod of his head or a flick of his eye. He was eighty-four years old, and still absolute boss. Now married to his third wife, his twenty-third child had just been born. He was the patriarch, the tribal leader. The five houses here were all McLean houses. With the exception of his own wife and several sons' wives, everybody here was Malcolm's child or grandchild. Beside these who had remained at the family seat, there were numerous others of his progeny in other parts of the bay. For instance, Murdock McLean at North West River was a son, and Hannah Montague, my fishing companion of the fits, was Malcolm's eldest daughter by a pure Eskimo mother. Hannah's grandchildren were in the North West River school side by side with one of Malcolm's young daughters, a blooming and beautiful girl of seven, named Bella—which is to say that Bella was in school with her father's great-grandchildren, her half-sister's grandchildren, and she was older than these, her own great-aunts.

Bella was at home, since school did not keep in the summer. She and I being old friends, she took me by the hand and led me up the path to the fine old McLean house where Mrs. Malcolm was overjoyed to see somebody from away, and treated me like visiting royalty. Tea was served on a spotless linen cloth from fine china cups, with gleaming silverware. The house was furnished with substantial birch tables and chairs and bedsteads, thick Hudson's Bay blankets like fur, a polar bearskin on the floor, good cupboards, generous-sized stoves, everything needful, and all about were voices, chatter, laughter, people, and every one of them a McLean. Malcolm came in for a moment, tall, straight, a man made strong by the years. He bowed to me slightly, a grave, proud gesture filled with traditions and obligations for guest as well as host. The only fitting return would have been a deep, deep curtsy to the floor.

I wished I might know some of the secrets locked forever under that thatch of white hair. His history was the bay's history in essence. His settlement had similarities to the headquarters of an ancient Scottish clan. True, no one here except Malcolm knew what a Scottish clan was, probably. But, seeing this place, I realized for the first time what clanlike divisions the bay contained. Pearl River was all Chaulks, Kenemich was all McLeans, Mulligans River was mostly Baikies except for a Campbell, Traverspine was all Michelins, Mud Lake was mostly Blakes, and Sabasquasho another branch of Michelins.

The rivermouths represented families where men bred themselves whole tribes. Of the old originals there were few left alive now, but among them were Uncle Joe Michelin, who was Robert's father and had seventeen living children, Annie Baikie's Eskimo grandmother, and Malcolm.

At nineteen Malcolm had come here from Scotland to be a "servant" of the Hudson's Bay Company in the fur trade. A Hudson's Bay Company advertisement puts his case like this:

To take the King's shilling, and "go for to be a soldier" of England was almost treason among the Highland clans. And the press gang had made the Royal Navy something to be shunned by the Scotch lad of that day. . . . So the ambitious sought opportunity in the great commercial companies in the Colonies. From the earliest days, the Hudson's Bay Company was largely staffed and officered by Scotsmen.

There were hundreds of Eskimos in Hamilton Inlet in Malcolm's early days; in fact, one of its original names was Esquimaux Bay. Malcolm helped around the post, learned blacksmithing, coopering, trapping, dog-driving, sailoring. With the river gangs he went to the height-of-land supplying the Indian fur posts the Company maintained then two and three hundred miles in the bush. After some years, with no choice except Indian or Eskimo, he took an Eskimo woman and began the Kenemich settlement as a trapper, hunter and fisher, supplying himself from the land with all the necessities he could, and trading furs and fish to the Company for those he couldn't. That union of Scotch and Eskimo blood and culture, with Indian skills that Malcolm had learned in the bush thrown in for good measure, was the basis of present-day Hamilton Inlet charm and uniqueness. It was the history of most of the clan-families.

All Malcolm's children learned to read, write and figure. In some families this knowledge lapsed because the mother had no civilized learning. But Malcolm (as did Joe Michelin) taught his sons and daughters, and even today possessed the old Bible and three other books he had brought from Scotland as a boy.

If he needed a boat, he built one (his shed was stocked with moulds of various models); if he needed a house, he built that too; when he needed food, he shot it or raised it if he could. For a while he took to raising sheep, and thirty years after leaving Scotland he made from memory a spinning wheel, carder and a loom for weaving homespun. As a boatman on the bay old Malcolm used to be a great hand to carry sail. Murdock has told me that when he was a boy sailing out to the seal nets with his father, he sometimes begged the old man to take a reef, but Malcolm at the tiller did not even answer. Nowadays Malcolm asked no favors from any one, and accepted nothing from the mission except medical aid, which he paid for, in cash, immediately.

The Kenemich was a good river for salmon and still is. Every year they sell a sloop-load of casks filled with salt salmon to the Company. Winters they have their own private river to trap, and valleys they know in their Mealy Mountain back yard where caribou use.

The loading of the scow went slowly because the hay all had to be carried aboard by hand, dumped down the hatch and stowed, and besides that some of the McLean men had to be spared for loading several thousand feet of lumber onto a motorboat that had come over from North West River. Malcolm had a gasoline saw with which he got out lumber for the timber company that had once operated here. They hired Malcolm to do this because their franchise stipulated that they must saw a specified quantity of timber yearly or lose their rights. It was the fields the lumber outfit had cleared for their horses that Malcolm and his sons were now haying for the mission.

While I was hanging around, I went to have a look at the ruin of the old steam sawmill by the river, a huge, sagging building that Jack said was haunted. I stumbled over tons of old iron, broken beams, rusty boilers, seeing evidence of hasty departure years before. On the saw table was a great log with the circular ripsaw stopped midway of its length, just as the timber crew had left it one autumn day long ago when they deserted aboard a passing ship, oppressed by the prospect of the long winter here, cut off from the world. It did seem ghostly in there, and I enjoyed it better walking the sun-and-shade sand of the winding river, wishing I could follow it all the way back into the mountains.

Arch Goudie's old motorboat was loaded at last with lumber for the new house he was putting up by degrees at North West River, and he set off across the bay. But it was late evening by the time we were ready.

A head wind slowed us, and our tons of hay sank us fairly deep too. As it grew dark, low clouds rolled in, shutting out the stars. We would be most of the night crossing to North West River at this rate.

Jack, with his sharp eyes, saw a tiny light shine and go out a long way off our starboard bow. "Stop the motor," he said to me, and we lay broadside to the seas, rolling, listening. We knew that every boat in the bay carries a shotgun in hope of picking up a meal of ducks en route. Far away we heard the gun boom three times—the local S. O. S.

Arch's open boat was wallowing in the trough under a tremendous load of lumber, a dark mass half sunk. "Engine's broke down," he shouted through his cupped hands. We could make out bundles of boards alongside him, boards he had jettisoned already but kept a line to, hoping to save them. Even so, his boat was half full, and he stood to the knees in water, taking more with every roll. He grinned up at us, showing his white teeth. "Thought I'd have to heave the lot pretty soon," he said. "I been listening for you a long time."

The dark wet wind blew cuttingly, nature versus Arch's dream of a new house. We tossed and wallowed alongside while he passed up boards, and the scow dipped her great clumsy sides and pulled them out again with a sucking sound that was peculiar to her. She was so roughly built, with big gaps in her inside sheathing, that every detail of her construction was naked and open to the eye; the spruce hewn knees, the knotty spots in her ribs, the oakum sticking through her seams. She'd been built one winter under Jack's direction by men of the village, who had never seen anything quite like her. And she was strong and crude, and, truth to tell, a bit clumsy, but we all loved her because she was a home product. At a time like this, surrounded by blackness, those honest axe cuts in *Capella*, as Doctor Paddon had christened her (Latin for capers and frolicsome goats), and those crooked timbers caused by lack of a straighter tree, made you think of the labor that had gone into her, and seemed a comforting assurance, illogically enough, against a watery grave.

The lumber was all piled on deck at last and lashed down. Since Arch still couldn't get his engine going, we gave him a line and started off very slowly, with the deckload catching the wind and his motorboat thrashing along behind.

"I'm going to be building a house myself pretty soon," said Jack.

"You and Annie?"

"Yes, me and Annie."

"I'm so glad. I hoped you would."

Spray was flying over the deck as we crawled toward a few stars under ragged clouds in the west. Jack stood at the tiller, grim as an iron post, in a frayed sou'wester and flapping oilskin pants, sparks streaming from a sodden cigarette in his mouth. And the motor went *pung, pung,* and the scow creaked and corkscrewed in the faintly revolting and ridiculous manner of a fat old lady attempting the *cancan.*

I burrowed into the fragrant hay below decks, glad to be dry, and lay drowsing and thinking how masculine the bay was, and the raw night wind. No wonder Jack was grim. It was no wonder, after the impersonal cold wetness of the bay and the woods, that men of this land loved their women in a very special way as they loved their homes and firesides and life itself. After all this wide blackness how gratefully they must accept the feminine, the intimate, the small and pretty and individual. Imagine how a touch of tenderness must seem to them.

I went to sleep and woke only as we came into the river. It was black as pitch now, an hour before dawn. Some thoughtful soul had left a lamp in the hospital window, which helped us to get our bearings as we crossed the river bar. But probably Jack would have managed it anyway, for he had cat's eyes on the water.

Pay day was over now, but I had had my money's worth.

CHAPTER XXVIII

THE WIRELESS, in one of its generous moods, reported that we were to expect a visit, even though we had no ham with which to welcome the visitors. Sir Wilfred and the Q. M. (Queen Mother, the mission's pet name for Lady Grenfell) were at Indian Harbor in *Strathcona*. Our friend the crack Canadian surgeon, Doctor Mount, was there again this summer on one of his "pleasure cruises" that changed lives. For three years he'd wanted to set eye on The Eden of the North, so they were going to bring him up the bay. They also sent word of another matter that gave me chills as I recalled it.

It was spring, just before the ice broke up, and I was standing in Doctor Paddon's office downstairs with a surgical book in my hand. The chapter entitled "Treatment of Inguinal Hernia" contained three treatises on different methods of complicated surgical repair, each a major operation and so impossible for me to comprehend, let alone perform, that they made me mad. Getting mad stopped the pages from rattling anyway.

My eye lit on a three-line squib tucked in like an afterthought at the end of the chapter: "TAXIS: the manual reduction of a ruptured inguinal hernia is now considered obsolete and dangerous, and should never under any circumstances be practised."

That was helpful! The only remedy I could attempt was obsolete, dangerous, and must never be tried under any circumstances. But did the book know about Donald Baikie, a thirty-six-year-old trapper, in the ward with a strangulated hernia? He was drawn and gray, unable to speak, and though I had injected one-quarter grain of heroin, not knowing what else to do while I came down to the doctor's office for a bit of browsing among his bookshelves, he still whimpered with the pain.

Donald had a wife and three children at Mulligan's River, thirty miles down the bay. Donald took after the Scotch side. He looked like a thoroughbred Scotsman, and he had the old Scottish obstinacy that characterizes those stony rovers that you find in every corner of the earth. Even this morning he had refused to get into the komatik box and be driven to the hospital; he said he'd get his rupture back in again somehow; he always had before. However, he collapsed this time while his brothers Jimmie and Earle were driving him up the bay, began to bawl out and then lapsed into unconsciousness.

When we had been undressing him for bed, his beard was frozen fast to the fur of his dickie hood. I took the scissors and snipped a piece of his beard off. "How long ago did the rupture happen?" I asked his brothers.

"Some time yesterday. He was hauling his sled in the woods, and it took him till night to get home. We been all day comin'."

He lay there moaning, retching spasmodically, with all the terrifying symptoms of acute intestinal obstruction. I didn't know what to do. So I had put hot-water bags to his clammy feet, given him the small shot of heroin, and come down to the office to think and study as calmly as possible. Shutting the surgical volume, I put it on the shelf. To try to push the rupture back might be obsolete, but if it had been done once it was worth trying again.

"Round up your relatives, will you?" I asked Jimmie and Earle. So they brought in sister Annie, sister Mae McLean, and another married brother and married sister who lived at North West River. "Now look," I said. "I don't know how to handle this very well. It needs a doctor and an operation. But I'm going to give him anesthetic and try to push the rupture back by every means I know. He may die while I'm doing it, but he'll surely die if he stays the way he is. Are you willing to have me try?"

"You might as well," said Jimmie.

"I'm willing and I won't blame you," said Mae.

"Go ahead," the rest agreed.

Sarah Jane and Pearlie and I got him onto the operating table and under general anesthesia. I had never even prepared a hernia patient for operation, because we have men orderlies to do that in the hospitals where I trained. I had never seen a manual reduction, because doctors don't do them. I had never had anything to do with hernia except to assist a surgeon in those impossible-for-me operations and to nurse various vociferous patients afterwards.

From the gas and congestion, Donald's entire abdomen was distended tight as a drum so that he looked like a pregnant woman. I drummed on it, because that is what doctors always do, though any one can see at a glance that such stretched parchment will resound. In the right groin was a reddish blue swollen mass, bigger than my two fists. You would not believe the body could accommodate such distention without bursting somewhere. Interference plainly intensified the danger of breaking the nipped intestine—my great fear, and the reason for the labels "obsolete and dangerous."

Hernia, as most people know, occurs because of an atavistic weakness of the abdominal wall, a weakness bequeathed to us from prehistoric time, along with appendices, wisdom teeth, and various other troublemakers. There are two weak spots, one on each side of the lower abdomen, where the muscle sheath can be forced apart by severe strain of the lifting muscles. The intestine, under pressure, forces itself through the muscle sheath. The skin is not punctured, of course, but when once the wall has been breached, so to speak, the condition is liable to repeat itself. Repeated friction causes the aperture to become inflamed and calloused; then comes the day when the intestine bulges through, is held fast by the calloused ring, and cannot be pushed back. Strangulation ensues, *i.e.*, the kink becomes shut off, there is complete blockage, everything in the vicinity swells and makes the tightness tighter, putrefaction sets in, the man is to all intents and purposes cut in half, and his hours are numbered.

I inserted a stomach tube, which brought up some gas and relieved the distention somewhat. I fastened Donald to the table face up, then tipped the head of the table way down almost to the floor so that he hung by the backs of his strapped knees in what is known as the Trendelenburg position. This made all his organs fall toward the chest cavity, and exerted a pull on them from within while I pushed on the bulge from without. The anesthesia relaxed all his muscles too, which helped. I felt something move under my hand, but in the midst of all that swelling I couldn't tell exactly what it was.

I was horribly uncertain whether it was kill or cure, and was disappointed to see no change in the immediate look, but, as his general condition was no worse, I decided the intestine must have gone back. Had it burst, there would have been a quick change of symptoms, temporary relief perhaps, certain peritonitis, finis. Still holding firm, I put on a pad like a truss, and bandaged it very tightly in a "thigh spica," which is a figure-eight bandage around abdomen, back and upper leg.

He was in his bed, mumbling a bit of nonsense as the anesthetic wore off, when, wonder of wonders, the gray began to recede from his face, with pink taking its place. I spent a bad night expecting the worst, but in the morning he was definitely improved.

"Feeling better?"

"Fine."

"No pain?"

"Not much. What did you do?"

"Just pushed it back."

"I tried that, but it wouldn't go."

"Oh well, you just didn't know how, that was all."

His hands began straying around. "By the Lord!" and his face clouded, "what d'you chop my beard off for?"

"I did it just to be mean."

He grinned sheepishly, ashamed that he had been so touchy. "You did not."

"It was frozen to your hood and I was in a hurry."

The second day he insisted on getting up, but I insisted on his staying down, and I won. The third day he got up and went home. "I'm getting me up a woodpile," he said, "and I can't stay in bed all my life." I put the fear of God into him, and told him the woodpile would kill him sure if he didn't let somebody else get it up. "You sit around and take it easy till summer, when you get operated on. It's your duty, never mind whether you want to or not. I suppose you want to leave your wife and little ones for somebody else to take care of?"

He hung his head and didn't stick his chin out quite so far. As a matter of fact he had had the scare of his life this time, for he realized that he'd been unconscious some hours, out of control, with his prized obstinacy not working. That joggled him.

I seized the opportunity. "If this ever happens again, you'll be a goner. You'd never listen to the doctor, would you? You thought other people went to hospital, not you. In the summer you get this operated on, and you'll be strong for the rest of your life. But if you don't, mark my words, you'll be crippled while you live, and that won't be long."

"I give up," he said. But I noticed that for the trip home he wouldn't sit in the komatik box, "the woman's box." He made his brothers leave it behind. "Oh, we'll pick it up in the summer some day. What odds, b'y."

And now Sir Wilfred and Doctor Mount were bringing Donald up the bay with them. Donald had bent his neck and gone to Indian Harbor where Doctor Mount, with Doctor Paddon assisting, had operated on the hernia. I was wondering how the case had turned out.

Tooting her whistle, the little black steamer dropped anchor in the river one afternoon. The summer staff piled into a motorboat and went out to her immediately, but I couldn't go till a few minutes later, when I grabbed a small boat and rowed out. It was as thrilling as ever to be seeing Doctor Mount again, for a nurse has it positively incorporated into her bloodstream that a brilliant surgeon is God's finest creation. Millionaires are all right because they sometimes finance researchers who are all right too because they make new knowledge available to surgeons. Authors are tolerable because they occasionally dramatize a surgeon so the public can faintly comprehend his worth, but for pure art and god-like power the man who grabs destiny by the tail and gives it a twist is the surgeon himself.

Doctor Mount was leaning on the rail as I made fast, his bright eyes never missing anything. "Here's the sailor lass again," he said. "You handle a lot of things, don't you?"

He indicated Donald, who was walking fretfully up and down the deck anxious to get ashore, looking hale and sturdy and beautifully obstinate. "We piled bricks on him to keep him in bed." Doctor Mount took me aside and sat me down on a nice clean flour barrel. "Glad to see you. I wanted to tell you about this man Baikie. He had the worst hernia I've seen, and I've seen a lot of them. Full of adhesions. Two hours it took me, two hours, think of it!"

"Yes," I said. "He'd been in bad shape for years."

"Miss Austen, I saw those charts of his history and the record of that manual reduction you did on him. How'd you ever manage that?"

"I really don't know."

"That was some going, Nurse, some going."

"Thank you," I said, and a surge of feeling made my eyes water and my chin tremble. It wasn't pride—it was a fierce gratitude that my hands, my acts, my training had just now picked me up and made me part of the wonder of the world. "Take a brace," said Mount. "Here's the chief."

And then I was shaking Sir Wilfred's hand. "Greetings, Miss Austen," he said warmly, and had a good look at me. "Harry, you've been praising her, confess now. When will you learn that nurses are more efficient on a steady diet of blame?" and his eyes twinkled and he kept on shaking my hand.

CHAPTER XXIX

LABRADOR is a land of heartwarming summer reunions that happen but once a year. It was great fun to see aboard *Strathcona* again the skipperman Will Simms, whose appetite for fresh eggs had already led him to investigate our henhouse; and Professor Sears of Amherst, Massachusetts, a good photographer and an agricultural expert able to advise us about all sorts of knotty problems. People here had named him Mr. Flycatcher, because he sometimes went about with a butterfly net collecting rare specimens.

Sir Wilfred was going through the hospital admission and out-patient books with me, which contained a record of all cases, their treatment, and results obtained. This man of many parts, whose small medical mission for fishermen had grown so vast that he could not personally manage it all any more, who spent his winters in England and America lecturing, writing, deciding policies, put his finger on one name after another in the big book. Here was Wilfred Grenfell, M.D., and never mind the *Sir*.

"Si Turner, axe cut, eh? General anesthetic, stitches, tendon uninjured. You were lucky. In hospital three weeks. Can he snowshoe all right?"

"Yes, perfectly."

"This Broomfield, I arranged about his pension, and put his wheelchair ashore at Rigolet this trip. H-m, May Shepherd, she was operated on at Indian Harbor last summer, if I remember. Is she well now? Good. Goudie, Goudie, which

Goudie is that? Oh, yes, his father was with me when we ran on a reef off Okkak once. Is he still living? Henry Jessup still has that chronic backache, eh? What did you do for that?"

"Well," I said hesitantly, "I didn't know what to do. I just gave him rhubarb and soda."

"Best thing. Used to give it to him myself. Poor old Sarah Gear has T. B. I see. Her husband's one of the best boat caulkers that ever was. Is he able to work?"

"He's a good help with the boats in summer, and very willing, but it's hard for him to get around in winter."

"Well, see that they get everything they need. M-m-m, you've delivered a lot of babies, haven't you? Placenta prævia, eh? How's my old friend Grandma Baikie?"

Doctor, lawyer, merchant, chief, that was Sir Wilf. He wanted to know about everything, he wanted to see the hayfield and the farm and the hens; and what about the water supply and what about the cellar for the new teachers' cottage, and how many cabbages had been planted in this village this spring? Not from any ulterior motive, but just because he was interested. He wanted to see the patients, he wanted to see little Ethel's burn-scars. He was not like some great men who have no time. Whether he was with a botanist, an aviator, an expert on cooperatives or Diesel engines, he wanted to know all about it, and he set right to work finding out. He was learning more new things, every day, on the side, at the age of seventy, than many a student whose sole business is learning.

"And this child Ethel, how did she get burned so badly?"

"Her nightdress caught afire from the stove."

"Who put it out?"

"Her mother tried to, but she caught afire too, and burned

her hand and arm. Her ten-year-old brother, Chesley Shepherd, threw a bucket of water on them both."

"Oh, Shepherd, Valley's Bight. I know Peter Shepherd, went deer hunting once with him over back of Double Mer twenty-five years ago. A great talker. How is he?"

"He's fine, and still hunting deer. I spent a night there early in the spring."

"How large an area was burned?"

"About a third of her body. Her whole upper leg and side was a third-degree burn."

"Come, come, tell me about it. Don't make me question you."

"Well, Pete brought his wife and Ethel up here on the last ice. Ethel had been unconscious for about two days. She has been here now three months. The shock had almost killed her. I gave her saline and stimulants, and fed her with a tube, and tried every kind of dressing I could think of, hot baths, foments, wax dressings. She remained unconscious for another three days. The mother had to go right back with Pete, because the ice was getting bad and they had children at home and work to do. I was dressing her scorched hand and arm before she left. Pete was in the ward, looking out the window, when suddenly he said, 'Look, Lou, there's the horse!'

"She was so excited, never having seen one before, that she got right up from the table and went to the window. All the dressings rolled onto the floor, but she didn't even notice. 'Oh, Pete,' she said, 'what a size! I didn't s'pose he'd look like that.' She thought it was wasteful of me to throw the dressings away and start over with sterile ones.

"Every time I changed Ethel's dressings, I put her in a

warm bath, because I didn't dare expose such a large area all at once. I often thought it was a blessing she was unconscious and couldn't feel anything. But she came to finally."

"Third-degree burns in the groin. Did that scar tissue contract her leg?" Sir Wilfred asked.

"I made a splint."

"You yourself?"

"Yes, I'd seen the men split out and whittle fur boards to stretch skins on, so I carved one out of spruce till it fitted her from heel to hip. It wasn't very big even when it was finished."

"Have you it here? I want to see it."

He took the splint in his hand. "Well, well, it isn't very big, is it? Tell me some more. I have to lecture all winter, you know."

"She's had daily extension," I said, "and then massage and exercise while we've been gradually dispensing with the splint. It's only the last few days that we've left it off entirely. She had only been talking a little while, you understand, two and a half years old, and her speech was completely gone. She had to learn all over again. The first thing she said was *Mally;* that was her name for me, a far-fetched contraction of Miss Austen, I suppose, and that's what she still calls me. She is also having to learn to walk again, step by step, precisely as though she had never known. She can only take a couple of steps even now, and we help her and stand her up to chairs as you would a tiny baby. It was six weeks before Mrs. Shepherd found out that Ethel was alive.

"Ethel had suffered such shock and pain that everything made her afraid. But she was too weak to cry or scream. Her hands just trembled and her eyes dilated. As she grew stronger, she screamed with terror one day, all unhinged by the shock, I thought. Or remembering, perhaps. But I noticed her great big eyes were following something with horror. It was a fly, but to her it seemed to be a monster. I killed it and showed it to her dead, but she shrank away trembling and gasping. She got a fly-phobia. We haven't many flies, but we can't keep every single one out. I told her, 'Don't be silly, don't be afraid. It won't hurt you. Look, the fly walks on me, and doesn't hurt.' But that made no impression. Every time a fly got into her room, she lay and trembled as though begging for mercy with her great shuddering eyes.

"So I tried a different tack. I had to. I said, 'Oh, I hate flies. When I was little, I used to hate them the same as you do. We both hate them, don't we? I'll tell you what we'll do: when you see one, you call me, and I'll kill him. We'll fix 'em, you and I together.' She had a part now, and was not alone. It was she and I together. I didn't know whether it would work. Honestly, she had been so nearly dead and gone out of this world, she couldn't seem to get used to it again.

"But it was miraculous how she would call, 'Mally, fly,' and after several weeks she took genuine enjoyment in it. She'd even call, 'Mally, fly,' as a ruse to get me to come and talk to her. Well, I think that's about all there is to it. You know even better than I do what a dirty sore a burn always is. It seemed as though it would never stop sloughing, but it's clean now, and almost healed. In another month she'll be fit to go home. To tell you the truth, I'll miss her."

"Come along," said Sir Wilfred. "I want to have a look at Ethel."

She was in her crib looking at a scrapbook. He examined

her scars, and when I had replaced the dressings, he said, "You know, I think we ought to have a picture of Ethel, and us too."

He picked her up and carried her down into the sunshine, where we had several pictures snapped.

The following summer Sir Wilfred showed me one of them and told me he had used the lantern slide of it in all his lectures. He said it was the most appealing picture he had ever used, and that the response it had brought from people everywhere was going to save a good many other Ethels.

CHAPTER XXX

IT WAS RIDICULOUS how busy I kept. I used to have dreams that I was in a boat, sailing, sailing all day long across a calm sea with nothing to do, nothing at all but watch the boat dip over the sea and the clouds float past the peak of the sail. The breeze would be always fair, and we never would have to tack.

For three days and nights, ever since Alice Pottle had been brought across the river on a stretcher, threatening to throw an eclamptic fit and to produce a baby at one and the same time, I had had little rest. Alice possessed a varied assortment of ills such as high blood pressure, a bad heart, terrific albuminuria, and, doubtless, a number of other things that I knew nothing about. On the third day she was in labor, gasping for breath on account of her heart, threatening to pass away at any moment, when another baby case arrived and I had two on my hands at once.

The second one was May Baikie, who had come up the bay in a boat with her husband, Jimmie. It was nice timing, I had to admit. She was in strong labor now, and the baby wasn't long in being born.

But following that, she nearly bled to death with an adherent placenta. At the end of an hour, I saw that I'd have to do a manual removal, an exceedingly dangerous procedure which I disliked very much. Lucky for me, my midwife friend, Mrs. Hicks, was visiting in the village, and I was able to send for her to take care of Alice in the next room. That dependable little busybody, how I blessed her when she bustled in, bubbling over with importance. Mrs. Pottle's face was badly swollen, and she was mad for breath. She needed extreme quiet, but it was difficult to give it to her.

I sent for May's husband, Jimmie, sterilized afresh with greatest care, prepared Sarah Jane as my anesthetist, and was starting in on May when Jimmie arrived.

I was too frazzled to spare him. "She may die. She's quite pulseless. I wanted you here, right there in *that* corner."

He was speechless.

I had to watch Sarah Jane and the ether like a hawk, for twice on the table May stopped breathing, but we brought her round again. I kept wishing I had had a decent night's sleep. When I had finished and was treating her for shock and hemorrhage, Jimmie whispered, "Is she dying?"

"No," I said, "she's living." I must have said it sharply, for long after that Jimmie used to josh me about it and repeat our cryptic conversation around the bay.

May kept on living, too, but not without a continuous eight hours of nerve-wracking assistance, during which time Alice's baby girl was born, and a huge schooner poked its snout over the horizon and tied up at our wharf with a load of mission freight to be landed instantly. With Jack away at Indian Harbor, nobody seemed to know anything about storehouse keys, trunks, lists, requisitions, except me. *Can you give us firewood and machine oil? Where'll we put this ton of flour? What'll we do with this smashed one? Where's the hand barrows? Why didn't ya build the storehouse another mile away from the dock? How about planks for that hole in the wharf?*

I gave that schoonerman as good as he sent. Finally he calmed down. He had supplies to deliver to Cartwright. He had to sail to Boston, back to the Labrador, and back again to Boston before the autumn gales. "We got to have more help. We'll be here two days at this rate. We got to have men to work all night, and get out of here."

Across the river at the Indian encampment there were nearly thirty men. They seemed a logical bet. I sent Johnnie Montague, who spoke Indian, to ask them. He returned with the information that they would work, but only under one condition. Their pay must consist of a good feed of baked beans. There was nothing we possessed that they would work for except baked beans. So we put on a huge mess of beans, both in the hospital and the boarding cottage kitchens, and stoked up the fires.

In the ward, when we'd begun to get things faintly organized again, Sarah Jane said, "I'm going downstairs and get us a cup of tea."

It seemed a good idea, since none of us had had any lunch, and sleepiness always makes you hungry. Mrs. Hicks and I were finishing up some cleaning, and I said, "Come on, Mrs. Hicks, we'll carry this down while we're going."

This was a great galvanized tub of bloody water. We each took a handle and started down. Midway, my handle came off, and the whole mess cascaded down the stairs with a shattering crash. I was on the lower side, of course, and got drenched.

We picked a dry stair and sat looking at each other. I was too tired to be exasperated.

"It's a great world, isn't it, Mrs. Hicks?"

"Sometimes I ain't sure," she said.

"Shall we sip a cup of tea, or do you prefer arsenic?"

"I likes tea, Miss."

I kicked the tub a few more steps to the bottom, and we went and drank our tea. Sarah Jane, the faithful one, set to with mops and pails cleaning the stairs and the flooded room below. For all of me, they would never have been cleaned. I'd had about all I could take.

In the evening after the Indians had come across in their canoes and started unloading, I could hear blocks squeaking and freight rattling into the storehouse. Mrs. Hicks stayed with us to help with the two mothers, neither of whom could be left alone. In May's case particularly, I feared the possibility of a second hemorrhage. At midnight, leaving Mrs. Hicks on watch, I set the alarm for two o'clock, since May and Alice would be needing treatment then. I really didn't need to set the alarm, for I've always been able to set myself and wake at a given hour no matter how tired. But I was dizzy for sleep this night. In order that the mothers might have quiet, the two newborn babies were in my room tucked in baskets by the dresser where I could hear them if they cried. *If they cried* is putting it mildly. One of them had cried ever since it was born. The textbooks would give you to understand that the newborn infant infallibly sleeps the first twelve hours, but that is in textbooks. Anyway, I was climbing into bed, thinking maybe I could put a pillow over my ears so as *not* to hear, when the sound of a motorboat exhaust came in from the bay. My Lord! I thought, is there no end to things around here? It was a cold night. A lantern glowed beside the schooner where they were tying up, and next I heard the thump of rubber boots on the steps. I threw on my flannel bathrobe and went down.

It was then, of all times, that we met. He had dark eyes, and his hands were blue with cold. He was an American, had been wop at Indian Harbor whence they had just arrived, and he was to be the new schoolteacher here for the winter. Jack, who was pulling off his boots by the stove, said with a jerk of the head, "This is Bud."

I should like to say that this pronouncement shivered my timbers from stem to gudgeon, or at least that I was concerned with the figure I must be cutting in a huge old pink flannel wrapper with my hair tied up in a knot on top, but unfortunately my mind was preoccupied with the idea of slumber. I concluded, not without a moment's hesitation, that I ought at least to get them some tea and a redberry sandwich. I nodded to the new man as I rummaged in the cupboard.

He nodded in return, awed, no doubt, by the spectacle in pink. "How do you do, Miss——"

What did it matter whether he knew my name or not? He'd find it out soon enough. They were cold and sleepy, and now, after the long, long trip, they would have to go to work on freight. None of us paid much attention.

"Have a good trip?" I asked to be polite.

"Not bad," said Jack. "No worse than usual."

"Well, you know where the new man's bed is. You'll show him, Jack?"

"Sure. What use are beds to us, with all that freight piled on the beach?"

"Good night then."

"Good night."

Just then there was a commotion. The Indians said it was 12:30 and they were tired of working and it was time they had their beans. We rousted out Sarah Jane, and she, Jack, Bud and I served up thirty whopping plates of baked beans with bread and butter. Then the Indians, who had agreed to work all night, said they didn't feel like unloading any more, and paddled back across the river to their tents, calm, aristocratic, untouched by the fever of civilization. The skipper of the schooner was fit to be tied.

I couldn't help that. I went up to my room. Alice's baby was still squalling, with short pauses for breath. I sat on a chair and dully thought of Chekhov's story, "Sleepy," in which Vaka, a nursemaid, worn to the bone, solved just such a situation as this by strangling the howler. Rather than that I changed the babe, put it in the linen closet, which contained a window and was across the hall from me, told Mrs. Hicks about it, and, hopping into bed, was asleep in two minutes. So much for the romantic encounter with the dark stranger from the States. But there was a sequel.

CHAPTER XXXI

THE NEW CHAP roamed around poking his nose into everything and making little canoe journeys in all directions whenever he could escape from the hard work that was steady diet
around here. He made a lot of desks for the school out of
packing cases, and kites for the boys, which they had never
seen before. We went duck hunting several mornings, and I
was educated enough by this time to show him how you went
about it. He liked to listen to the book of records Polly had
bequeathed me when she left for her home in Massachusetts,
and gradually we became good friends.

When the coast station at Indian Harbor had closed for the
season, and Doctor and Mrs. Paddon were settled at North
West River for the winter, Doctor Paddon said I ought to
have a couple of days off. I thought so too.

It was mid-September, and the mission motorboat was
taking a crew of trappers up Grand River as far as the first
portage-falls on the initial leg of their journey. Jim Pottle
ran the engine, Bud went, and eight trappers with such mountains of flour and traps and rifles and gear that we had to tow
their four canoes. The trappers were gay in their new pants
and old hats and the shirts their wives had been sewing,
and colored Hudson's Bay sashes that they used for tump-
lines. They were happy to be starting on their annual sojourn
in the woods—just as they would be happy to come home

again. They told us tales of lakes and rivers they knew, and they alone. And as they talked, the old restlessness stole over me. Last year I had seen them go and felt the pull of that adventure. Now they were friends, and I was going a little way, but must return.

We camped at Muskrat Falls some twenty miles up the river and helped them carry loads across the portage, and in the evening beside campfires heard more stories of rapids white as snow and lakes so big the farther shores were dim. "My Lord, b'y, you never see that country in to the head of Mackenzie's Lake, did you? There's islands green as hay-fields, and brooks comin' down out of the hills right full of mink. I got me a tilt on a point where the big firs grow, and a beach of sand. I'd build me a house there for good and all, but for the flies in summer and the long haul. My kin'-oo will be wore to the bare ribs, likely, when I get there. I should have put new canvas on 'er, but——"

In the morning we stood on the windy beach above the falls waving good-bye. The broad water was torn with white-caps among which the heavy canoes rolled and skittered. The men were digging their paddles hard and had no time for waving. A long way off they landed and got out their tracking lines. Then slowly they disappeared around a bend. Behind us and over our heads the trees sighed loudly. We sighed too and turned back across the portage path.

So far away and lovely it seemed here, no house, no cares, just the river and the woods and sky and the sailing clouds. What a perfect place to camp and live a little! While Jim tinkered with the boat engine in the cove, Bud and I sat on a driftwood log below the falls. Our tent and blankets and gear were piled on the beach. A couple of campfires still smoked on the sand. There were great heaps of driftwood jammed up on the shores, enough dry wood to supply a house for years.

A longing that was mutual tugged at us both. And it was strong, one of those powerful magnets that alter lives. We were both of the kind, as witness our presence there, who believe the best ideas are the ones that are acted upon.

"You'd like to go, wouldn't you?" he said.

"Yes."

"You'll never be able to leave this country without knowing what's back in there. And neither will I. Let's go together. What do you say? We can't go now, but next fall."

"I like to wander," I said. "I've wandered halfway round the world—almost too far I sometimes think."

He moved over on the driftwood log and put his arms around me and kissed me. "I've been wandering alone too," he said. "But I've found what I was looking for, if you have. Have you found what you were wanting?"

I glanced at him sitting on the log, and realized that my past had been dull compared with the future. "I didn't know it," I said, "but I've been looking for you."

So we teamed up. That winter he taught school and I was nurse again at North West River. For me the work was much easier, since Doctor Paddon was there to run things, to make the trips and take the responsibilities. And Mrs. Paddon, a nurse herself and my true friend, was there beside me whenever the work grew heavy. I had time to sew and prepare our gear and see to the sleeping bags and the fur-hooded dickies. The first thing Bud had to do was to learn to snowshoe, for we knew that in the woods in winter trappers sometimes snowshoe thirty miles a day. I was good at it by this time, but he fell down five times on the first circle around the hospital. We practised and practised.

We sent out to the States for sheath knives and a new gun. Bud made a camp stove and paddles. We collected up a tent, canoe, flour bags of canvas, endless stuff. The winter and summer passed, and we were ready. I had worked two-and-a-half years for the mission, he one-and-a-half; we had done a good job and now we were on our own. A gay young trapper, whose son I had delivered, said we might go with him and live in his trap-line cabin 350 miles up Grand River; he would be glad of company during the long four months in the woods.

It was then that Robert Michelin came from Traverspine and told me, "I said I'd work for you, and now I'm going to do it."

All that old nightmare time of dysentery at Traverspine when his children couldn't hold their eyes open seemed a thing of by-gone ages. Nevertheless, he was determined he was going to help us get our canoe up through the worst rapids of the lower river. A riverman of unusual skill, he came with us for forty miles, leaving his boat behind, and working like a galley slave to get our loads along. When at last it was time for him to leave us, time for him to walk that rocky, rough, cliffy river shore for home, wading icy brooks, swimming the biggest ones on a log, no tent, no stove, I felt humbled and almost ashamed at the thought of all he was doing for us. "It is too much, Robert," I said. "You did not owe me anything."

"I've still got my kids, haven't I?" he said. He yanked his hat on tight and turned. "Good luck. So long." And he rounded a bend of the shore toward his boat and Traverspine. He got there too.

Our travels in the bush that winter are another tale. The life was hard and dangerous, but all the sweeter for that. At its farthest point, the farthest I have ever been, hungry, frost-bitten, with a pack on my back, I saw the inner wilderness and the long white lakes wrapped in midwinter savagery and beauty beyond the height-of-land.

When spring came to Hamilton Inlet again, Bud and I were off in a skiff with a tent and a sail to island glades and camping spots by coves, to duck-hunting marshes and salmon rivers marked on our own map for special habitation. We fished and sailed to our hearts' content, and lived on goose and duck and salmon as well as love. The sun was warm on the sandy beaches where nobody lived way up Grand Lake by the channels of Nascopi rivermouth. When rain pattered on the tent or bread was browning in the pan, we remembered the itinerant Newfoundland minister who had instructed us at our marriage ceremony to repeat after him the words, "according to God's 'oly hordinance," for it seemed that we lived now as never before according to divine command. We discovered that each of us had always wanted to live this way from our childhood on; and we discovered such existence is a part of life's goodness that surpasses expectations.

We live in the States now, and are still teamed up. Three personal and extremely important baby cases, concerning which I was able to give a lot of unasked advice, have come my way since those Labrador days of caring for other people's families and travelling the bush. It is a great joy that I don't have to give my blue- and my brown-eyed boys and the hazel-eyed girl back to somebody else every time they recover from an ailment. As the bends in the river and the dogteam trips are part of me, so are these three.

In the evening when we five sit by the fire, it is our fire, and thus different from all others. If you like, you may say that my adventuring is over.